The First Crusade
and the idea of crusading

By the same author:

The Crusades: A Short History
(1990, The Athlone Press; re-issued by Continuum 2001)

The First Crusade
and the idea of crusading

JONATHAN RILEY-SMITH

continuum
LONDON • NEW YORK

Continuum
The Tower Building, 11 York Road, London, SE1 7NX
370 Lexington Avenue, New York, 10017-6503, NY
www.continuumbooks.com

Paperback edition first published in 1993 by
The Athlone Press
Reprinted 1995

Published by Continuum in 2003

Copyright © 1986, 1993 Jonathan Riley-Smith

British Library Cataloguing-in-Publication Data
*A catalogue record for this book is available from
the British Library.*

ISBN 0-8264-6726-1

*Printed and bound in Great Britain by
Bookcraft (Bath) Ltd, Midsomer Norton, Somerset*

For R.C. Smail

Lingua sapientium ornat scientiam.
Proverbs 15:2

Contents

Acknowledgements

My first debt of gratitude is to my publisher whose genial compliance with regard to another contract enabled me to finish this even sooner than I had hoped. I owe much to the Librarians and staff of the British Library, the London Library, the libraries of the universities of Cambridge and London and of Royal Holloway College, the Warburg Institute and, above all, the Institute of Historical Research. I have to thank the editors of *Studies in Church History* and *The End of Strife* for permission to incorporate parts of my articles on the persecution of the Jews and martyrdom, which are listed in the Bibliography. My wife Louise, Dr Norman Housley and Mrs Susan Edgington kindly read the typescript and offered good advice, as did Dr Bernard Hamilton, Dr W.G. Waddington and Dr Roy Porter on particular points. Janet Daines typed the final version. Janet Fahy drew the maps. This book is dedicated to the historian to whom I owe most.

Introduction

The prevailing view of the origins and early history of crusading thought owes most to Carl Erdmann's *Die Entstehung des Kreuzzugsgedankens*. Although published fifty years ago, the influence of this brilliant book is now stronger than ever, for the recent appearance of an English edition has made its message available to a wider public.[1] Most studies of the subject in the past half-century have drawn on it or have reached similar conclusions to it, although naturally some of them have differed from it on points of detail,[2] and now Ernst-Dieter Hehl has modelled himself on Erdmann in writing a clever and learned exposition of the Church's attitude to war in the period following the First Crusade.[3] There is, in fact, general agreement that the crusade was the climacteric of a movement in which the eleventh-century Church reformers, locked in conflict with ecclesiastical and secular opponents, turned to the knights of the Christian West for assistance. Pope Urban II's message to the faithful in 1095, in which he summoned them to fight in aid of the eastern Christians, is believed to have been a synthesis of ideas and practices already in existence – holy war, pilgrimage, the indulgence – although it was not fully understood by those who responded to it, many of whom were anyway motivated by a desire for material gain. But it is supposed that crusading theory did not reach maturity until the 1140s. By then the traditions had been reinforced by the work of apologists like Pope Innocent II, St Bernard of Clairvaux and, above all, the great canonist Gratian, who, drawing on elements already present in crusade propaganda, had demonstrated definitively that the Church, and especially the popes, could authorize holy war on God's behalf.

So goes the standard modern interpretation. It is worth noting that it is from English scholarship that most dissent has come. Mr Cowdrey has questioned Erdmann's suggestion that Pope Urban's main preoccupation was with aid to the Greeks not with the liberation of Jerusalem, the goal of which was, according to Erdmann, secondary and devotional.[4] Dr Blake has drawn attention to the way ideas also developed under the stresses imposed by the campaigns themselves, 'a pattern of events, seen progressively emerging into a coherent experience'.[5] Professor Gilchrist has argued that the influence of the theologians of violence on Urban II was slight.[6] In this book I wish to challenge another generally held assumption. Because Erdmann ended his work with a discussion of the First Crusade it has been supposed that he dealt adequately with it: Hehl, for instance, devoted comparatively little space to it before moving on to the period that followed. Erdmann, in fact, concentrated on the background to the crusade, not the crusade itself, and in the course of the subsequent discussion the sources for it and the spate of commentaries that followed it have been neglected. So I have examined all the material for the First Crusade afresh. I am inclined to think that Urban's original message was conventional in the sense that it was not unlike many put forward by Church reformers at the time. For various reasons, above all because he presented Jerusalem as a goal and appealed to the French and because opinion among the ordinary faithful was moving in his direction, the laity's response was far more positive than it had been to earlier summons of this sort. The concepts to which Urban gave expression, moreover, were transformed by the dreadful experiences of the army on the march and the euphoria that followed the liberation of Jerusalem into a new association of ideas, crude and semi-popular, which found its way into the narrative accounts of eyewitnesses. This was refined by the next generation of writers, especially by three French monks, Robert the Monk, Guibert of Nogent and Baldric of Bourgueil, who represented it to the clerical public in relatively sophisticated and theologically acceptable terms. They put the miracle, as they saw it, of the success of the crusade into the context of providential history and they chose to treat the crusaders as temporary religious, professed into what looked to them like a military monastery on the move. Their picture of the crusade accorded with the ideals of the eleventh-century reformers, whose chief aim had been to infuse secular life with monastic values. That is briefly the story told in this book.

Before launching into a discussion of the First Crusade it might be helpful to sketch in the background to it, especially since in the response of the faithful to Urban's preaching the aspirations of churchmen and laymen suddenly coincided. Behind this meeting of minds there were movements of opinion on both sides which had their origins in the violence of tenth-century France.

French society had been extremely violent, although the way this violence had been bred is still not very clear to us. Society had been dominated for a long time by the needs of war and the enjoyment of plunder, first as the Carolingian empire had expanded and then as it had become subject to invasions from without. In a graphic phrase, a historian has described the moment when the empire ceased to grow and its warriors became involved in the defence of France as one in which the whole military system began to turn 'inward upon itself'.[7] Invaders came less and less – after 1000 not at all – but in many parts of France, instead of disbanding, the local armed companies turned their attention to the ordinary villagers in the neighbourhood. Based in castles, which were now springing up everywhere, these warrior companies, reluctant to lose a standard of living built on looting, forced the peasantry to produce more and more for them, thus indirectly bringing about a sort of rural economic revolution. The anarchic violence, springing from the very success of the Carolingian war machine, flourished unchecked because political power in France had fragmented. The king no longer exercised direct control over most of the provinces, where the dukes and counts, descended from Carolingian officials, now governed without reference to him. From 1028 these great magnates ceased even to come regularly to royal assemblies; neither did the bishops, who could see little advantage in attendance on the king. Meanwhile in the chaos many of the dukes and counts themselves lost control of their own regions. Men were likely to look for security – if such a word could be used – only to the local castellan and his predatory band. In the early eleventh century, in a revealing change in the use of language, the word *dominus* (lord), first used only of God, the king and the bishops and then in the tenth century extended to counts, came to be applied to these garrison commanders and marked public recognition of their right to judge and tax those living in or passing through their territories. The castellans and their *milites* (knights), as their followers came to be called, were now the only authorities many men knew. And since their word was law and there was nobody to restrict them, violence proceeded unchecked.

The Church had been faced by a violence that it knew was wrong and by an anarchic society in which it could not expect to find the security it needed to flourish. It had, therefore, taken the leadership of a movement for the 'Peace of God', which canalized popular concern about the endemic violence and tried to substitute the sanctions of the Church and popular disapproval for the enfeebled controls of the king. The movement had first emerged in southern France in the late tenth century. Assemblies of free men, not unlike the old Carolingian public courts, met around piles of relics collected from all the local churches and in the presence of this supernatural power decreed the immunity of religious sanctuaries and the protection of the clergy and the poor from violence and exploitation. They aimed to compel all knights to swear oaths to respect the peace provisions. The peace movement, at first openly opposed to knighthood in all its forms, engendered a hatred of knights, justifiable in the circumstances, which was powerfully expressed at the Council of Limoges in 1031, when God's anger was invoked 'upon all knights, upon their arms and their horse'. But the bishops and monasteries were themselves lords with their own knights, while the Church itself, in the name of the peace movement, was prepared to organize military actions against peace-breakers. While they condemned knights in the strongest terms, therefore, churchmen were prepared to find a more positive role for them.[8]

At this time a movement for the reform of the Church was getting under way. The reformers were inspired by monastic values, and the dominance among them of ideas associated with the great Burgundian abbey of Cluny and its dependencies meant the influence of churchmen who went further than those engaged in the peace movement and believed that a certain accommodation ought to be made with the world to convert it to monkish ideals. It is hard to exaggerate the effort they put into the transformation of the whole Church, including, of course, ordinary lay men and women. Living in a much richer age, and one marked by ambitious building projects, it is easy for us to underrate the widespread construction of parish churches, which constituted one of the greatest achievements of the central Middle Ages. In village after village there came to tower over the very insubstantial dwellings of the villagers a building which was by any standards large and elaborate. The establishment of these churches ranks with the building programmes of the Roman empire and yet was carried through at the expense of a relatively poor society. In the end the evangelization of the faithful would lead to an understanding of the role of laymen as a distinct vocation in itself, but at this stage it was enough for the reformers to maintain that the laity had God-given functions to perform, functions that could include fighting to protect the Church.[9] This attitude seems to have reached Rome with Pope Leo IX (1049–54), who came from Lorraine, where reform ideas flourished, and as deacon and bishop had been associated with the use of the militia of his church of Toul. Within two months of his consecration a Lateran synod summoned the Roman militia to fight against his opponents in the region. In 1053 he himself took command of an army raised to campaign against the Normans in southern Italy and after its defeat he fostered the cult of the martyrdom of those of his troops who had fallen in battle. His army, summoned to a war which he stressed was defensive, was a papal army, led under a papal banner, and the soldiers in it were offered remission of penance and absolution from their sins. He was criticized for this at the time, but his successors also resorted to violence in defence of the Church. Nicholas II (1059–61) turned to the same south Italian Normans for military support and for the next few decades the Normans were active defenders of the papacy. Alexander II (1061–73) granted the first indulgence for war to fighters in Spain in 1063 and may well also have given them the right to bear a *vexillum sancti Petri*, a banner of St Peter, which was a mark of papal approval for a military venture. Banners of St Peter were increasingly sent to those favoured by papal support, among them Count Roger of Sicily, conquering Sicily from the Muslims, and Erlembald, the military leader of the Pataria, an association of clergy and lay people fighting for reform in Milan.[10]

In an atmosphere of crisis generated by the Investiture Contest the pontificate of Gregory VII (1073–85) was marked by important advances in the authorization and direction of war by the papacy. Gregory's uncompromising commitment to reform led to conflict in Italy and Germany, where a party of nobles rebelled against King Henry IV and dragged the papacy into war with him. With reform leading to hostility and then to open conflict, Gregory turned to scholars for justification for his conviction that violence could be used in defence of the Church and could be authorized by it. He seems to have relied especially on a group of men gathered round one of his most ardent supporters, Countess Mathilda of Tuscany: Bonizo of Sutri, John of Mantua and Anselm of Lucca. Of these Anselm was to have the most influence. In a work called the *Collectio canonum*, written in *c*.1083 and probably commissioned by Pope Gregory himself, he put forward a strong theoretical justification for

Christian holy violence with reference to precedents and authorities, drawn especially from the Fathers, above all St Augustine of Hippo. Almost everything the militant reformers wanted in the way of justification was to be found in Augustine's writings but, although Augustine had worked out a satisfactory and comprehensive Christian justification of violence, he had never collected it into a single work; rather it was scattered throughout an enormous *corpus* of material, ranging over forty years of writing. It was Anselm's achievement to have extracted these passages and to have collected them together in easily digestible extracts, with the contradictions ironed out. He was thus able to present a coherent body of thought emanating from one of the most powerful intellects Christian civilization has produced. And among Augustine's ideas cited by him was that of warfare approved of and even directly commanded by God, who could intervene physically on behalf of his chosen instruments of force. The concept was, of course, to be found in the Old Testament accounts of the victories of the Jewish people and would have been very familiar to anyone accustomed to the psalmody of the divine office.[11]

At the same time as he sought authoritative justification from scholars Gregory VII approached laymen for support, putting forward the idea of a body of knights scattered throughout western Christendom at his personal disposal, bound to him by duty to the Church and to him as its head. Although he occasionally used the term *milites Christi* of these men, he more commonly referred to them as *fideles* or *milites sancti Petri*. In this he was imitating a standard practice by which the vassals of a bishop were called the *fideles* of the patron saint of his cathedral.[12] And he was only doing what was becoming popular with other churchmen: from the monastic reformers and the papacy the movement of turning to the laity for material aid had been spreading rapidly through the Church as individual members of the clergy encouraged local lords to defend the Church with arms. It was in their interest, just as much as it was in the pope's, to justify the use of force. Concerned, moreover, to improve the morals of their flocks and recognizing that anyway they could do little to change their way of life, they were coming to popularize theology in terms that ordinary laymen would understand, which meant reconciling it with the heroic and martial ideals of knighthood. A famous example was Gerold, the earl of Chester's chaplain, who

did his best to turn the men of the [earl's] court to a better way of
life by putting before them the examples of their ancestors. . . . To
great barons, ordinary knights and noble boys he gave salutary
counsel; and he collected tales of combats of holy knights from
the Old Testament and from modern Christian stories for them to
imitate. He told them vivid stories of the conflicts of Demetrius
and George, of Theodore and Sebastian, of Duke Maurice and the
Theban Legion and of Eustace, supreme general and his companions, who won through martyrdom the crown in heaven.[13]

The reformers turned towards the laity with a pyrotechnical display of hyperbole. It is hard to say how wide a currency their
pronouncements on the Church and violence had. They certainly
aroused fierce opposition from the supporters of King Henry IV.
That they may have been too radical for many, perhaps the majority
of, intelligent churchmen is suggested by the contradictions in the
treatment of violence in the work of one of the greatest contemporary canonists, Ivo of Chartres, who wrote his canon law collections
on the eve of the First Crusade and probably at the request of Pope
Urban II himself. Ivo quoted extracts from rather earlier works,
including the statement that penance must be performed for killing
even in a just war, alongside texts on the justification of force which
echoed Anselm of Lucca and precedents in support of war against the
pagans. He gives the impression of being a moderate man trying
unsuccessfully to reconcile the new radical programme with an
older, more ambiguous *corpus* of ideas.[14] It is important to stress,
however, that for twenty years before the First Crusade popes and
senior churchmen had occasionally let fly references to a 'knighthood of Christ', 'knights of Christ' or 'knights of God' fighting wars
'in defence of righteousness'.[15] An early example of this hyperbole
was Gregory VII's reaction to the news of Turkish advances in Asia
Minor after the defeat of the Greeks at Manzikert in 1071. There
survives a series of letters from him on the subject, dating from
February to December 1074. In the name of St Peter he twice
summoned the *fideles sancti Petri* and all who wished to protect the
Christian faith to give their lives to 'liberate' their brothers in the
East. Such a service would be service of Christ and defence 'of the
Christian faith and the heavenly king'. 'Eternal reward' would result
from such a labour and death on it would be death for Christ, more
glorious than death for the fatherland. He himself would lead the

expedition as *dux et pontifex*, leaving Henry IV of Germany, with whom he was soon to be in bitter conflict, to protect the Church. The dowager empress Agnes of Germany and Countess Mathilda of Tuscany would accompany him. He even suggested, echoing perhaps the 'Sibylline prophecies', about which more below, that under his leadership an army of 50,000 might push on to the Holy Sepulchre in Jerusalem. Strictly speaking, what he proposed was not the same thing as the crusade preached by Urban II twenty-one years later. It was an extension of the service of St Peter, which he was already advocating, rather than of the service of Christ, which was to be a feature of crusading. There was no indulgence, no vow was required of the volunteers, and the protection of the Church was not offered to them, their lands and families. After December 1074 Gregory never referred to these plans again. But they demonstrate not only how exaggerated his language could be, but also how easy it was for a reformer to transfer the associated ideas of brotherly love, physical liberation and military force to an eastern theatre of war and how quickly, once he began to think of the East, his mind would turn to Jerusalem.[16]

It cannot be said that before 1095 the appeals of the reformers to the laity had been outstandingly successful. Only a few laymen, scattered throughout Europe, had become *fideles sancti Petri* or had answered the Church's call for physical aid in other ways. It was only with the response to the preaching of the crusade that this particular message of the reformers seems to have really got across. To understand why, we must consider the world lay men and women shared with churchmen. It goes without saying that although western Europe was enjoying economic expansion it was still relatively poor and insecure and that the poverty and insecurity were exacerbated not only by a dependence on primitive methods of cultivation but also, in a period of rapid population growth, by systems of inheritance which were bound to leave many individuals in difficulties. Where, as in northern France, primogeniture was developing, younger sons had to find some means of supporting themselves. Where, as in Italy, Burgundy and southern France, partible inheritance prevailed, the prosperity of a family collectively occupying a holding depended on self-discipline and the practice of a crude birth control, for which the only workable measure was celibacy; if all else failed, a member of such a family could choose to opt out by emigration, thus reducing the number of mouths dependent on the holding for food.

But if families added to the problems of both rich and poor in a period of expanding population, they also helped to alleviate them, for the acknowledgement of ties of kinship was an important stabilizing factor. A difficulty, it has often been pointed out, is that families are 'silent', since matters that were well-known to relatives were never written down and are therefore lost to us. But three features of family attitudes are clear and are relevant to us. The first was the acceptance within a group of variable size – at this time far larger than later in the Middle Ages – that it was kin, that the members of it were 'friends', a commonly used term for relatives, perhaps the best, perhaps the only 'friends' a man or woman might have, who were obliged to protect one another and guard each other's interests. The second was the prevalence of the blood feud, in which members of kin would spring to the defence of a relative or avenge him. The third was a consciousness of the family estate, the patrimony, on which the family interest concentrated, around which it coalesced and which, in some cases at least, it farmed collectively.

Another stabilizing factor in an insecure world, and one in which the patrimony and the vendetta again bulked large, was feudalism. By the late eleventh century feudalism, in the sense of a system of contractual relationships in which men were bound to one another by ties of protection, tenancy and service, was prevalent in France, northern Italy and England and was spreading in Germany. The importance of it from our point of view was that western Europe was permeated with ideas of lordship, since so many men were either lords or subject to them. And lordship signified rewards and mutual loyalty, expressed as far as the inferior was concerned in obedience. Lordship, like the family, gave an individual the sense of belonging to a group – in this case the lord and his vassals, a nexus which was treated as though it were a family and like a family imposed on its members the obligation of the vendetta – and the certainty of protection and help in time of trouble. Indeed without family or lord (or vassals) a man's life must have been virtually unendurable.[17]

In many areas society was still dominated by the castellans and their knights; and therefore it was still violent. Violence often breeds a romanticism which at this time was expressed above all in the *chansons de geste*, in verse which, although apparently composed by the clergy, was intended for popular consumption and reflected popular tastes. The *chansons* we know are nearly all in forms that date only from the twelfth century, by which time they must have been subjected to all sorts of new influences, particularly crusading itself, but there are three features which seem to have been always with them: the role of Charlemagne as a great and good emperor presiding over a golden age; a concern with war and the martial virtues of bravery, honour and fidelity, combined with a love of travel in knight-errantry; and the theme of Christian heroism in battle for the faith against pagans. It is as though society was yearning for a means of expressing its beliefs in the only way it knew.[18]

In fact the secular world was being touched by the reform movement. In France the aggressive violence of the castellans and their followers had peaked in the 1020s. Thereafter there was a perceptible shift towards public demonstrations of piety and it seems that by the late eleventh century nobles with a reputation for devoutness and an interest in church affairs were becoming quite common. One of them was Anselm of Ribemont, who was to die on the crusade and was the founder of the monastery of Ribemont and a benefactor of the religious communities of St Amand and Anchin; he had a devotion to St Quentin, the patron of the region in which he lived, and was a friend of the archbishop of Rheims.[19] Arnold of Ardres, another crusader, was believed by his descendants to have been extremely pious.[20] These are only two examples among many and it is easy to demonstrate that, at least at the level of consciousness, we are dealing with genuine feelings of piety. The plethora of new monastic foundations in the late eleventh century, multiplying the numbers of religious many times, could not have occurred without the support and endowments of men and women who may never themselves have intended to enter the religious life. They exhibited, of course, the conspicuous generosity of the age, which reflected social practices and expectations as much as religious feeling. But nevertheless society did think it important to contribute extravagantly to the good works of the Church.

The devotions increasingly popular with the laity were positive responses to the evangelical zeal of the reformers and reflected attitudes shared by them all towards the material world, which they despised as a shadowy unreality. Behind the façade it presented lay verity: heaven and hell, angels and saints on one side, the devil and his attendant demons on the other, striving for their souls. Every now and then these warring hosts would invade the natural stage, proving to men the existence of that long struggle which nature masked; and every now and then God, omnipotent and interventionary, would step in and by means of signs and miracles would change the course of events in this dimension. The natural world, itself miraculous since it stemmed from God's act of creation, was important only in so far as it gave men signs of what was in reality happening behind it, revealing to them the significance of these supernatural events. Nature was to be interpreted, not explained. The world, moreover, was a source of constant temptation to sin, which was one reason why monasticism, representing an abandonment of it, was so attractive to postulants and benefactors alike. If there was an aim that united laymen and religious in the eleventh century it was to avoid the consequences of the sinfulness they witnessed around them and felt within them, either by escaping from its more open manifestations or by seeking 'remission' of it.[21] And if someone chose to remain a layman he could help to realize the second of these goals by involving himself in those good works that assisted him on the path to an inner conversion or were demonstrations of it. The most popular form that good works took – one that reflected ancient penitential practices – was the pilgrimage. The popularity of pilgrimages also stemmed from the fact that Christianity had been grafted on to a pagan world of nature rites and local deities, and so the devotions of the faithful and the cosmology shared by simple and learned alike had combined to create popular religion's chief characteristic, which was that it was cultic. Christ and the saints were not only struggling on mankind's behalf behind the scenes; here on earth they had left behind them echoes of their sacred power in the objects they had touched while living and in their relics, those pieces of skin and bone which, it was believed, would be reassembled on the Last Day to share in the Beatific Vision. Relics had been treasured from the days of the early Church, but in western Europe enthusiasm for them had increased greatly in the ninth century, partly because ecclesiastical legislators had laid down that all altars should contain them, partly because of the emergence of avid collectors and the accumulation of great collections in many Carolingian churches and monasteries. The eleventh, twelfth and thirteenth centuries marked the height of veneration of them and witnessed the construction of elaborate shrines at the cult centres. Like the ancient pagan gods and goddesses, many of whose attributes they had inherited, the saints were believed to hold in special affection places where they had resided while in this world or churches which had their relics, and they were believed to favour those who visited them with their powerful intercession with God. In the tenth and eleventh centuries, perhaps in reaction to the anarchy, the miracles recorded as being performed by them were predominantly those in which, often in violent ways, they protected the property and territorial claims of the monasteries or churches in which their relics rested. By the late eleventh century this defensive function was beginning to give way to one of healing the guardians of the shrines or the pilgrims who visited them, but it is important to stress the vengeful, protective character of the miracles associated with the cult centres, which not only, of course, reflected the expectations of the devout, but also imbued them with the notion of supernatural violence on behalf of holy places. The heightened feelings of veneration towards relics helps to explain extraordinary measures like the pious theft of relics, justified if successful by the conviction that the saint involved wanted his bones transferred to a new site, and the public humiliation of relics, undertaken when a monastery which had been deprived of property or privilege wished to frighten its oppressor and punish its saint who had failed in his role as protector.[22]

With hindsight it is easy to see how Urban II's background made him the ideal man to reconcile the perceptions of the reformers with those of an important section of the laity. His time, perhaps ten years, as monk and prior of Cluny must have exposed him to the Cluniac views on the functions of knights. His career in Italy and Germany as cardinal and papal legate under Gregory VII had given him the chance of absorbing the latest ideas of the reformers. But most important of all, perhaps, was the fact that, being born into the petty nobility of Champagne, he was qualified to know the minds of the lay knights of France.[23] It is surely no coincidence that his summons to them was couched in terms they understood, giving them a devotion to perform which was in tune with their own aspirations.

Chapter 1

Pope Urban's message

Urban spent the year from August 1095 to September 1096 in France. He had returned to his homeland primarily to oversee the reform of its Church, but he had also come with the intention of preaching the crusade and soon after his arrival he seems to have conferred about this with Adhémar of Monteil, the bishop of Le Puy who was to be his personal representative in the army, and with Raymond of St Gilles, the count of Toulouse. On 27 November 1095 he proclaimed the crusade to a large but mainly clerical gathering at Clermont. He then journeyed through central, western and southern France, skirting the areas under the direct control of the king, whom it would be difficult to meet while his appeal against a sentence of excommunication imposed on him for adultery was under consideration. There is evidence that he preached the crusade at Limoges at Christmas, at Angers and Le Mans in February 1096 and at a council held at Nîmes in July, but he must have preached elsewhere as well. Possibly at Le Mans in February, certainly at Tours in March, he presided over ceremonies during which knights took the cross. By the time he left France the enterprise was already under way.[1]

The crusade was his personal response to an appeal which had reached him from the Greeks eight months before. In March 1095 he had been presiding over a council at Piacenza, when there had arrived an embassy from Constantinople to ask for aid against the Turks. Urban replied by encouraging 'many to promise, by taking an oath, to aid the emperor most faithfully as far as they were able against the pagans.[2] The close connection between the events at Piacenza and Clermont was noticed by a contemporary,[3] but it would be wrong to suppose that a spontaneous reaction at Piacenza started a chain of thought in Urban's mind that ended with Clermont. In fact his response was probably premeditated. Since the beginning of his pontificate he had been involved in negotiations with the Greek emperor Alexius over relations between the churches of Rome and Constantinople and over military aid from the West to

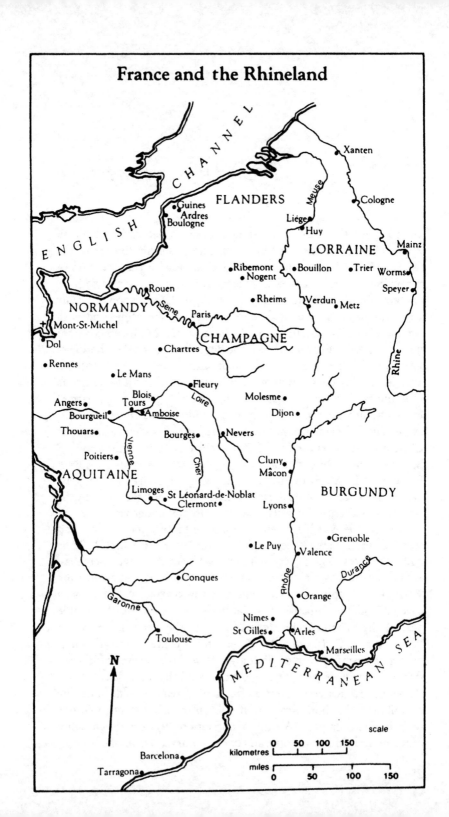

France and the Rhineland

the Byzantine empire, which had now lost most of Asia Minor. It has even been suggested that his announcement of his intention to visit France as early as July 1089, at a time when he was deeply involved in these negotiations, may be evidence that he had been considering calling for French volunteers for a long time.[4] It is certainly possible that his appeal had been thought out long before 1095 and that it was only then that he knew himself to be politically strong enough to deliver it, for the decline in the fortunes of the anti-pope and the western emperor and the increasing prestige of the reform papacy were becoming apparent to all and were confirmed by the impressive gathering of bishops and representatives of secular authorities at Piacenza.

It is obviously important to try to recapture as accurately as possible his message to the faithful, a harder task than one might think, because it means concentrating on material written before memories were distorted by the news of the crusaders' liberation of Jerusalem in July 1099: we cannot, for instance, put much trust in four eyewitness accounts of his sermon to the council of Clermont which were written from memory after 1099.[5] We have the texts of two decrees of the council and a description of a third;[6] and a later reference to a ruling made by the pope at Clermont on the status of the churches in conquered territory.[7] We have some fragmentary reports of the other sermons he preached in France, particularly the one at Angers,[8] six letters from him in which reference is made to the subject and some material concerning the decisions he made and the discussions he had in Italy between his return in September 1096 and his death on 29 July 1099, before the news of the final success had reached him. We also have a fair number of deeds of gift, sale or mortgage composed for departing crusaders and some letters written on their behalf while on the march.

Urban considered himself, and was considered by others, to have authorized the war in his capacity as pope. He referred to Adhémar of Le Puy as his legate 'in our place' and his inspiration was recognized by the crusade leaders, who wrote to him about the war 'which you began' and 'which is your own'; they asked him to join them in Syria so that they might have him 'after God as our aider and helper'; once the crusade had been completed, they wrote, 'all the world will be obedient to you'.[9] But he also claimed to be acting on Christ's behalf and he resorted to the kind of expostulatory language already used by Gregory VII and other reformers. He employed, in fact, language he had already used himself in other contexts, for the association of God and God's will with military triumphs against the Muslims had been a feature of his letters from the beginning of his pontificate. On the fall of Toledo:

> we rejoice with a most joyful heart and we give great thanks to God, as is worthy, because in our time he has deigned to give such a great victory to the Christian people.[10]

On Pisan victories:

> In our time the ordering of God's majesty has deigned to make renowned the glory of the city of Pisa . . . with triumphs against the Muslims.[11]

On Christian advances in Sicily and Spain:

> God, the ruler of all things, whose wisdom and strength, when he wishes, *taketh away kingdoms* and *changeth times*.[12]

It is worth asking if his references to crusading were in this respect any more exaggerated than earlier papal war propaganda. Although the idea of the crusade as Christ's own war, divinely commanded through the agency of the pope, was a powerfully developed theme in three reports of his sermon at Clermont, all written, it will be remembered, after the crusade had triumphed,[13] the language in his own letters was in comparison relatively restrained. He wrote of the crusaders as being inspired by God and as agents of God, who fought for them. Engaged 'in the service of God', they acted out of love for God. He told them, it is clear, that they were followers of Christ.[14] There is no contemporary evidence that he referred to them as *milites Christi* (knights of Christ), although surely he must have done so: the terms *exercitus Dei* (army of God), *exercitus Domini* (army of the Lord, which is synonymous with *militia Christi* or knighthood of Christ) and *milites Christi* were to be in use in the crusading army in Asia.[15] In the charters of departing crusaders the authority for the expedition was sometimes said to be God[16] and the crusade was known throughout France as the *via Dei* (way of God).[17] The concept of divine war for Christ was clearly present, but it was expressed no more stridently, perhaps more moderately, than it had been by Gregory VII. The difference was that it was now popular. Were it not for the response of the faithful and for later writings it might strike one as being fairly conventional and, although hyperbole, less hyperbolic than some other contemporary expostulations. I am inclined to believe that the authority of Christ, the most characteristic feature of crusading, was originally introduced in a conventional, even a muffled, way and that it was the extraordinary series of events that followed which convinced the crusaders that they really were engaged in a divine enterprise.[18]

Urban had no doubt that war against the Muslims in the East would be just and in this he reflected the thinking of his time and his own predilections: he had, of course, already supported wars against Muslims in Spain and Sicily. Given the theoretical studies of the reformers on violence, he had, moreover, a much firmer intellectual basis for his conviction that his summons to war had a just cause than had any of his predecessors. But we also find in his appeal an emphasis not prominent in Anselm of Lucca's transmission of the writings of St Augustine. For Augustine violence was justified in response to injury; for Urban this response took the form of a war of liberation. It is no exaggeration to say that 'liberation' was the word most frequently used by him when justifying the need to crusade. In this, of course, he, a Cluniac monk, reflected the monastic idealism of the reformers, among whom there had developed an exaggerated notion of liberty, bred in the great exempt monasteries from which reform ideas had sprung, where freedom from local ecclesiastical and secular control had been guaranteed by papal privilege. 'Liberation' had meant freedom under the popes – for dependence on the papacy was the corollary to such freedom – and it was the battle-cry of the most important reforming party.[18] The eleventh-century sources are full of the words *libertas* and *liberatio*, referring to a liberation conceived of in material, even legal, terms, although it was believed to have important consequences for the development of the spiritual life. Gregory VII had already referred to the need to 'liberate' the eastern Christians[19] and sooner or later the reformers were bound to turn from the struggle to 'liberate' Latin Christians to the plight of their eastern brothers, many of whom laboured under more grievous yokes than those imposed by any western king. Urban called for a war of liberation with two purposes. The first was the freeing of the eastern churches in general and the church of Jerusalem in particular from the oppression and ravages of the Muslims;[20] the second was the freeing of the city of Jerusalem from the servitude into which it had fallen.[21] So one aim was the liberation of people, the baptized members of the churches,[22] the other was the liberation of a place. It is clear that Urban saw the liberation of Christian people in the wider context of the liberation of the Church as a whole; in fact he referred to the crusaders going 'for the liberation of the Church'.[23] This was fairly conventional: the reformers had tended to associate the general needs of Christendom with their wars of liberation fought in Germany and Italy and Urban himself was later to state that by his victories in Sicily Count Roger had 'spread greatly the Church of God into Muslim territories' and, with reference to Spain, that

we ought to make many expressions of thanks to the mercies of God that in our time the Church has been enlarged, the domination of the Muslims has been reduced, the ancient honour of episcopal sees has been, by the gift of God, restored.[24]

In one eyewitness account of his sermon at Clermont he was made to compare the general benefit to the Church of the Carolingian wars of conquest with that promised by the crusade.[25]

His preoccupation with Spain before 1095, moreover, made it impossible for him to treat the crusade to the East in isolation. From the 1060's the reform papacy had been closely involved in Spanish affairs and the reconquest of Toledo by Alfonso VI of León in 1085 had caused a sensation. The subsequent appearance in Spain of the North African Almoravids, more intimidating to the Christians than the Moorish *taifa* kingdoms had been, created an anxiety which Urban shared.[26] But it was to the north-eastern corner of the peninsula that his attention had been particularly directed. The ancient Roman and Visigothic city of Tarragona, 50 miles down the coast from Barcelona, was a ghost town in the no-man's land between Christian and Muslim Spain. Every now and then the Christian counts of Barcelona had planned to restore it, and the Aragonese advance down the tributaries of the Ebro, which had begun in 1078, had at last opened the way for its reoccupation. Almost as soon as he came to the papal throne Urban enthusiastically took up the cause. He persuaded Count Berenguer Raymond of Barcelona to reoccupy the city and hold it as a frontier post and he authorized him to do so. It is not clear that Tarragona was actually occupied at this time – it did not pass fully into Christian hands until 1120 – but the activity reflected in Urban's letters around 1090 shows how seriously he was taking the matter. Count Berenguer made all his land, and specifically Tarragona, over to the pope as a *terra sancti Petri* (land of St Peter). Urban translated Bishop Berenguer of Vich to the newly established archdiocese of Tarragona and defined his rights as archbishop. He fostered colonization. In 1089 he encouraged the secular and religious leaders of the region to help in the rebuilding of the town, which was to be 'a wall and ante-mural of Christianity against the Muslims', and he introduced the language of indulgences, about which more below, enjoining them to do this 'in penitence and for the remission of sins'. He suggested that those who planned to make penitential pilgrimages – even to Jerusalem which, interestingly enough, he mentioned – should commute their penances to work on and contribute financially to the restoration of the city, and he assured them of the same indulgence as that which they would have gained by fulfilling the pilgrimage. In 1091 he repeated for the count of Urgel's benefit his assurance that those who aided the city, which he believed had begun to be restored, would have 'indulgence of your sins'.[27] At the time he preached the crusade, therefore, a military project involving the occupation of a frontier post in Spain, on land which was his own, and its defence against the Muslims, ordered by him and associated by him with an indulgence, was in train and it is not surprising that he was reluctant to allow diversion of effort from it. Some time after the Council of Clermont he wrote to the Catalonian counts of Besalú, Empurias, Roussillon and Cerdaña and their followers, who had taken the cross for Jerusalem, encouraging them to stay to help defend Tarragona and unequivocally associating this with the crusade.

If the knights of other provinces have decided with one mind to go to the aid of the Asian church and to liberate their brothers from the tyranny of the Muslims, so ought you with one mind and with our encouragement to work with greater endurance to help a church so near you resist the invasions of the Muslims. No one must doubt that if he dies on this expedition for the love of God and his brothers his sins will surely be forgiven and he will gain a share of eternal life through the most compassionate mercy of our God. So if any of you has made up his mind to go to Asia, it is here instead that he should try to fulfil his vow, because it is no virtue to rescue Christians from Muslims in one place, only to expose them to the tyranny and oppression of the Muslims in another.[28]

In 1099 he forbade Archbishop Bernard of Toledo, who had taken the cross and had reached Rome, to proceed to the East: he had already asked Bernard to take in hand the direction of the restoration of Tarragona.[29]

As far as the liberation of people was concerned, therefore, Urban regarded the new crusade to the East as part of a wider movement of Christian liberation and did not distinguish it from the Spanish Reconquest. This, which made an impression on at least one contemporary commentator, was reiterated by him in a letter of 1098 in which he wrote that 'in our days [God] has fought through Christian men in Asia against the Turks and in Europe against the Moors'. It was also made clear in the decrees of a council he held in Rome in April 1099, at which the crusade appeal was renewed and it was laid down that an arsonist's penance should be 'that he remains in the service of God in Jerusalem or in Spain for one year'.[30]

The other goal of the crusade was the liberation of a specific place. Wars with such an aim were, of course, as old as war itself and the letters of Urban are full of references to other campaigns of this sort: '*Toletana* [Toledo] *est ecclesia liberata*'; '*Siciliae insulam . . . liberavit*'; '*Oscam* [Huesca] . . . *urbem Saracenorum tyrannide liberatam*'.[31] But Jerusalem was special. A natural centre of interest to Christians, it had been elevated further by the heightened veneration of relics, the popularity of cult centres and the growth of pilgrimages. There had already been a revival on a large scale of pilgrimages from the West to Jerusalem, the overland route to which had been partially cleared by the conversion of Hungary to Christianity and the Byzantine victories over the Bulgars and Muslims in the late tenth century. Large numbers of people were regularly departing for Jerusalem with the encouragement of the monasteries[32] and there was traffic right up to the eve of the crusade and beyond. Six months before the Council of Clermont Count Roger of Foix was making preparations for a pilgrimage, while a knight called Odard, who endowed the abbey of Jumièges in the spring of 1098, appears to have just returned from Jerusalem: he must have travelled out and back peacefully as a pilgrim at the very time his fellow knights were battering their way through Asia Minor and suffering before the city of Antioch.[33] In fact the attitude of eleventh-century Christians towards Jerusalem and the Holy Land was obsessive. Jerusalem was the centre of the world, the spot on earth on which God himself had focused when he chose to redeem mankind by intervening in history; at the same place, at the end of time, the last events leading to Doomsday would be enacted. In this respect a prophetic tradition, culminating in the re-working around the year 1000 of the Late Roman Tiburtine Sibylline writings, seems to have been very influential. Before the world's end, it was said, a last emperor would be crowned in Jerusalem. This legend had been the subject of discussion in Italian circles, both papal and imperialist. We have seen that in 1074 Gregory VII had proposed to lead an army to the East which might push on to the Holy Sepulchre. On the other side, the imperialist Benzo of Alba had been moved to advise Henry IV of Germany to go to Jerusalem where, after conquering his enemies and the pagans, he would stand in glory.[34] Jerusalem and the land around it, moreover, was a relic, having absorbed the *virtus*, the sacred power, of the prophets and holy men of Israel, the apostles and first Christians and above all Christ himself, the incarnate God. He had walked there. He had been baptized in the waters of the Jordan. He had been crucified on Golgotha, where the ground had soaked up his blood. He had been laid to rest in the Holy Sepulchre, from which he had risen. In an age in which, as we have seen, men felt strongly the cultic power of those localities where saints had lived or where their relics rested and in which the ideals were set by monks whose lives and interests were bound up with the maintenance of such shrines, Jerusalem was bound to outshine all others, even such great depositories of relics as Rome and Constantinople. Beyond this, the Holy Land was the physical inheritance, the patrimony, of Christ. No passage of scripture was to be more often quoted in connection with crusading than the opening words of Psalm 78 (79): 'O God, the heathens are come into thy inheritance'.

In the context of eleventh-century thought and devotion the view which prevailed until recently, that Urban's primary aim was to help the Greeks and that in his mind Jerusalem was secondary, in the sense that the restoration of the eastern church in general would lead to its liberation in the end,[35] is untenable. It is not justified by the evidence for his preaching,[36] and it is impossible to believe that a man like him, trained in the monastic life, could have mentioned Jerusalem without conjuring up images of Zion and the holy city that would have impinged strongly on his consciousness by virtue of their constant repetition in the psalmody of the divine office. There is, in fact, evidence that as the news of the crusade's successes began to reach the West he himself was drawn to join it[37] and that he began to have even wilder ambitions, including the conquest of Egypt.[38] That the goal of Jerusalem was central to the crusade from the first is confirmed by the charters of departing crusaders, in which the holy city is so clearly and uniformly at the centre of the stage that it is impossible to believe that in this respect Urban's message was being distorted. Many charters contain references to Jerusalem as the goal of the impending expedition.[39] Two give its liberation as the aim.[40] I know of only one in which mention is made of the sufferings of the Christian people in the East.[41]

It was the goal of Jerusalem that made the crusade a pilgrimage. There is no doubt that Urban preached the crusade at Clermont as a pilgrimage[42] and many of the measures he took brought it into line with pilgrimage practices. He extended the protection of the Church to crusaders, decreeing that their property was to be inviolate until their return. This protection was associated specifically with the Truce of God, the means by which the Peace of God movement had prohibited all violence at certain times, but it must also have been linked to existing pilgrimage regulations,[43] as may have been the pope's insistence that parishioners get permission from their parish priests and young men the agreement of their wives before departure.[44] He also introduced a vow to be taken by the participants, which was signified by the wearing of a cross.[45] He must have come to the conclusion that some sort of vow was necessary by the time of the Council of Piacenza in March 1095, because there, as we have seen, he exhorted westerners 'to take an oath' to help the Greeks.[46] Whether this was to be a full vow in the technical sense, or simply a looser oath of association binding members of the company together, is not clear. But it is certain that the vow introduced at the Council of Clermont was a *votum*, a proper vow, made to God, to fight for him on a journey to Jerusalem; only there could it be fulfilled.[47] Although there survive no formal regulations in canon law as early as this, it is clear that by the late eleventh century at least some pilgrims had been making vows before their departure – a great German pilgrimage to Jerusalem in 1064–5 had consisted of *c.*7000 persons, who had made vows which they regarded as being fulfilled on their arrival in the holy city[48] – and in the twelfth century crusade and pilgrim vows were equated with one another and were, as far as we can tell, indistinguishable. It is, therefore, safe to assume that the crusade vow came into being as a consequence of the crusade being treated as a pilgrimage and it is easy to see how the giving of pilgrim status to crusaders in this way made it possible for the pope to control them to some extent, since pilgrims were treated in law as temporary ecclesiastics, subject to church courts.[49] Indeed the fact that this was a public vow enforceable by the Church was soon to be stressed. In October 1097 the clergy accompanying the crusade appealed for the excommunication of those who had not left for the East as they had promised, and in the following January they formally excommunicated those westerners who had not joined the army and asked their colleagues in the West to do the same. In September 1098 the leaders at Antioch were worried by a rumour that Urban had allowed those who had not carried out their vows to remain at home: perhaps he had dispensed those too poor to go, as his successor Paschal II did, or those who were not physically suitable, as did Archbishop Manasses of Rheims. But the fears of the leaders were misplaced. Before his death Urban seems to have ordered the enforcement of the vows with the sanction of excommunication, and this was repeated by Paschal II and carried through by the diocesan bishops.[50]

The fact that the crusade was a pilgrimage was well understood by those taking the cross, as their charters to religious houses demonstrate. One of them described the crusade entirely in pilgrimage terms:

> Considering that God has spared me, steeped in many and great sins, and has given me time for penance, and fearing that the weight of my sins will deprive me of a share in the heavenly kingdom, I, Ingelbald, wish to seek that sepulchre from which our redemption, having overcome death, wished to rise.[51]

And two brothers stated that they were going to Jerusalem

> on the one hand for the grace of the pilgrimage and on the other, under the protection of God, to wipe out the defilement of the

pagans and the immoderate madness through which innumerable Christians have already been oppressed, made captive and killed with barbaric fury.[52]

The crusaders on the march regarded themselves as pilgrims and observed the liturgical exercises traditionally associated with pilgrimages.[53] They were, however, taking part in an odd sort of pilgrimage, because they were engaged in a military campaign[54] and, more importantly, because the needs of war meant that this pilgrimage was preached as one only for healthy young men. At Clermont Urban tried to limit the types of person taking part. The old, the infirm and women were not suitable, although women apparently could go with their husbands and brothers provided they had permission from the church authorities. The wording in the sources is woolly; the prohibitions, at least as far as the laity were concerned, were not absolute.[55] Nor could they be. Pilgrimages had always been open to all kinds of person, especially the penitent; and recently the sick were increasingly going on them to be cured. It is true that the Holy Sepulchre, like St Peter's in Rome and St James's in Compostella, was not renowned for healing miracles, being a goal for penitents rather than the sick, although people went there to die.[56] But there can be no escaping the fact that a pilgrimage of the young and healthy and masculine broke with established practices. There was no way in which the pope could absolutely forbid any of the faithful to go, if they were not monks or clerics, and this partly accounted for the Church's failure to control recruitment and the large numbers of the unsuitable who did join the expedition.

Urban's introduction of the cross to be sewn on the crusaders' clothing must also have been associated with the pilgrimage to Jerusalem, but in addition it was a manifestation of a powerful theme in contemporary devotional writings: the importance of the cross to Christians.[57] The pope, who had already in 1093 referred to Muslims as 'enemies of the cross',[58] directly equated the wearing of it with one of Christ's most striking precepts, 'If any man will come after me, let him deny himself and take up his cross and follow me' (Matthew 16:24 or Luke 14:27), which he appears to have linked to another, 'Every one that hath left house or brethren or sisters or father or mother or wife or children or lands, for my name's sake, shall receive an hundredfold and shall possess life everlasting' (Matthew 19:29). In September 1098 the leaders of the crusade in Syria referred to him as 'You who by your sermons made us all leave our lands and whatever was in them and ordered us to follow Christ by taking up our crosses'.[59]

Urban appealed particularly to the French and in doing this he broke with the recent practice of popes and harked back to the policies of his eighth- and ninth-century predecessors. It is true that as he began to realize how great was the enthusiasm elsewhere he was prepared to encourage other nationalities to join, except, of course, the Spaniards. He expressed approval of the zeal shown by his partisans in Bologna;[60] and a concern for maritime support must have led to his despatching a high-level delegation, consisting of the bishops of Grenoble and Orange, to Genoa as early as July 1096 after the Council of Nîmes.[61] He sent appeals to Pisa and Milan in 1098 and 1099 when further reinforcements were needed.[62] But his choice of Clermont for his first summons and his itinerary after the council show that his primary concern was to recruit Frenchmen, something that was natural in a man of his origins, born into the class and region from which much support for the crusade was to come.[63] He himself wrote that 'we visited Gaul and urged most fervently the lords and subjects of that land to liberate the eastern churches',[64] and a contemporary report of his sermon at Angers in February 1096 confirmed that his appeal was directed especially to the French: 'The pope ... came to Angers and exhorted our people to go to Jerusalem'.[65] A later account of his sermon at Clermont made him remind his audience of the exploits of past Frankish rulers like Charlemagne and Louis the Pious.

> May the stories of your ancestors move you and excite your souls to strength; the worth and greatness of King Charlemagne and of Louis his son and of others of your kings, who destroyed the kingdoms of the pagans and extended into them the boundaries of Holy Church.[66]

That he did address the council in such terms is likely, given the style of exhortation to be found in a letter he wrote to the king of Hungary in 1096, encouraging him to take up arms against the anti-pope.

> Raise, O king, the glorious standard of the catholic faith, which

ought to share the victory and glory with the secular banners of your kingdom. . . . Be mindful . . . of the religious prince Stephen, who was the first of your family to receive the faith from the Holy Roman and Apostolic Church.[67]

He stressed that the crusade was an enterprise for the laity, knights and footsoldiers. Priests, clerks and monks were not to go without licence from their bishops and abbots. In fact he did not want monks to go at all: he made this very clear at Clermont and he later explained why.

We were stimulating the minds of knights to go on this expedition, since they might be able to restrain the savagery of the Muslims by their arms and restore the Christians to their former freedom: we do not want those who have abandoned the world and have vowed themselves to spiritual warfare either to bear arms or to go on this journey; we go so far as to forbid them to do so.[68]

One interesting feature of his summons is that it was addressed not just to the great magnates but also to their followers.[69] Urban clearly had in mind the castellans and their knights and this must have led to the comparison, which was almost certainly included in his sermon at Clermont, between old reprobate warriors and new Christian knights.[70] His message was given further point by the fact that the Council of Clermont under his presidency renewed the Peace of God decrees. The more one considers the question the more clearly it appears that Urban was deliberately appealing to those elements in French society which had been so disruptive in the past and were not to be brought to heel until the twelfth century.[71] This marked, as we have seen, the culmination of a movement by the Church towards the laity which had begun a century earlier. Urban stated explicitly that participation in the crusade would be an act of merit, that is to say something that would contribute to a man's salvation. He called it a *recta oblatio* (a right kind of sacrifice) and an act of devotion for the salvation of the participant's soul.[72] It was meritorious because the crusaders would be obeying Christ's injunction to take up their crosses and follow him and because they would be expressing in this their love of God and their neighbours.[73] So the Church was beginning to suggest not simply a role for the laity that operated through grace, but was putting forward the crusade as a way of the cross, a path to salvation which, it had previously been thought, only religious could be sure of taking.

The idea that war could be meritorious had been occasionally voiced since the eighth century, particularly in references to the dead in wars against infidels or enemies of the Church as martyrs; and statements of this sort had become perceptibly more common since the middle of the eleventh century.[74] But crucial to Urban's thinking, with its emphasis on love, was probably Anselm of Lucca's inclusion in his *Collectio canonum* of extracts on the subject from the writings of St Augustine, who had justified violence as an expression of Christian charity. To Augustine the intentions of those who authorized violence and of those who participated in it had to be in favour of justice, which worked through love of God and one's neighbour. It followed that just violence had to have love for those on whom it was meted out as the mainspring of action. The intention of just violence was to make the offender happy; it was often, indeed, more loving to use force than indulgence and Augustine wrote of the way parents could express their love for their children by correcting them and of the violence sometimes needed in healing the sick or in rescuing men against their wills from physical danger. The scriptures were combed by him for references to acts of violence or justifications of it, motivated by love and perpetrated by Moses and Elijah, St Paul, a loving God and even a loving Christ, who scourged the stall-keepers from the Temple and blinded St Paul on the road to Damascus. In his public statements Urban did not follow Augustine as far as speaking of the crusade as an expression of love for the enemies, the Muslims; he stressed instead love of Christian brothers and the risking of life to save them, possibly because his audiences simply would not have comprehended the more rounded theological view.[75]

He also proposed the crusade as a severe and highly meritorious penance, as can be seen in his grants of the indulgence. In recent years historians have tried to trace a direct line of development from his formulae to the mature indulgences of Pope Innocent III, with their emphasis on God's mercy and their promise to sinners of the remission of the temporal punishments for sin imposed by God in this world or in purgatory, through the mediatory Power of the Keys, and they have concluded that Urban's indulgences were confused and contradictory. But it is unlikely that the pope was unclear about what he was granting and there is no sign of confusion among the clergy who wrote the crusaders' charters for them: they believed that participation in the crusade would 'remit sins' and help to save a man's soul.[76] Urban's pronouncements become clear once one gives up trying to reconcile them with the new theology of penance that became popular in the course of the twelfth century. A starting point for him was the already slightly old-fashioned idea that penance could be 'satisfactory', which meant that the performance of it could counterbalance sin and purge the sinner of it, so that through self-imposed punishment he could repay God what was due. A penance as severe as the crusade could be entirely satisfactory, counterbalancing all previous sin and making good any previous unsatisfactory penances. Almost a century after the Council of Clermont this interpretation of the crusade indulgence could still be given by a senior churchman.

> By the privilege of the apostle Peter and the general authority of the Church, the Lord has set forth the word of reconciliation in this sign [of the cross], so that the adoption of the way to Jerusalem should be a complete penance and sufficient satisfaction for sins committed.[77]

In c.1135 the historian Orderic Vitalis had given precisely the same explanation of Urban's indulgence to the first crusaders.

> The pope urged all who could bear arms to fight against the enemies of God, and on God's authority he absolved all the penitent from all their sins from the hour they took the Lord's cross and he lovingly released them from all hardships, whether fasting or other mortification of the flesh. As a wise and kind doctor he had the foresight to see that those who pilgrimaged would be most severely tried by many and daily perils on the way and would be troubled each day by many kinds of accident, happy and sad, through which the willing servants of Christ would make amends for all the filth of their faults.[78]

So Urban's indulgence was no more than an authoritative declaration that the crusade was so severely penitential an exercise that it would be satisfactory penance for all previous sins. And this seems to be confirmed by his indulgence for those he wanted to remain fighting the Moors in Spain. It looks as though these men were assured of a plenary indulgence only if they died, which makes sense if one takes into account the fact that the restoration and defence of Tarragona was obviously a far less demanding enterprise than the march to Jerusalem.[79] Seen in this light, his formulae are no longer ambiguous.

> Whoever for devotion only, not to gain honour or money, goes to Jerusalem to liberate the Church of God can substitute this journey for all penance.[80]
> We acting as much on our own authority as on that of all the archbishops and bishops in Gaul, through the mercy of almighty God and the prayers of the catholic church, relieve them of all penance imposed for their sins.[81]

Nor does his use elsewhere of the phrase 'for the remission of all their sins'[82] seem any longer to be in conflict with the references to penance in these formulae, since sins were obviously remitted by fully satisfactory penances. In fact Urban's indulgence was fairly conventional, even a little old-fashioned, and, although it seems to have come to many of the faithful as a surprise, it was not unprecedented: over thirty years before Pope Alexander II had granted a very similar one to Christian warriors in Spain, perhaps to those who were fighting to recover the town of Barbastro.[83]

From the point of view of churchmen in reforming circles in Italy, nothing Urban proposed was particularly novel, except perhaps for the idea of an appeal of this sort being aimed at the French; and even here the novelty was relative only to the previous two centuries, which had seen the rise of the rulers of Germany and the breakdown of central authority in West Francia. In some ways, indeed, the pope's appeal was less radical than those that had been made by reformers in the recent past. That is not to say, of course, that it struck his audience as being a conventional one – patently it did not – but the excitement he aroused is really only evidence of the backwardness of much of western Europe and the difficulty the reformers had had in getting their message into the Christian provinces. Given his earlier concentration on the Spanish Reconquest, Urban must have regarded his proposal as being a reasonably moderate if ambitious expression of ideas already exhaustively discussed in the highest church circles.

But never before had a holy war been proclaimed by a pope on Christ's behalf, the participants in which were treated as pilgrims, took vows and enjoyed indulgences. The war preached at Clermont really was the First Crusade. It is often said that in doing this Urban created a new 'synthesis', which is acceptable provided one realizes that some of the elements, particularly the crucial concept of fighting for Christ, were very embryonic and were to be transformed in the minds of the crusaders as they suffered in Asia. It was not until after the crusade was over that a coherent and internally consistent body of thought was to be distilled.

Chapter 2

The response of lay people

Urban made quite strenuous efforts to publicize his proclamation of war. A letter of his to the people of Flanders is dated very soon after the Council of Clermont.[1] He followed up his tour of France, as we have seen, with embassies or letters to Genoa, Bologna, Pisa and Milan, and the crusade was on the agenda of councils he held at Bari in October 1098[2] and Rome in April 1099.[3] At Clermont and possibly again at Nîmes he encouraged all the bishops present to preach the cross in their dioceses.[4] Hugh of Die, the archbishop of Lyons and an enthusiastic reformer, certainly promoted the crusade and so did several other bishops,[5] but not all appear to have carried out the pope's instructions energetically. Very few copies of the Clermont decree on the crusade indulgence survive, which suggests that few of the bishops took the trouble to have it copied. One of those who did, Lambert of Arras, has left us his own account of the council, in which no reference is made to the crusade at all: for Lambert the most important result was naturally the pope's confirmation of the standing of his own bishopric.[6] And there is no record of the crusade being discussed at the Council of Rouen of February 1096, which republished many of the Clermont decrees.[7] Enthusiasm was generated by the sermons of freelancers like Peter the Hermit and by monks, who were often active recruiting officers: the abbot of Maillezais seems to have been prominent as a preacher;[8] Duke Robert of Normandy was persuaded to crusade by 'certain religious';[9] and there were religious houses which were agencies of recruitment, perhaps because they were enthusiastic or rich or business-like enough to be centres for the disposal of property and the raising of funds: Cluny and St Vincent of Le Mans stand out.

In whatever way the news was spread – one contemporary exclaimed that it travelled so fast that there was no need for preaching[10] – there is little doubt that it passed quickly from Clermont into areas which were not visited personally by the pope. As early as 11 February 1096 King Philip of France and his brother Hugh of

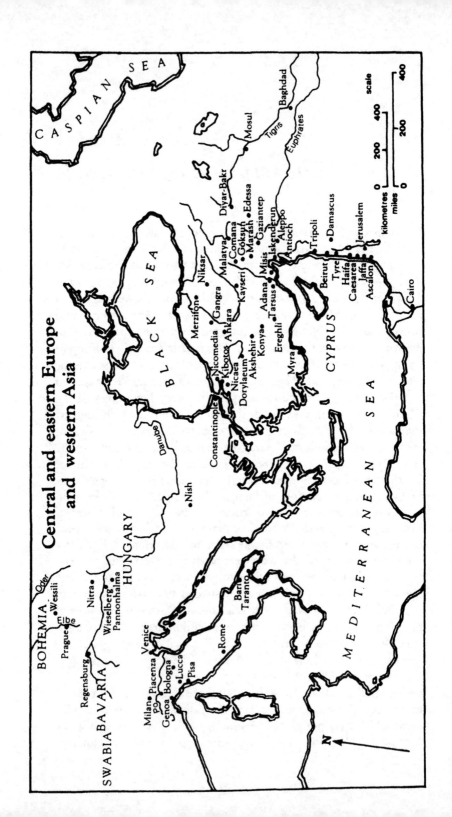

Central and eastern Europe and western Asia

Vermandois held discussions about the crusade in Paris with some of the greater nobles.[11] The message was all the more forceful for being proclaimed in the flickering light of a remarkable sequence of natural wonders, which began before Clermont, continued during the preaching in 1096 and then, after a break, resumed in the autumn of 1097, enveloping the crusade in a magical penumbra. Our evidence for these occurrences comes from reports written after the crusade had been successful and it was natural, given contemporary cosmology, for men to search for portents of such a great event. But even allowing for that, the skies seem to have been unusually disturbed because of a gradual increase in solar activity, leading to the period of heightened disturbance which is now known to have lasted from *c*.1120 to *c*.1280. This gave later writers the opportunity to dwell on the way nature foretold the liberation of Jerusalem.

In the time of the emperor Henry IV . . . according to the prophecies in the Gospels, everywhere *nation* arose against *nation and kingdom against kingdom*; and there were *great earthquakes in divers places, and pestilences and famines and terrors from heaven and great signs*. And because already in all nations the evangelical trumpet was sounding the coming of the Just Judge, the universal Church beheld throughout the whole world the portents in prophetic signs.[12]
When it was God's will and pleasure to free the Holy Sepulchre, in which his son had lain for the sins of men, from the power of the pagans and to open the way to Christians desiring to travel there for the redemption of their souls, he showed many signs, powers, prodigies and portents to sharpen the minds of Christians so that they should want to hurry there. For the stars in the sky were seen throughout the whole world to fall towards the earth, crowded together and dense, like hail or snowflakes. A short while later a fiery way appeared in the heavens; and then after another short period half the sky turned the colour of blood. Many dreams and visions were experienced, too many for anyone to count.[13]

The sequence opened on 4 April 1095, seven months before the Council of Clermont, when a meteor shower was seen throughout France.[14] On 11 February 1096, when the king, his brother and the magnates of the kingdom were meeting to discuss the crusade, there was an eclipse of the moon, during which it turned red. This was followed in March by a 'sign in the sun' and by an aurora which so frightened people that litanies were said in the churches. In August there was another eclipse of the moon.[15] There was then a gap until the autumn of 1097, when a comet was sighted. In February 1098 the sky glowed red. In the following autumn there was a great light seen in the sky, which appeared to be on fire all one night. In December there was an eclipse of the sun and in February 1099 another red aurora filled the eastern sky.[16] From the autumn of 1097 onwards signs in the heavens were also observed by the crusaders in Syria, as we shall see. Meanwhile a severe drought, which had lasted for several years and had been responsible for a succession of bad harvests and famine in France, ended abruptly in 1096 with a wet spring followed by a magnificent harvest.[17]

Against this spectacular backdrop the preaching of the crusade went ahead and the news of the preaching spread. In France, western Germany and Italy there was a large response. There can be no doubt that there was a hysterical element in it, whipped up by demagogues like Peter the Hermit, who claimed to have been summoned to preach the crusade by Christ himself and brandished a celestial letter of commission.[18] The hysteria may have fed on eschatological expectations, drawing on the popular prophecy of the last emperor in occupation of Jerusalem before the Last Days. It manifested itself in visions,[19] in brandings of crosses on the flesh of a significant number of crusaders,[20] and probably also in the behaviour of Count Emich of Leiningen, the most merciless persecutor of the Rhineland Jews in the early summer of 1096. A Jewish writer reported that

> [Emich] concocted a tale that an apostle of the crucified one had come to him and made a sign on his flesh to inform him that when he arrived in Greek Italy [the crucified one] himself would appear and place a kingly crown upon his head, and Emich would van-quish his foes.

This is obviously a reference to the prophecy of the last emperor, in whose reign, it was believed, the Jews would be converted to Christianity.[21] That Emich claimed to have had a vision is confirmed in the account of him by the German abbot Ekkehard of Aura. 'Emich . . . like another Saul, called, it is said, by divine revelations to religious practice of this sort [the crusade].' Ekkehard's comparison of Emich with Saul suggests that he thought him very unstable. To the Jewish chroniclers he was merciless and wicked. Ekkehard reported that even before the crusade he was 'notorious for his tyrannical behaviour' and that after his death in 1117 his ghost was believed to haunt the region of Mainz imploring alms and prayers from the faithful so that he might be released.[22]

Enthusiasm for the crusade, moreover, was to be found in classes that Urban had not intended to arouse. I have already drawn attention to the curious kind of pilgrimage he preached, because he aimed his message specifically at knights and tried to limit the crusade to them, and to the fact that since it was a pilgrimage it was impossible for him to prevent women, children, the old and the sick vowing to go if they were determined enough. What is more, the preaching of the crusade coincided with outbreaks of ergotism or *ignis sacer*, an unpleasant disease that was caused by eating bread made from mouldy rye. Epidemics in France often resulted in mass pilgrimages. Urban appears to have taken steps to alleviate the suffering caused by the illness during his visit to France and he must have known that a mass, even a hysterical, response to his call was likely.[23] He had put the responsibility of controlling recruitment on the parish priests, whose advice must be sought by everyone intending to take the cross,[24] but the parochial system was not yet adequate to cope with the task. A rich noblewoman called Emerias of *Alteias* took the cross and went to ask her bishop for his blessing before her departure. He suggested that it would be better for her to establish a hospice to care for the poor. She agreed to this commutation of her vow, but it is noteworthy that she seems to have had little difficulty in making it in the first place and it was only the bishop who was able to persuade her to change her mind.[25] It is, therefore, not surprising that the crusade contained large numbers of women and children and poor people.

It is difficult to believe, however, that hysteria affected more than a minority of crusaders. Millenarianism was certainly a subject of discussion, as is demonstrated by contemporary references to the Muslims as attendants of Antichrist and a number of allusions to the Last Days and to signs and portents of them, but the evidence is not copious enough for us to suppose that eschatological ideas were widespread.[26] And although we should never underestimate the importance of the non-combatants and the poor we should not overestimate it either. We shall see, for instance, that the so-called peasant armies were run by knights and probably contained almost as many knights as the other armies did.

There is, in fact, a significant body of material dating from the eve of the crusade which purports to reveal the feelings of the magnates, castellans and knights on taking the cross. It is made up on the whole of their charters in favour of churches and monasteries. In it a serious and purposeful devotion on the part of would-be crusaders comes across, suggesting that the south Italian Norman Tancred's reaction to the news of the preaching of the crusade, described by his biographer Ralph of Caen, was typical.

Frequently he burned with anxiety because the warfare he engaged in as a knight seemed to be contrary to the Lord's commands. The Lord, in fact, ordered him to offer the cheek that had been struck together with his other cheek to the striker; but secular knighthood did not spare the blood of relatives. The Lord urged him to give his tunic and his cloak as well to the man who would take them away; the needs of war impelled him to take from a man already despoiled of both whatever remained to him. And so, if ever that wise man could give himself up to repose, these contradictions deprived him of courage. But after the judgement of Pope Urban granted remission of all their sins to all Christians going out to fight the gentiles, then at last, as if previously asleep, his vigour was aroused, his powers grew, his eyes opened, his courage was born. For before . . . his mind was divided, uncertain whether to follow in the footsteps of the Gospel or the world.[27]

It seems to have been a pious desire to arrange for adequate intercessory prayer, combined no doubt with apprehension, that led crusaders to make gifts to religious houses before they departed and testamentary provisions in favour of religious communities should they die. In a generous donation to the cathedral of Le Puy, for instance, Raymond of St Gilles stipulated that for as long as he should live a candle should burn continually before the statue of the Virgin Mary at Le Puy; after his death the Office of the Dead was to be sung once a year for him there and in other churches subject to the cathedral; and for the rest of time a daily prayer was to be said on his behalf. Hugh of Apigné surrendered a tithe to the nuns of St George of Rennes on condition that they commemorate the anniversary of his death. Anger fitz-Robert gave a rent to the monks of St Vincent of Le Mans for the benefit of his soul and that of his father.[28]

The charters also reveal the crusaders' concern, which was to be shown by their successors in the movement and was perhaps already a traditional preparation for pilgrimage, to leave their affairs at home in the best possible state by resolving any disputes in which they happened to be involved, particularly with churches. Anselm of Ribemont ended a quarrel with the monastery of St Amand over mills and their use of water and the rights of a new settlement he had established, a quarrel that had led to his anathematization by the abbot and the formal humiliation of the monastery's relics. Baldwin of Guines appears to have at last allowed the transfer to the church of Watten of four prebends at Licques endowed by his father. Raymond of St Gilles resolved a dispute with the abbey of St Gilles in the pope's presence at the Council of Nîmes, and he made his large endowment to the cathedral of Le Puy

for the redemption of my crimes and those of my parents and for the honour and love of St Giles, whom I have frequently offended by many kinds of injuries, so that his feast may be celebrated annually in the church of Le Puy and at other churches subject to her.[29]

Sometimes these renunciations of injury were part of an agreement from which the crusader benefited financially. Godfrey of Bouillon mortgaged or sold all his allodial properties to the bishops of Liége and Verdun in arrangements which brought to an end long-standing disputes with them in return for cash for himself and his brother Baldwin. Count Guy of Chalon-sur-Sâone visited the community of Paray-le-Monial and formally renounced exactions he had been accustomed to demand in return for a good mule. Hugh of Juillé agreed to sales made by his father to the abbey of St Vincent of Le Mans in return for 20 *solidi*.[30] Of course the abandonment of a technical or unjustifiable claim in return for cash was a good first step in raising money, but that there was more to at least some of these arrangements than mere financial expediency is suggested by four of them. The lord Nivelo was given £10 by the religious of St Père of Chartres in return for the renunciation of rights he had maintained, like a typical castellan, by force. He agreed to the formulation of his surrender in an abject way.

I Nivelo, raised in a nobility of birth which produces in many people an ignobility of mind, for the redemption of my soul and in exchange for a great sum of money given me for this, renounce for ever in favour of St Peter an oppressive behaviour resulting from a certain bad custom, handed on to me not by ancient right but from the time of my father, a man of little weight who first harassed the poor with this oppression. Thereafter I constantly maintained it in an atrociously tyrannical manner. I had harshly worn down the land of St Peter, that is to say Emprainville and the places around it, in the way that had become customary, by seizing the goods of the inhabitants there. This was the rough nature of this custom. Whenever the onset of knightly ferocity stirred me up, I used to descend on the aforesaid village, taking with me a troop of my knights and a crowd of my attendants, and against nature I would make over the goods of the men of St Peter for food for my knights. . . . Everyone ought to note that I made satisfaction to St Peter for such abominable past injuries and that I will forever desist from causing this restless trouble, which is now stilled.[31]

Bertrand of Moncontour had retained in his possession two-thirds of the property with which his father had endowed Trinity of Vendôme. Now he gave it up in return for 1,800 *solidi*, but also because 'he believed that the Way of God [the crusade] could in no way benefit him while he held these proceeds of theft'.[32] Similarly, Hugh Bochard renounced his usurpation of a peasant's holding which belonged to St Philibert of Tournous in return for £4 and a mule and because 'he feared punishment for this sin and wished to go to Jerusalem'.[33] Three knights of the castle of Mezenc, Peter *Bastarcius*, Pons and Bertrand, had been extremely violent and oppressive towards villagers of the abbey of St Chaffre of Le Monastier. They renounced their depredations in return for cash and also because they had vowed to join the crusade. They were given absolution by the bishop of Mende and by Bishop Adhémar of Le Puy himself, who was 'astonished at their cruelty, but absolved them from their crime on account of the fact that they were going on the expedition to Jerusalem and on account of their contrition'.[34]

The evidence of the charters suggests, therefore, that the response of the knights to Urban's call was idealistic. But of course the surviving charters concern only a fraction of the crusaders and the question anyway arises whether documents written by fairly well-educated clerics mainly for the benefit of their own communities are misleading. Many of the ideas expressed in them cannot be supposed to reflect accurately the notions of a largely uneducated class. It is, for instance, highly unlikely that Nivelo, who made his mark and so presumably could not write, recognized an apposite quotation from St Gregory I which appeared in the preamble to his charter. It is true that most contemporary commentators, who were, of course, propagandists for the movement, portrayed the crusaders in a highly favourable light as idealists who had renounced wordly things. But theirs was not the only view. When, according to one story, St Ambrose appeared to an Italian priest and asked him why there had been such a great response to Urban's appeal, the priest replied that he was troubled, because

different people give different reasons for this journey. Some say that in all pilgrims the desire for it has been aroused by God and the Lord Jesus Christ. Others maintain that the French lords and most of the people have begun the journey for frivolous reasons and that it was because of this that setbacks befell so many pilgrims in the kingdom of Hungary and in other kingdoms. And for that reason they cannot succeed.[35]

According to Ekkehard of Aura:

It was easy to persuade the western Franks to leave their farms. For Gaul had been afflicted for some years, sometimes by civil war, sometimes by famine, sometimes by an excessive death-rate. Finally a plague . . . had terrified the people to the point at which they despaired of life. . . . Of other nations or persons not covered by the papal edict, some confessed that they had been summoned to go to the Promised Land by certain prophets recently arisen among them or by signs in the heavens and revelations; others that they had been compelled to take such vows by all kinds of personal disadvantages. In fact many of them were burdened on the journey with wives and children and all their domestic goods.[36]

Urban may well have drawn the attention of his audience at Clermont to the possibility of amassing wealth; certainly the decree on the crusade indulgence issued by the council, with its limitation of the remission of penance to those who crusaded 'for devotion only, not to gain honour or money', is evidence that the pope and the French bishops were aware that some at least would take the cross for material reasons, while apparently the pope had to make a ruling on future conquests, stipulating that the churches which were restored would appertain to the principalities established by the crusade. The meaning of this ruling is not clear, since it seems to imply the sort of lay dominance over churches that would have been unacceptable to reformers. Perhaps Urban considered this to be a theoretical question, because he must have assumed that there would be an active Byzantine participation in the conquests and therefore the extension of Greek, rather than Latin, civil power. But the issue became a live one once Antioch had been taken by the crusaders without Byzantine assistance, and the decision at Clermont was confirmed by a 'council' held in the newly occupied city, presided over by the papal legate, Adhémar of Le Puy.[37] Even the propagandists agreed that the crusading armies contained adventurers and charlatans, although most of these were not knights. There is, however, evidence for a materialistic element among the knights as well. Wolfker of Kuffern, a German nobleman, and Achard of Montmerle, a young castellan who was to be killed near Jaffa, had clauses written into their mortgages to cover the contingency that they might settle in the East.[38] Norgeot of Toucy crusaded without making his peace with the abbey of Fleury, on a village of which he, like Nivelo and Peter *Bastarcius*, had imposed unjust exactions. Dying on a later pilgrimage to Jerusalem, he confessed his sins to the patriarch and was told that penance was fruitless unless he made restitution. So he sent letters to his wife and men to renounce his claims.[39]

A number of knights, moreover, failed to fulfil their vows. Some may have had good reasons. Count Helias of Maine, for instance, who was reputed to be very devout, took the cross but then refused to depart when he learnt that King William of England was determined to seize his county. He apparently converted the defence of his lands into a personal crusade, although our evidence for this comes from the pen of Orderic Vitalis, writing forty years later in the light of the tendency to transfer crusading ideas to other theatres of war that, we will see, followed the triumph of the liberation of Jerusalem.

I wished to fight the pagans in the Lord's name, but now I see that I must wage a war nearer to home against enemies of Christ. Everyone who resists truth and justice shows himself to be an enemy of God, who is truth itself and the sun of justice. . . . I will not abandon the cross of Our Savour with which I have been signed in the manner of a pilgrim, but I will have it put on my shield, my helmet and all my arms and I will imprint the image of the holy cross on my saddle and bridle. Fortified by this sign I will proceed against the enemies of peace and right and I will defend by force the lands of Christians. And so my horse and my arms will be marked with a holy image and all foes who attack me will be fighting against a knight of Christ. I trust him who rules the world to know the secrets of my heart and I will wait, through his clemency, for a better time to fulfil my vow.[40]

But many others had no good reason for staying behind and from the autumn of 1097 onwards the existence of this potential relief force became something of an obsession with those who were directly engaged in the toil and dangers of the campaign. We have already seen that the bishops in the army excommunicated them and expressed the hope that their brothers in the West would do the same and that in September 1098 there was astonishment at an unjustified rumour that Urban had dispensed them from their vows. It is impossible to guess at the numbers involved – although those on the crusade clearly believed that there were many of them – but the size of the crusade of 1101, in which many of them took part, suggests that they were numerous.

'Honour and money': the narrative accounts of the crusade echo the wording of the Clermont decree. There can be little doubt that a desire for earthly glory, present or posthumous, did motivate the knights. It was bound to do so, given their backgrounds and the traditions of knight-errantry already growing among them, although it is impossible to quantify its effects. A man might take the cross to acquire honour, or he might take it when his honour was impugned, as did Arnulf of Hednith, who was to die at Antioch and had left England after being falsely accused of treason.[41] Honour was certainly gained, as we shall see. As for money, we shall also see that for understandable reasons – above all the need to live – the crusaders became obsessed by loot but that there is little evidence for them returning home rich in anything but relics, which is not surprising when one considers the expenses in which they found themselves involved. It is striking that the Clermont decree did not refer to land, even though it had certainly been a subject of discussion at the council. In this respect Georges Duby's suggestion that in areas, such as the Mâconnais, where the custom of partible inheritance predominated the crusades benefited families by taking off members and thus reducing the numbers of co-heirs has been remarkably influential, considering that Duby merely proposed it in passing and produced in evidence the example of only one family.[42] And the value of this and other arguments for land-hunger as a motivating force must be weighed against the fact that after the capture of Jerusalem and the victory over an Egyptian army on 12 August 1099 most crusaders decided to return home. The largest party was said to have numbered 20,000; this estimate probably exceeded all the crusaders at that time in Palestine, but it underlines the point that the bulk of the survivors left for the West. Fulcher of Chartres, the chaplain of the first king of Jerusalem, reported that in 1100 there were no more than 300 knights and the same number of foot left to guard Jerusalem, Jaffa, Ramle and Haifa. This figure did not include the substantial bodies of horse and foot commanded by the already great feudatories in Galilee and Hebron and perhaps in Nablus, and the settlers in northern Syria;[43] nor should the evidence of rapid settlement around al-Barah in Syria and during the advance on Jerusalem be ignored, although this latter occupation left little mark on the system of land-holding and was perhaps only remembered in some of the place names on the road from Ramle to Jerusalem.[44] But even so there can be little doubt that most crusaders did not settle in the East. At one time I thought that a study of the evidence for those who did might provide some clue to motivation and I was persuaded that, although there were a few examples of an apparent desire for material gain, most cases for which we have evidence – admittedly a very small and unrepresentative group – reveal either idealism or the close emotional ties of dependence that led the members of the household of a magnate like Godfrey of Bouillon to remain at his side.[45] But I am not at all sure that my investigation was relevant, given the stresses the crusaders had suffered since leaving Europe. It is straining credulity to believe that those who laid siege to Jerusalem in 1099 felt as they had when they had left home in 1096. Three years is a long time and three such years must have left their mark on all the survivors of them. To understand the decisions made in 1096 it is

more sensible to look realistically at the expectations of those who
took the cross and the conditions in which they did so.

The distance involved in a campaign from western Europe into
Asia must have been well known, given the large number of pilgrimages to the East in the eleventh century and the many western knights
who had served with the Byzantine forces, like Peter of Aups, to
whom the crusade leaders gave custody of a city they took in Asia
Minor, or even further afield, like Hugh Bunel, who turned up to
help Robert of Normandy during the siege of Jerusalem after twenty
years in Islamic territory, whence he had fled after murdering Mabel
of Bellême in 1077.[46] It would have daunted poor men, although it is
clear that many of those who started with nothing hoped to live off
alms from the faithful as far as the borders of Christendom; the rich
helped the poor; money was collected in Europe and on the way; the
armies marched into the Balkans with treasure transported in
waggons.[47] But the prospect for knights was rather different. Even
poor knights could already travel quite widely in western Europe, in
the tradition of knight-errantry, enjoying the hospitality of others
of their class; but that is not in the same category of adventure as
that envisaged in 1095–6. War was an expensive occupation and a
properly equipped knight, with armour, arms, war-horses, pack-
horses and servants, had to plan for a costly journey. It has been
estimated that a German knight called upon to serve the emperor in
Italy in the middle of the twelfth century would have needed to put
by for such a campaign twice his annual income.[48] One can only
guess by what factor a French knight intending to campaign in the
East in the late eleventh century would have had to multiply his
income, but a factor of 4 or 5 would surely not be unreasonable; in
the light of this the traditional picture of landless knights or younger
sons blithely departing is absurd. Richer men could take the poorer
into their employment, as Bohemond of Taranto took his nephew
Tancred, who was already well-equipped, into his service.[49] All
knights could expect to benefit from alms and subventions collected
on the way. But, apart from the possibilities from loot, that was the
limit of their expectations. Later crusades were helped by more
efficient means of financing, including secular and ecclesiastical
taxation and the moneys raised from the redemption of crusade
vows, but at this time every crusader had to make his own arrangements for the meeting of his expenses, which in an agricultural
society could only mean the disposal of, or the raising of loans upon,

property. It could involve measures like those described in a charter of Henry IV of Germany in which reference was made to Godfrey of Bouillon and Baldwin of Boulogne who, 'seized by hope of an eternal inheritance and by love, prepared to go to fight for God in Jerusalem and sold and relinquished all their possessions'.[50] The pope and the bishops of Clermont, in fact, legislated to excommunicate those who stood in the way of 'gifts and redemptions' (in other words sales and mortgages) negotiated by departing crusaders.[51]

Another factor must also be taken into account. The crusade was preached at a time of severe agricultural depression caused by a succession of bad harvests due to drought. The run was broken by a marvellous one in 1096, after a wet spring that seemed like a physical expression of God's approval of the enterprise, but this came too late for many of the crusaders, who had already been engaged in selling and mortgaging their lands, although it meant that the purchasing of supplies for the march came at a time when corn was plentiful.[52] It is possible that the complaints of the monastery of Göttweig that Wolfker of Kuffern had gone back on his agreement to mortgage property to it and had negotiated a *pariage* agreement with another lord reveals a change of mind following the lifting of the depression and an easing of the market, although the case involved Germany, not France.[53] At any rate the consequences for those busy raising money early in 1096 were extremely serious and were exacerbated by the facts that the sales and mortgages were so numerous and the number of individuals or institutions capable of providing ready cash on a large scale so few that the value of goods in France actually fell.[54] Extraordinary measures were taken to raise cash by those who acted as financiers. The bishop of Liége, who was admittedly securing peace for his territory and was also involved in other transactions, raised money for the castle of Bouillon by stripping the reliquaries in his cathedral and in the churches of his diocese of their jewels; King William II apparently ordered similar measures to be taken in England to raise 10,000 silver marks for five years' enjoyment of his brother's duchy of Normandy.[55]

A commitment to crusade, therefore, involved heavy expenses and real financial sacrifices, and the burdens on families were even heavier if several members chose to go. This was common. Eustace and Baldwin of Boulogne and Godfrey of Bouillon, Adhémar of Le Puy and William Hugh of Monteil, Bohemond of Taranto and his nephews Tancred, Robert and William are well-known examples.[56]

But the list is, in fact, almost endless: Ralph of Gael and his son Alan;[57] Conon of Montaigu, incidentally Godfrey of Bouillon's brother-in-law, and his sons Goscelo and Lambert;[58] Hugh of St Pol and his son Enguerrand;[59] Walter of St Valeri and his son Bernard;[60] Baldwin of Guines and his four sons, one of whom, Fulk, was to remain in Palestine;[61] Geoffrey of Roscignolo and his brothers;[62] and the brothers Albert, Conrad and Frederick of Zimmern;[63] Arnold, Arveis and Peter Tudebode;[64] Bartholomew Boel and Fulcher of Chartres;[65] Lethold and Engilbert of Tournai;[66] Franco of Malines and Sigemar;[67] Godfrey and Henry of *Ascha*;[68] Aubrey, Ivo and William of Grandmesnil;[69] Peter of Stadenois and Reinhard of Toul;[70] Pons and Peter Rainouard;[71] Ralph and Odo of Beaugency;[72] Walter Sansavoir, Simon and William;[73] Itier, Hugh and Norgeot of Toucy;[74] Hugh and Ansellus of Méry;[75] Dodo and Leofranc Donat.[76] Among those intending to go but for whom we have no evidence of actual participation were the father and son Roger and Robert and the brothers Geoffrey and Guy, Peter and Pons of Fay, Pons and Bernard, and Raymond, Gerald and Pons.[77] I have put down here only the closest relatives; the point would become even more striking were I to add more distant ones.

There were various options open to knights who wanted to raise money for their crusades. They could tax their tenants, as did the Swabian with expensive tastes Frederick of Zimmern, who was dissatisfied with what his father had given him.[78] But not much evidence for this very obvious measure is to be found, perhaps because the shortages in France were so acute that there was little to be got that way, at least until the late summer of 1096. They could, as we have seen, renounce claims they had been making on rights or property in return for cash. Most usual was the mortgaging or selling of property, including fiefs and allods, those freeholds which were so valuable to families, but which were more easily disposed of than fiefs.[79] It was not for nothing, however, that a contemporary crusade hymn stated 'There we must go, sell our fiefs, gain the Temple of God, destroy the Muslims'.[80] The disposal of property, particularly if it were patrimonial, was something that involved the interests of all members of a crusader's family, and sometimes these interests surface in the documents. William of Vast's mortage included a clause that permitted his sisters or relatives to redeem the land if he could not. A mortgage made by Anselm of Ribemont could be redeemed by his wife, son or any heir. Astanove of Fezensac's would be redeemed by his brothers and subjects if he returned; if he should die – and he did – the property was to go entirely to the canons of St Mary of Auch. Fulcher of Faverges's mortgage could be redeemed by him or by his brothers. Bouillon could be redeemed only by Eustace of Boulogne besides Godfrey of Bouillon himself. On the other hand, Achard of Montmerle's sister agreed that his mortgage could be redeemed only by him personally. Peter and Pons of Fay sold a shared property to the monastery of St Chaffre; Pons died before departure, but his heir sold the half he inherited to St Chaffre anyway, presumably in fulfilment of the obligation, although he was well paid for it. Stephen Bonin gave his half of a shared allod to the cathedral of St Vincent of Mâcon; his brother Leodegar, who confirmed this, later sold the other half to the cathedral with the consent of yet another brother, Hugh. The family of the knight Guy of Sarcé – that is his mother and his brothers Nicholas and Payen – appear to have insisted on the sale of one of his fiefs to the abbey of St Vincent of Le Mans, even though the monks would have preferred a mortgage. Gerard Le Duc, his brother Berenger and his sons Guy and Geoffrey surrendered claims they had to some land in return for 5 *solidi* from the monks of St Vincent of Le Mans; the sum went entirely to Guy, the eldest son, who was going on crusade, although the younger son was given an additional 6 *denarii*. The wife, son and two brothers of Robert the Vicar agreed to the sale of his property to St Vincent of Le Mans, and one of the brothers guaranteed the services already owed for this to the lord. Geoffrey Chotard's brothers agreed to his grant of exemption from passage duty to the abbey of Marmoutier. Hugh of Apigné's nephew agreed to his gift of a tithe to St George of Rennes. The mother and brothers of Geoffrey and Guy agreed to their sale of an allod to St Victor of Marseilles. The father of Albert, Conrad and Frederick of Zimmern gave them money for the journey. The mother of Reinold sold property to the abbey of St Peter of Helmarshausen to provide her son with cash. The crusade of the brothers Dodo and Leofranc Donat was financed by their sister Saura and her son Bertrand of St Jean, who bought land from Dodo and entered into a mortgage agreement with Leofranc. Countess Ida of Boulogne helped her sons to raise funds. Hugh of Chaumont mortgaged his fief and castle of Amboise, but he was also helped by a large cash gift from his uncle Godfrey of Chaumont.[81] On the other hand the abbey of St Père of Chartres had to pay sums of money to Nivelo's relatives for their agreement to his renunciation of the rights he had claimed; so had Trinity of Vendôme and St Chaffre of Le Monastier to the relatives of Bertrand of Moncontour and the relatives and fellow knights of Peter *Bastarcius*, Pons and Bertrand; and the measures taken by departing crusaders could become the subjects of litigation if disputed by members of their families.[82] The picture that emerges, however, is one of relatives making substantial sacrifices to provide cash for crusaders. There really is no evidence to support the proposition that the crusade was an opportunity for spare sons to make themselves scarce in order to relieve their families of burdens. The evidence points, in fact, to families taking on burdens to help individual members fulfil their vows.

In the light of the evidence it is hard to believe that most crusaders were motivated by crude materialism. Given their knowledge and expectations and the economic climate in which they lived, the disposal of assets to invest in the fairly remote possibility of settlement in the East would have been a stupid gamble. It makes much more sense to suppose, in so far as one can generalize about them, that they were moved by an idealism which must have inspired not only them but their families. Parents, brothers and sisters, wives and children had to face a long absence and must have worried about them: in 1098 Countess Ida of Boulogne made an endowment to the abbey of St Bertin 'for the safety of her sons, Godfrey and Baldwin, who have gone to Jerusalem'.[83] And they and more distant relatives – cousins, uncles and nephews – were prepared to endow them out of the patrimonial lands. I have already stressed that no one can treat the phenomenal growth of monasticism in this period without taking into account not only those who entered the communities to be professed, but also the lay men and women who were prepared to endow new religious houses with lands and rents. The same is true of the crusading movement. Behind many crusaders stood a large body of men and women who were prepared to sacrifice interest to help them go. It is hard to avoid concluding that they were fired by the opportunity presented to a relative not only of making a penitential pilgrimage to Jerusalem but also of fighting in a holy cause. For almost a century great lords, castellans and knights had been subjected to abuse by the Church. Wilting under the torrent of invective and responding to the attempts of churchmen to reform their way of life in terms they could understand, they had become perceptibly more pious. Now they were presented by a pope who knew them intimately with the chance of performing a meritorious act which

exactly fitted their upbringing and devotional needs and they seized
it eagerly.
But they responded, of course, in their own way. They were not
theologians and were bound to react in ways consonant with their
own ideas of right and wrong, ideas that did not always correspond
to those of senior churchmen. The emphasis that Urban had put on
charity – love of Christian brothers under the heel of Islam, love of
Christ whose land was subject to the Muslim yoke – could not but
arouse in their minds analogies with their own kin and their own
lords' patrimonies, and remind them of their obligations to avenge
injuries to their relatives and lords. And that put the crusade on the
level of a vendetta. Their leaders, writing to Urban in September
1098, informed him that 'The Turks, who inflicted much dishonour
on Our Lord Jesus Christ, have been taken and killed and we
Jerusalemites have avenged the injury to the supreme God Jesus
Christ.'[84] It is probable that even intellectual churchmen, who after
all had been brought up in the same world as the laity, could not
resist playing on these sentiments in order to arouse their listeners.
Baldric of Bourgueil, a learned French monk-bishop who was writing his *Historia* nine years later, gave a version of a sermon preached
beneath the walls of Jerusalem in the summer of 1099. The words are
his, but the sentiments might well have been expressed by preachers
in 1095–6.

Rouse yourselves, members of Christ's household! Rouse yourselves, knights and footsoldiers, and seize firmly that city, our
commonwealth! Give heed to Christ, who today is banished from
that city and is crucified; and with Joseph of Arimathea take him
down from the cross; and lay up in the sepulchre of your hearts an
incomparable treasure, that desirable treasure; and forcefully
take Christ away from these impious crucifiers. For every time
those bad judges, confederates of Herod and Pilate, make sport of
and enslave your brothers they crucify Christ. Every time they
torment them and kill them they lance Christ's side with Long-
inus. Indeed they do all these things and, what is worse, they
deride and cast reproaches on Christ and our law and they
provoke us with rash speech. What are you doing about these
things? Is it right for you to listen to these things, to see these
things done and not to lament them? I address fathers and sons
and brothers and nephews. If an outsider were to strike any of

your kin down would you not avenge your blood-relative? How much more ought you to avenge your God, your father, your brother, whom you see reproached, banished from his estates, crucified; whom you hear calling, desolate, and begging for aid.[85]

The trouble with this sort of imagery was that it not only aroused the faithful; it inspired them to do things responsible churchmen did not want them to do. And the opening act of the crusade demonstrated clearly the dangers of presenting a complex moral idea to laymen in such simple terms.

The first bands of crusaders started to leave western Europe in the spring of 1096. In doing so they ignored the wishes of the pope, who had called for departure on the Feast of the Assumption, 15 August,[86] and they left at a time of food shortage, before the good harvest of the following summer. The most famous of the early leaders, Peter the Hermit, had preached in central France and had collected a substantial following before moving on to the Rhineland in April. In advance of him and apparently on his instructions, a large body of foot, which included only eight knights and was under the command of Walter Sansavoir, marched into Hungary on 21 May and proceeded in a comparatively orderly fashion to Constantinople, where it was joined by parties of Italian pilgrims, who had journeyed separately. Peter, who had gathered more recruits in the Rhineland, had a much more troubled crossing of the Balkans, for which the indiscipline of his followers, anxious about provisions, was largely responsible – at Nish they were thrashed in a brush with Byzantine forces – but he joined Walter at Constantinople with most of his army on 1 August. The crusaders were ferried across the Bosphorus on the 6th, but differences soon came to the surface between the French and the Germans and Italians, who elected their own leaders. The army had advanced to Kibotos, from where in the middle of September a party of the French raided as far as Nicaea. The Germans sought to emulate them by establishing a base close to Nicaea, but they were surrounded by the Turks and forced to surrender; those who agreed to apostasize were sent to the East, but all who refused were executed. When the news of this disaster reached the main body of Christians, Peter the Hermit was absent in Constantinople and Walter Sansavoir's pleas for caution were not heard. Advancing into the interior on 21 October, the crusaders were ambushed by the Turks and annihilated. Meanwhile three other armies got no further than Hungary. A force of Saxons and Bohemians under a priest called Folkmar was broken up at Nitra. Another undisciplined band under a Rhineland priest called Gottschalk was forced to surrender at Pannonhalma. And a large army of Rhinelander, Swabian, French, English, Flemish and Lorrainer crusaders under Count Emich of Leiningen was halted at Wieselberg where, after taking six weeks to construct a bridge over the river in front of the town, its first assault ended in panic and flight.

In what has been called 'the first holocaust', most of these armies had begun their marches by persecuting European Jews. Between December 1095 and July 1096 there took place a series of events so distressing to the Jewish people that rumours of them reached the Near East in advance of the crusade, breeding messianic fervour in the Jewish communities there; dirges in honour of the German martyrs are recited in the synagogues to this day. The first outbreaks seem to have occurred in France soon after the crusade was preached, evidence of them being a letter written by the French communities to their Rhineland confrères, warning them of the impending threat. It is possible that persecution was widespread in France, although the details of it are lost, apart from two references to an anti-Jewish riot which broke out among men gathering to take the cross in Rouen.[87] Much more evidence is available about events in the Rhineland. On 3 May the storm broke over the community at Speyer, where Emich of Leiningen's army had gathered. Emich marched north to Worms, where the massacres began on the 18th, and then to Mainz, where he was probably joined by more Swabians under Count Hartmann of Dillingen-Kybourg and by an army of French, English, Flemish and Lorrainer crusaders. Between 25 and 29 May the Jewish community at Mainz was annihilated. The movements of the crusaders, at no point very clear, now become impossible to trace with certainty. Some marched north to Cologne, where the Jews had already been dispersed into neighbouring settlements. Throughout June and into early July they were hunted out and destroyed. Another band of crusaders seems to have marched south-west to Trier and then to Metz, where the massacres continued.[88] During May a separate crusading army, probably Peter the Hermit's, forced almost the whole community at Regensburg to undergo baptism.[89] The communities at Wessili and Prague also suffered, probably from the attentions of Folkmar's followers.[90] It is usually assumed that these armies consisted in the main of undisciplined hordes of peasants, in contrast to the armies of knights who left Europe later in the year. It is true that contemporaries were inclined to explain their excesses and failures in terms of the large numbers of ordinary people, poor, women and children in their ranks. They must have been accompanied by more non-combatants than those which departed later, and there were certainly disreputable elements and the adherents of strange sects.[91] But they were not nearly as unprofessional as they are assumed to have been. We know little about Folkmar's or Gottschalk's. Walter Sansavoir's was made up almost entirely of footsoldiers. Peter the Hermit's strikes one as being an old-fashioned armed pilgrimage, with a strong ecclesiastical contingent in it. Peter had great difficulty in controlling his forces in the Balkans and in Asia Minor,[92] but his later career on the crusade was to show that he was far from being simply an incompetent rabble-rouser. His captains, Godfrey Burel of Étampes, Raynald of Broyes, Walter fitz-Waleran of Breteuil and Fulcher of Chartres, all seem to have been experienced knights: Fulcher was to end his days as a great lord in the county of Edessa.[93] Attached to Peter's army, moreover, was a strong force of Swabian nobles under the Count Palatine Hugh of Tübingen and Duke Walter of Tegk.[94] Emich of Leiningen's forces were not negligible either. Emich was a major south German noble. So was Count Hartmann of Dillingen-Kybourg. They were probably accompanied by the counts of Rötteln, Zweibrücken, Salm and Viernenberg and the lord of Bolanden.[95] The army of French, English, Flemish and Lorrainer crusaders which met Emich at Mainz was, according to one report, large and well-equipped.[96] It was under the leadership of a remarkable group of men, Clarembold of Vendeuil, Thomas of Marle lord of Coucy, William the Carpenter viscount of Melun and Drogo of Nesle.[97] One is inclined to wonder, in fact, whether these men led a French advance party. After the break-up of Emich's forces they joined Hugh of Vermandois, the brother of the king of France, and continued their journey to the East. Clarembold of Vendeuil[98] and Thomas of Marle had distinguished crusades and Thomas had a colourful and violent career before he died as count of Amiens in 1130.[99] William the Carpenter, who had already fought in Spain, was panicked into flight from Antioch, but eventually settled as a fief-holder in the principality of Antioch.[100] Drogo of Nesle, of a well-known French family, joined Baldwin of Boulogne, following him to Edessa and then to Jerusalem.[101] It is not possible to adhere to the comforting view that gangs of simple peasants persecuted the Jews and failed disastrously in the Balkans. These armies contained crusaders from all parts of western Europe, led by experienced captains.

It is clear that over and over again worry about supplies led them to act rashly in the Balkans, although this anxiety was natural in armies that were probably very large indeed.[102] They entered Hungary with plenty of cash,[103] but they had set out too early, before the good summer harvest which provided their successors with ample supplies of corn for the early stages of the march, and before the Byzantine government, which had not expected to see western troops so early in the year, had properly prepared the route. An obsession with cash, in fact, showed itself in their treatment of the Jews as they left western Europe. Although most of the examples of avarice described in the Hebrew sources for the persecutions were attributed not to the crusaders but to the bishops, their officials and townspeople, who took bribes in return for promises of protection which they failed to carry out, it is certain that the crusaders made financial demands of the Jewish communities in the cities on their line of march and it is apparent that these were extortions backed by threats of force. When Peter the Hermit reached Trier in early April he brought with him a letter from the Jews of France asking their co-religionists everywhere to give him provisions; in return, it said, Peter promised to speak kindly of Israel. His arrival and preaching terrified the community at Trier, which suggests that there was an anti-semitic tone to his sermons. The Jews of Mainz hoped in vain to pacify Emich of Leiningen by offering him similar letters and also money. Perhaps in the erroneous belief that canon law permitted the expropriation of the goods of infidels, crusaders joined the local inhabitants in looting Jewish property in the towns where the massacres took place; at Mainz the Jews delayed their enemies for a while by throwing money out of the windows to distract them.[104] One near-contemporary was in no doubt that the pogroms were inspired by greed. Writing of the disasters in the Balkans, he commented,

> This is believed to be the hand of the Lord working against the pilgrims, who sinned in his sight with their great impurity and

intercourse with prostitutes and slaughtered the wandering Jews, who admittedly were contrary to Christ, more from avarice for money than for the justice of God.[105]

In the pogroms, however, there is more evidence for the desire to convert, even by force, than to loot. Everywhere attempts were made to force Christianity on the Jews, who had heard that the crusaders intended to offer them the choice of conversion or death and that they desired to 'cut them off from being a nation': a Christian writer confirmed that the crusaders' aim was 'to wipe out or convert'.[106] Synagogues, Torah scrolls and cemeteries were desecrated. At times the Christians employed terror tactics: during the persecution at Mörs, near Cologne, they covered their swords with the blood of animals to frighten the Jews into thinking that killings had already taken place. In every settlement subjected to the persecutions Jews were slaughtered when they refused to convert and so desperate did they become that they died at their own hands or at those of members of their communities to avoid defilement. Those who submitted to baptism were spared.[107] Abbot Guibert of Nogent's autobiography contains the story of a learned monk whose life began as a young Jewish boy in Rouen. He was saved by a son of the count of Eu, who took him to his mother, Countess Helisende. She asked the child if he desired baptism and when he was too frightened to demur had him immediately christened. He was given the name of William and was sent as an oblate to the monastery of St Germer of Fly to prevent him returning to his parents.[108]

Forcible conversions were, of course, directly contrary to the injunctions of canon law, about which educated churchmen were in no doubt. For centuries the principle had been repeatedly enunciated that infidels, and particularly Jews, should never be forced to the faith but could only be persuaded by reason. To Albert of Aachen, writing of the persecutions of 1096, 'God is a just judge and orders that no one be brought unwillingly or by force under the yoke of the catholic faith'.[109] According to Cosmas of Prague, '[the bishop of Prague], seeing that [the forcible baptisms] were against canon law and led by zeal for justice, tried vainly, because unaided, to forbid them lest the Jews be baptized against their wills'.[110] In fact most of the bishops made some effort to protect the Jews, taking them into their fortified palaces and, at Speyer, Mainz and Cologne, dispersing them in their villages in the countryside. The bishop of Speyer was outstandingly successful: he made no effort to interfere with the Jews' religion and he took strong measures against the townspeople. The bishop of Prague also took a strong line, but with less success. The archbishop of Mainz began well, but weakened in the face of the mob, and he then tried to exploit the Jews' fears to convert them, as did the archbishop of Trier. Individual priests at Mainz and Xanten also tried to take advantage of the situation to gain converts, although that is obviously not the same thing as baptizing by force.[111]

The senior clergy knew their church law and it is unlikely that any responsible crusade preacher ever suggested to the faithful that they were embarking on a war of conversion. Although it is possible that popular preachers were not so restrained – we have seen that Peter the Hermit may have been indulging in dangerous rhetoric – and the idea of the expansion of Christianity was certainly current, the crusade was not regarded by most of those who took part in it as a missionary war.[112] There were, however, two states of mind, which come across strongly from a reading of the sources and provide an explanation for the pogroms.

The first was a difficulty the crusaders had in making any distinction between Jews and Muslims as enemies of the faith. In France they were reported saying that 'It was unjust for those who took up arms against rebels against Christ to allow enemies of Christ to live in their own land'.[113] At Rouen men who had come into the city to take the cross began to say 'We wish to attack the enemies of God in the East, once we have crossed great tracts of territory, when before our eyes are the Jews, more hostile to God than any other race. The enterprise is absurd.'[114] Jews were held to be enemies of the Church within the territories of Christendom and it was this which presumably led a later writer to comment of the south Italian Norman crusaders that they 'held Jews, heretics and Muslims, all of whom they called enemies of God, equally detestable'.[115]

The second was a commitment to a war of vengeance. There was a manifest desire for revenge upon the Jews for the crucifixion, which one contemporary understood to be the purpose of the crusade.[116] Crusaders in the army of French, English, Flemings and Lorrainers which met with Emich at Mainz claimed that the pogrom was the start of their service against the enemies of the Christian faith, and German crusaders announced their intention of clearing a path to Jerusalem which began with the Rhineland Jews: a count called Dithmar was reported saying that he would not leave Germany until he had killed a Jew. The Jews had heard that it was believed that killing them would gain indulgences and that their co-religionists were slain in the name of Christ.[117] Residual feelings of vengeance may even have manifested themselves towards the end of the crusade, although we shall see that the Jews in Palestine were not treated as badly as their confrères had been in Europe: it was the crusaders who were now an alien minority and feelings of animosity towards Jews must have been overshadowed by fears of the Muslim powers. But it was reported that Tancred chose to ransom Jews for 30 pieces of silver each.[118]

It is clear that in respect of the desire for vengeance a significant number of crusaders did not distinguish between Muslims and Jews and could not understand why, if they were called upon to take up arms against the former, they should not also persecute the latter. If they were to make good and avenge injuries to Christ which included the occupation of his land four and a half centuries before, why should they not also avenge the crucifixion, an injury to Christ's person? The Jews reported French crusaders arguing that 'we are going to a distant country to make war against mighty kings and are endangering our lives to conquer kingdoms which do not believe in the crucified one, when it is actually the Jews who murdered and crucified him'.[119] In the minds of the crusaders, in fact, the crucifixion and the Muslim occupation of Palestine could become confused. In an extraordinary scene in the *Chanson d'Antioche*, the greatest of the vernacular epics of the First Crusade, Christ was pictured hanging on the cross between the two thieves. The good thief commented,

'It would be most just, moreover, if you should be avenged
On these treacherous Jews by whom you are so tormented.'

When Our Lord heard him he turned towards him:
'Friend,' said he, 'the people are not yet born
Who will come to avenge me with their steel lances.
So they will come to kill the faithless pagans
Who have always refused my commandments.
Holy Christianity will be honoured by them
And my land conquered and my country freed.
A thousand years from today they will be baptized and raised
And will cause the Holy Sepulchre to be regained and adored . . .

Know certainly
That from over the seas will come a new race
Which will take revenge on the death of its father.'

It has been suggested that this scene was added to the *Chanson* in
c.1180 by the poet Graindor of Douai, who went on to write of the
destruction of Jerusalem by the Romans as an earlier act of vengeance for the crucifixion, an idea echoing an eighth-century legend
which was referred to in a barbarously forged papal encyclical, a
piece of crusade propaganda which seems to have emanated from the
south French abbey of Moissac at the time of the preaching of the
First Crusade, and was incorporated into the twelfth-century poem
La Venjance Nostre Seigneur.[120] But the idea that Christ himself had
called for vengeance was certainly circulating at the time of the First
Crusade, for a Jewish writer reported crusaders saying to Jews,

> You are the children of those who killed the object of our venera-
> tion, hanging him on a tree; and he himself had said: 'There will
> yet come a day when my children will come and avenge my
> blood.' We are his children and it is therefore obligatory for us to
> avenge him since you are the ones who rebel and disbelieve in
> him.[121]

The Church had an answer to this distortion of its message, but it
was inadequate to deal with the forces unleashed by its own preaching. As early as 1063, at the time of the planning of the Christian
advance on Barbastro in Spain, Pope Alexander II had been obliged
to write to the Spanish bishops, forbidding attacks on Jews.

> The reasons [for the use of violence against] Jews and Muslims are
> certainly dissimilar. For one may justly fight against those who
> persecute Christians and drive them from the towns and their own
> dioceses. The Jews are prepared to serve Christians everywhere.

By the time of the First Crusade this letter had already been included
in the canon law collections of Ivo of Chartres; it was to pass into
Gratian's *Decretum*, the standard collection of canon law, and its
message was to be developed by later canon lawyers.[122] Force, Pope
Alexander II was stressing, could only be used to meet present injury,
and that injury had to be apparent and material: military aggression,

the occupation of Christian property or revolt. The Jews were not at present injuring Christians. Past acts, moreover, were relevant only in so far as their consequences still constituted such an injury: the occupation of Jerusalem by the Muslims in 638 was relevant only because Muslims still held it; the crucifixion was clearly not in this category. But in their eagerness to arouse the faithful to what was of its very nature a voluntary exercise – not subject to the demands of feudal service or conscription – preachers were prepared to make use of the idea of vengeance, which they knew would be attractive to their audiences. The trouble with the notion of vengeance was that it could concern abstract as well as material injury, 'shame' or 'dishonour', to which any past action, however distant, contributed. The vengeful do not forget; and if called upon to remember the dishonour to Christ of the occupation of Jerusalem 450 years before they were also reminded of the dishonour to him of the crucifixion, over a thousand years before. It was useless for churchmen to dwell on the criterion for Christian force of present injury when at the same time they drew the attention of their listeners to their obligations under the custom of the vendetta.

Chapter 3

Conditions on the march

The second wave of crusaders began to leave western Europe in the middle of August 1096, on or after the date fixed by the pope. They travelled in groups under the leadership of great magnates, around whom the lesser lords and knights gathered for the time being: Hugh of Vermandois, the king of France's brother; Godfrey of Bouillon, duke of Lower Lorraine; Bohemond of Taranto, the eldest son of Robert Guiscard, who had involuntarily disinherited him by granting him future conquests on the eastern shore of the Adriatic which the south Italian Normans were never strong enough to make; Raymond of St Gilles, count of Toulouse, who shared the leadership of the largest of the armies with the chief papal legate, Bishop Adhémar of Le Puy; Count Robert of Flanders; and Duke Robert of Normandy and Count Stephen of Blois. Between November 1096 and May 1097 these great men were arriving in Constantinople, where they were persuaded to become vassals of the Byzantine Emperor Alexius – full vassals in all cases save that of Raymond of St Gilles, who would only agree to a modified form of commendation – and to promise to restore to the emperor all lands they conquered which had once belonged to the empire.[1] From April 1097 they were being shipped across the Bosphorus and in early June they came together in one host before the city of Nicaea, which on the 19th surrendered to the Greek troops accompanying them. On the 26th they began to march out across Asia Minor and on 1 July they won a major victory over the Seljuq Turks at Dorylaeum. After two days' rest they took the road to Akshehir, Konya and Ereghli, where on c.10 September they routed a Turkish army blocking their way. Tancred, Bohemond's nephew, and Baldwin of Boulogne, Godfrey of Bouillon's brother, now broke away from the main army to raid Cilicia, taking Tarsus, Adana, Misis and Iskenderun. Baldwin went eastward to Gaziantep, Tilbeshar and Edessa, which he reached on 20 February 1098. After being formally adopted by its Armenian prince, he took over its government entirely on 10 March, establishing the first Latin state in the East. Meanwhile Tancred had rejoined the crusade, which had proceeded by way of Kayseri, Comana, Göksun and Marash to Antioch, which it had reached on 21 October 1097.

The siege of Antioch was to last until 3 June 1098. Within four days of their occupation of the city the crusaders were themselves besieged by a large Muslim relief army under Kerbogha, the Turkish governor of Mosul. Their situation was very serious and the Emperor Alexius, who had been following them with a Greek force and had reached Akshehir, turned back on hearing exaggerated stories of their plight from deserters. Inside Antioch the crusaders, heartened by reports of the appearances to visionaries of Christ, Our Lady, St Peter and St Andrew and by the discovery under the floor of the cathedral of an object they believed was the relic of the Holy Lance, decided to seek battle. On 28 June they sortied out of the city and put the Muslims to flight in an engagement which marked one of the climaxes of the crusade. The citadel, which had still been holding out, now surrendered to them and Bohemond claimed possession on the grounds that the Byzantine emperor had forfeited his right to Antioch by deserting them.[2] The crusaders decided to rest until 1 November, when they would resume their march, but they had now entered a doldrum. In a serious epidemic, probably of typhoid, before which the leading magnates dispersed, the crusade lost Adhémar of Le Puy, in many ways the only leader who was generally respected, and it became paralysed as the other princes, particularly Bohemond and Raymond of St Gilles, who spoke for the rights of the Byzantine emperor, quarrelled over the possession of Antioch and future plans. At length the ordinary crusaders, disgusted by their leaders' dilatoriness, took matters into their own hands, destroying the fortifications of Ma'arrat-an-Nu'man, Raymond of St Gilles's base in Syria, and threatening revolt in Antioch. Raymond set out from Ma'arrat on 13 January 1099, followed by Robert of Normandy and Tancred, and, at the end of February, by Godfrey of Bouillon and Robert of Flanders. Bohemond remained behind to guard Antioch. The crusaders were reunited before 'Arqah in the Lebanon before the end of March. Abandoning the siege on 13 May, they crossed the Dog River north of Beirut six days later and marched fairly rapidly by way of Tyre, turning inland north of Jaffa and reaching Ramle on 3 June. They arrived before Jerusalem on the 7th. Bethlehem had already fallen to Tancred the day before. The siege of Jerusalem lasted until 15 July, when the city was taken by assault and sacked. On the 22nd Godfrey of Bouillon was elected ruler. Almost his first task was to organize the defence of the new settlement against an Egyptian counter-invasion. On 12 August a large Egyptian army was surprised and destroyed near Ascalon and the westerners' possession of Palestine was assured for the time being.

Such is a bare outline of events. We are fortunate in having a wealth of evidence for them, provided by many contemporaries, but above all by some of the participants themselves. There are a few west European charters in which are recorded the last wishes of crusaders who had died on the march. There is a sequence of nine letters written by and for crusaders in the army. The first dates from *c*.24 June 1097, after Nicaea had fallen. Five, dating from October 1097 to probably April 1098, were written during the siege of Antioch. One was composed in July 1098, shortly after the Battle of Antioch, and another in the following September, after the death of Adhémar of Le Puy. There is then a gap of a year before the last letter, written at Latakia in Syria by Archbishop Daimbert of Pisa, who was on his way to Jerusalem, and Raymond of St Gilles, who had now left Palestine. Although presumably all these letters were penned by clergy, the majority were dictated by laymen: two were dictated by one of the princes, Stephen of Blois, and two by a charismatic figure of the second rank, Anselm of Ribemont. To them should be added a circular sent out by the town of Lucca in October 1098 in which was incorporated an account of events in Antioch during the previous spring and summer, dictated by a citizen who had just returned.[3] There are also four eyewitness narrative accounts, the anonymous *Gesta Francorum* and the *Histories* of Peter Tudebode, Raymond of Aguilers and Fulcher of Chartres, which are obviously related to one another, the first two very closely. Their relationship has presented scholars with great difficulties and the subject has recently been reopened in a way that calls into question the prevailing view that the first nine books of the *Gesta* were composed before November 1098, while the author, perhaps a Norman knight from southern Italy, was in Antioch. For our purposes, however, the question is not of great significance, since we are rarely in a position to distinguish movements of opinion finely enough for the exact date of individual passages of narrative to matter. What is important is that we have accounts written by men, including again a high proportion of laymen since perhaps the author of the *Gesta* and certainly a collaborator in Raymond of Aguilers's *History* were knights, who had experienced the crusade and composed their accounts soon afterwards: the author of the *Gesta* before 1104, perhaps much earlier; Fulcher of Chartres and Raymond of Aguilers before 1105; and Peter Tudebode before 1111. The value of their testimony is heightened by the fact that they were attached to several different leaders. The author of the *Gesta* was a follower of Bohemond and then Raymond Pilet and Raymond of St Gilles. Raymond of Aguilers was also in Raymond of St Gilles's company. Fulcher of Chartres was in the entourage first of Stephen of Blois and then of Baldwin of Boulogne.[4] It is hardly necessary to remind ourselves that these writers were interpreters as well as reporters of the extraordinary events they saw, but this is of value because they provide us not only with evidence for the activities of the crusaders, but also with their reflections on their experiences.

Contemporaries were unanimously of the opinion that the crusade, 'that glorious sweated labour',[5] was a very unpleasant experience indeed. 'My judgement is that this is unparalleled. There never had been among the princes of the secular world men who exposed their bodies to so much suffering, solely in the expectation of spiritual reward.'[6] It is not difficult to understand why, given the composition of the army and the route it took. It is hard to estimate its size even after the convergence before Nicaea, because it contained many non-combatants and because its numbers were never constant. Very heavy casualties were sustained in Asia Minor and at Antioch. There was a steady stream of deserters, a counter-flow back along the crusade's path,[7] while it was always being joined by new recruits. To give three instances. The knight Hamo of La Hune certainly did not leave France until Christmas 1096. When in June 1098 the Byzantine emperor heard the gloomy and erroneous report on conditions at Antioch and decided to withdraw from Akshehir to Constantinople, he was accompanied back by many crusaders, who had joined his army of relief; many of them could not keep pace with his retreat and died on the road, but two members of Bohemond's household were determined to make their way to Antioch to find Bohemond's body and give it a good burial; taking ship to Cyprus and from there to Suwaidiyah, the port of Antioch, they met 500 fully armed Frenchmen, who had just arrived. Crusaders were still

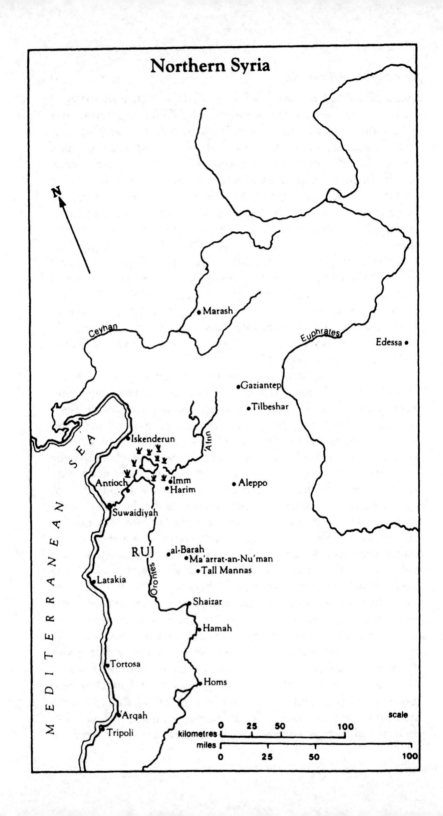

entering Palestine as those who had won Jerusalem were leaving for home in the autumn of 1099.[8] Nevertheless we ought to make some sort of estimate. It has been suggested that the host at Nicaea in June 1097 consisted of 4200–4500 cavalry and 30,000 infantry. Raymond of Aguilers, a chaplain of Raymond of St Gilles, gave the size of the army that besieged Jerusalem in July 1099 as 12,000 fighting men, of whom 1200–1300 were knights.[9] These figures included the arms-bearing poor, but there were also non-combatants who were, of course, able to perform many useful tasks.[10] If we add a further 25 per cent to the numbers given above, we arrive at figures of 43,000 for the army besieging Nicaea in June 1097 and 15,000 for that laying siege to Jerusalem two years later. The first may be a bit low; the second is credible. Both are no more than guesses.

It is, however, certain that large numbers of men and women set out to march from western Europe to Palestine without any proper planning or system for provisioning and it is not surprising that victuals and animals – horses and beasts of burden – were at the forefront of their minds from dawn to dusk. To feed themselves and their animals, and to provide themselves with fresh animals, they relied on three sources of supply. First, gifts were occasionally made to them by the Christians through whose territories they marched and in the later stages by terrified Muslim rulers. Secondly, they foraged, raiding the countryside around them. Thirdly, while they were in Byzantine territory the Greeks and once they were in Syria Armenians, Syrians and western traders occasionally brought them provisions. For much of the time, of course, they were out of touch with Christian suppliers and anyway they had almost invariably to pay for the supplies they got and the prices could be exorbitant.[11] They needed cash, therefore, which was an additional reason for looting the surrounding countryside and despoiling every army defeated and town or strongpoint taken: the message passed along their lines as early as the Battle of Dorylaeum – 'Today if God pleases we will all become rich'[12] – was probably an expression of anxiety. Plundering had to become a normal and absolutely necessary occupation, which explains the quarrels among them over booty, the anxiety of the leaders lest they turn aside for spoil in battle and even the carnage and sacking that followed the fall of Jerusalem. It had become almost a natural reaction for men who for three years had been enclosed in an alienated, suffering world of their own in which provisioning, by whatever means, had become paramount.[13]

With regard to supplies, the passage of the crusade can be divided into three stages. The first stretched from western Europe to Nicaea. The crusaders who left in the autumn of 1096 had the benefit of the good harvest at home, which meant that they had plenty of bread at first,[14] although their leaders must have been worrying already about cash: Godfrey of Bouillon apparently extorted subventions from the remnants of the Jewish communities of Mainz and Cologne.[15] They also benefited from the lessons learnt from the passage of the earlier armies through the Balkans. The leaders of the later armies seem to have issued strict instructions against plundering.[16] They purchased the supplies they could and only resorted to depredation on the few occasions when the arrangements broke down; that they did so at all is evidence for their concern about supplies.[17] They were provisioned by the Greeks once they had crossed the Bosphorus, although there was a severe shortage for a time in May 1097, which was energetically solved by Bohemond.[18] Before Nicaea food seems to have been distributed free to poor crusaders,[19] but it is clear that nearly all supplies had to be paid for, and this must have consumed most of the Emperor Alexius's generous gifts of cash to the leaders and to the poor when they were at Constantinople and again after the fall of Nicaea, although on that occasion the crusaders clearly did not believe that his donatives were the equivalents of what they would have got had they been allowed to sack the city.[20] Alexius also presented the leaders with horses, which must have been already welcome.[21]

The second stage of the crusade lasted for nearly two years, from the departure from Nicaea between 26 and 29 June 1097 to the conjunction before 'Arqah in mid-March 1099. It was marked by suffering and deprivation. From Nicaea the crusaders advanced across Asia Minor, far from any supply points. Mounts and pack animals were, of course, essential to them all, and it should not be forgotten that the knights were naturally concerned about the horses that gave them status and enabled them to fulfil their functions. Already by 1 July 1097 they were worried about their chargers, which were hungry and exhausted.[22] During the following month, as they passed across a devastated wilderness in central Anatolia, their horses and pack animals died like flies. Many knights were already without mounts; some rode oxen; goats, sheep and even dogs were put to use as pack animals.[23] By the time they reached Antioch there was an acute shortage of horses and it got progressively worse. At the beginning of the siege, in October–November 1097, there were perhaps 700–1000 horses left, of which the south French force of Raymond of St Gilles and Adhémar of Le Puy had only about 100. The crusaders' efficiency was being impaired since worry about their horses made them reluctant to risk them on raids. Raymond and Adhémar established a confraternity with a common chest, in which 500 silver marks were deposited, to provide their knights with money to replace their lost mounts. This measure was apparently successful and it is noteworthy that on three later occasions Raymond was able to provide other leaders with horses.[24] By June 1098 the number of horses in the whole army had shrunk to 100–200 and the weakness of these survivors caused anxiety during the Battle of Antioch; on Adhémar's orders they had been given a little extra food beforehand.[25] Most of the rest had died of cold and starvation; some had certainly been killed and eaten, although many knights refused to slaughter their horses and satisfied their hunger by bleeding them and drinking the blood.[26] Many more knights, among them well-known men who were powerful figures at home, now fought on foot or rode donkeys or mules: even Godfrey of Bouillon and Robert of Flanders had to beg for horses for themselves before the Battle of Antioch.[27] Anxiety about horses and pack animals became obsessive.[28] It was notable when they were taken on raids.[29] A skirmish outside Antioch was lost because a party of knights left the fight to chase a riderless horse.[30] Men would boast of their horses and gifts of them were worth recording and obviously reflected a man's prestige.[31] The crusade was still desperately short of them at the turn of the years 1098 and 1099.[32]

During the march across Asia Minor hunger struck in wastelands before Konya and afflicted Baldwin of Boulogne's force advancing through another patch of waste on its way into Cilicia,[33] but the crusaders reached Antioch in late October 1097 in a fairly good state. At first they found plentiful supplies in the region, which they supplemented with provisions brought by a Genoese fleet that docked at Suwaidiyah in mid-November.[34] A horde of around 40,000 men and women, however, could not remain encamped in one place for long before shortages would be felt. Supplies coming in by sea were infrequent and the 20-mile road from Suwaidiyah to Antioch was anyway dangerous.[35] The countryside around Antioch was stripped bare, or at least appeared to be so. The local inhabitants hid what goods remained, although the Muslims seem to have been able to smuggle adequate provisions into the city's defenders.[36] Before Christmas food was becoming very dear in the Christian camps and this provoked a foraging raid, organized by Bohemond and Robert of Flanders, which returned with practically nothing.[37] Raiding, in fact, became more and more pointless and the crusaders were obliged to search further afield, travelling in foraging parties 50 miles for food and establishing foraging centres at great distances from Antioch.[38] A picture of this constant activity is to be found in the poor servant Peter Bartholomew's account of his visions, about which more below. He was in the camp before Antioch on 30 December 1097. On 10 February 1098 he was in the Ruj, over 50 miles from Antioch, having accompanied a foraging expedition. By 20 March he was at Suwaidiyah. He then returned to the main camp and from there travelled to Misis in Cilicia, still on the business of procurement since his employer, William Peyre of Cunhlat, tried three times in April and May to sail from there to Cyprus. He returned to Suwaidiyah and went on to Antioch, which he reached before 14 June. So in six months he had travelled at least 340 miles in search of food.[39]

One predictable result of the long halt at Antioch was famine. Some of the poor had already starved to death at Nicaea.[40] At Antioch the prices of foodstuffs and bedding for horses rose to stupendous heights. The famine reached a peak as early as January 1098.[41] When the city was captured on 3 June there may have been a brief respite, but within days the shortages were acute and, shut in by the immediate investment by a new Muslim army, people were consuming leaves, thistles and leather.[42] The loot seized after the Christian victory on 28 June brought relief.[43] So did the supplies now being sent from Edessa by Baldwin of Boulogne.[44] But the easement was only temporary and the army was still haunted by starvation. In late November and early December, during the siege of Ma'arrat, which lay within the area already devastated by the crusaders' foraging parties, 10,000 men could be seen scattered across the countryside searching the ground for grains of corn and roots. It was reported that so desperate did the plight of the poor become that some even resorted to cannibalism, devouring the corpses of Muslims, even rotting ones.[45] Raymond of St Gilles's followers were still very short of food in January 1099.[46]

The third stage of the crusade, the march down to Palestine and then inland to Jerusalem, was a happier one. Local Muslim rulers hastened to make peace, pay tribute and open their markets.[47] From February the crusaders advanced down the coast, so that they could be supplied from the sea, particularly from Cyprus, although it cannot be said that the provisioning was always satisfactory.[48] In the early summer they could also live off the local harvests.[49] Although there was a severe shortage of water and a temporary shortage of food during the siege of Jerusalem,[50] the worst was now over.

It is impossible to begin to evaluate even the physical effects of three years of stress, two of which were marked by real deprivation, but the more obvious consequences included a heavy mortality rate: the entire entourage of the bishop of Foligno apparently died, leaving him alone in the Holy Land.[51] Death from starvation, of knights as well as the poor, seems to have been common at Antioch.[52] Illness, of course, stalked the crusade, affecting the rich as well as the poor. Raymond of St Gilles, who was elderly anyway, was seriously ill twice and it was said later that he was quite worn out by the expedition.[53] Stephen of Blois was probably ill at the time of his flight from Antioch, about which more below.[54] Guy Trousseau returned to Europe exhausted;[55] Hugh of Chaumont came home a sick man.[56] Typhoid[57] probably carried off Adhémar of Le Puy on 1 August 1098 and fear of it scattered the other leaders. Some idea of the effects of illness on manpower can be gauged from a letter written by Anselm of Ribemont to the archbishop of Rheims in November 1097, before the bad times had really begun. Anselm asked the archbishop to pray for the souls of thirteen men who had died. It is not clear what common factor bound them: they were either members of Anselm's own company – one of them had been his chaplain – or they were in some way known to the archbishop. Seven had died in battle; six had died of disease. So about half the mortalities in this little group were already not directly the consequence of fighting.[58] Hunger, the lack of proper cover during the winter of 1097–8[59] and the unhygienic environment of the camp and then of Antioch itself must have fostered disease. A link between hunger and ill-health is perhaps revealed in Peter Bartholomew's account of his experiences. In February 1098 he fell ill and began to lose his eyesight. This may have been a symptom of an insufficient diet, but he put it down to divine punishment for disobeying St Andrew's instructions to him to carry his message to the leaders of the crusade. He claimed that he was shy of approaching them in his poverty lest they should think that he was a hungry man telling them tales for the sake of food.[60]

There was also impoverishment and financial anarchy. At Antioch there was an acute shortage of cash.[61] It was the poor, with their ragged clothing and rusty weapons,[62] who suffered especially, providing the leaders with a constant cause for concern. While he lived, Adhémar of Le Puy encouraged the better-off to help them[63] and it became the custom to provide alms, often linked to fasts and penitential processions, for the poor before any important engagement and to do the same out of the spoils of victory.[64] But these measures alone could only be spasmodically effective and others came to be taken. After the Battle of Antioch, when there was plenty of loot about, the leaders decided to enlist all the poor they could into their service for wages.[65] On two occasions Raymond of St Gilles tried to organize large-scale foraging parties *causa pauperum* (for the cause of the poor).[66] At 'Arqah in the spring of 1099 it was decided to establish a common fund out of the tithes of all spoil; half was to go to the clergy and half to Peter the Hermit, who had been given general responsibility for the poor.[67]

But it was not the poor alone who suffered. I have already noted that some knights starved to death. Many had to sell their arms and become footsoldiers: the 'king' of the Tafurs, a well-organized body of poor, was supposed to have been a Norman knight who had no lord – in other words no benefactor – and had been reduced to the ranks.[68] Godfrey of Bouillon had to provide rations to two well-known but indigent knights, his relative and vassal Henry of *Ascha* and Count Hartmann of Dillingen-Kybourg, whom we have already met persecuting Jews.[69] There had, as we shall see, always been movement within the crusade as lesser men moved from one allegiance to another. By the spring of 1098 this was being encouraged by the growing obligation upon the leaders to take their fellow-crusaders into their service for wages, binding some men to them more closely than ever, but also drawing new men into their entourages. On 29 March Stephen of Blois wrote to his wife that 'many of our Frenchmen would have died of hunger if the clemency of God and our money had not helped them'. Raymond of St Gilles was also paying his followers. So were Godfrey of Bouillon and Robert of Flanders. So, among the men of the second rank, was Anselm of Ribemont.[70] It is not surprising that some of the leaders themselves were at times short of cash. They seem to have established a common fund to spread the burden: when a new siege fort, La Mahomerie, was constructed in March 1098 some of them sought to have guard of it, it was said, to benefit from the sums provided by the community for its defence; before Jerusalem engineers were paid out of the fund.[71] In January 1098 Bohemond was threatening to leave Antioch because he could not bear to see his men and horses dying of hunger and because he was not rich and did not have the resources to finance a long siege. Robert of Flanders and Godfrey of Bouillon were both impoverished in the following summer by the sums they had had to spend on their knights and, as we have seen, they had to beg for horses before the Battle of Antioch.[72] Godfrey was saved by his brother Baldwin, who sent money and horses from Edessa to all the leaders, but especially to him, to whom he made over the rich returns of the estates attached to the castle of Tilbeshar, although it must have been some time before Godfrey began to benefit from them.[73] This source of wealth must have contributed to his election as ruler of Jerusalem, since at a crucial stage he was able, as we shall see, to augment his following significantly.

It would be wrong to suppose that all suffered equally. There was money to be made out of the misfortune of men desperate for anything to eat.[74] There were also rich men, who somehow managed to preserve their wealth. At late as 29 March 1098 Stephen of Blois claimed to have doubled the money he had brought with him from France, although he associated this with his election as overall commander.[75] Raymond of St Gilles remained throughout the richest of the crusaders. He had more knights in his household than any other leader and he could pay them; for this reason he took guard of the fort of La Mahomerie. When Tancred was put in charge of the western sector of the siege lines at Antioch in early April 1098 and claimed that he could not take on this duty without payment – presumably to provide wages for his knights – Raymond gave him more than the other magnates. He provided Godfrey of Bouillon with a horse for the Battle of Antioch, as we have seen, and some months later he gave him another beautiful one in settlement of a dispute with him. In January 1099 he was able to offer the other leaders very large sums of money on condition that they entered his service for the march to Jerusalem. During the siege of Jerusalem he alone paid his engineers without recourse to the common fund.[76] It is not clear where his money came from, although it seems that his following was more efficiently organized than the others; at Antioch the Provençal contingent appears to have been better fed and one writer quoted a children's proverb: 'The Franks live for war; the

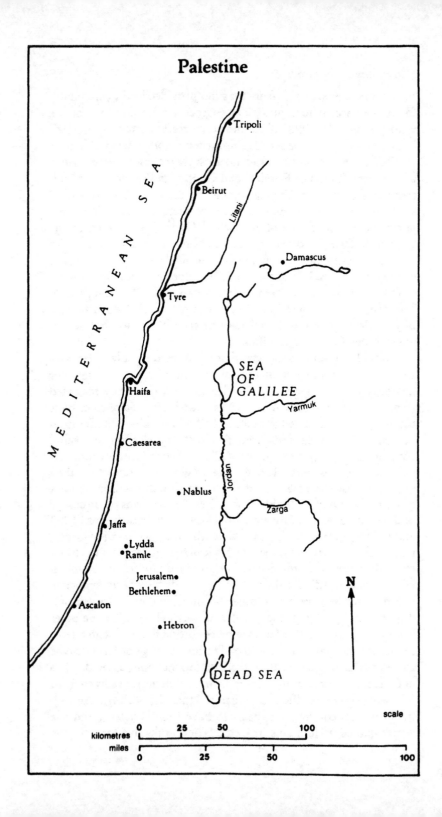

Palestine

Provençals for victuals.'[77] Perhaps Raymond made use of Byzantine funds; perhaps he also had at his disposal the Church's cash after Adhémar of Le Puy's death and the accretion of Adhémar's company. Some lesser figures, moreover, may have made at least passing fortunes, which they used to build up followings. For instance, Raymond Pilet, the Limousin lord of Alais[78] who was in Raymond of St Gilles's following, must have taken some valuable spoil in the Battle of Antioch, because soon afterwards, when the leaders announced their intention of taking poor men into their employment, he took into his service many knights and footsoldiers and led an expedition to Tall Mannas and Ma'arrat, about which more below. Thereafter he played a major part as a sub-commander.[79] Sudden accretions of wealth, of course, helped to fuel the inflation that accompanied acute shortages.

In these stressful circumstances it is not surprising that the crusaders were often very frightened. At times, indeed, they seem to have been almost paralysed by a terror that they themselves could hardly comprehend.[80] In the second week of October 1097, as they crossed the Anti-Taurus range of mountains between Göksun and Marash, the knights became demoralized at the prospect of the precipitous paths they had to traverse. Some of them offered to sell their armour at any price, some even abandoned it, to avoid having to wear or carry it during the crossing; by this time, of course, they had lost many of their pack-animals.[81] There were large-scale desertions during the siege of Antioch, many of the deserters being moved by fear of starvation.[82] When the crusade was bottled up in Antioch by Kerhogha's relief force it was gripped by such blind panic that there was the prospect of a mass break-out and on the night of 10 or 11 June 1098 Bohemond and Adhémar had the gates of the city closed.[83] It is worth noting that many of those whom later chroniclers, writing after the events in comparative comfort in Europe, vilified for cowardice and desertion seem to have been treated more charitably by their fellow-crusaders, who must have understood what pressures they had been under. Stephen of Blois returned to be a leader of the 1101 crusade. Peter the Hermit, who was brought back from attempted flight in disgrace, was shortly afterwards an ambassador to Kerbogha,[84] the official leader of the poor in the last stages of the crusade, a preacher during a great procession round Jerusalem before it fell and one of those responsible for organizing intercessory prayers in the Holy City at the time of the Battle of

Ascalon. William the Carpenter, who had shared Peter's flight and had been stingingly rebuked for it by Bohemond – there had been a similar incident involving William in one of the Spanish wars – settled with Bohemond in Antioch.[85] Ralph of Fontenelles (or Fontenay) in Anjou, who had fled with a party of Angevins from Antioch, returned to the crusade, settled in Palestine and later had property in the city-territory of Jerusalem and a fief between Bethlehem and Hebron.[86] The crusaders' acceptance of these men, when compared with the anger they expressed about those who had remained at home in the West and had not fulfilled their vows, suggests the bond of common understanding and a shared feeling of insecurity.

Nor is it surprising that in such strange surroundings the crusaders should have thought constantly of home. Both Anselm of Ribemont's letters to the archbishop of Rheims contained anxious requests that the archbishop protect his lands.

First [he wrote in November 1097] we remind you and beseech you in the Lord Jesus to see to . . . the sacerdotal and pontifical burden of providing for our land, so that the magnates are at peace with one another, the lesser men work in security at what they have, the ministers of Christ, leading quiet and tranquil lives, devote themselves to the Lord.[87]

Now [he reiterated in July 1098] we beg you to keep our land in peace and defend the churches and the poor from the hands of tyrants.[88]

On 29 March 1098 Stephen of Blois commanded his wife 'to act well and manage your land excellently and treat your children and vassals honestly'.[89] Thoughts of home were also revealed in other ways. When Robert of Flanders sent relics home from southern Italy he specified that they were to be given to the monastery of Watten, founded by his father. On crusade Raymond of St Gilles kept the feast of St Faith, whose famous shrine at Conques was in his dominions; when he was ill in August 1097 it was St Giles, whom he had been so concerned to pacify before his departure, who appeared to a Saxon count in the army with the assurance that he would not die; and in April 1099 the visionary Peter Bartholomew told him that he should take the relic of the Holy Lance to southern France and that he should build a church to house it at a place called Montjoie, 5 leagues from the cathedral of St Trophimus at Arles, because St Peter had promised it to his 'disciple' Trophimus (actually an Ephesian follower of St Paul), who was supposed to have been the first bishop of Arles.[90] Home naturally came into the minds of the dying: Riou of Lohéac sent from his deathbed relics to the church of St Saviour at Lohéac; Bernard Le Baile's last thought was for an endowment for his local priory of Aureil.[91]

It is clear that the crusade imposed on its participants extraordinary stresses. In an alien environment they experienced not only the perils of warfare, but also inflation, poverty, starvation, disease and death. They were often frightened and homesick. The knights among them were humiliated as they lost status without their arms and horses. Most of the leaders had nagging financial worries. It is not hard to understand their obsession with horses and their desire for loot.

The churchmen who wrote their sophisticated histories a decade later portrayed the crusade as a unique, unprecedented affair, a co-operative, democratic, or at least aristocratic, enterprise in which all, equally sharing the burdens and without any commander-in-chief, were inspired only by the Holy Spirit and by a desire for salvation.

Who has ever heard of so many princes, so many dukes, so many knights, so many footsoldiers, fighting without a king or emperor? In that army no one had command over another or ordered another about; no one arranged what seemed to be good to him alone, unless the common counsel of the wise decreed it and unless the people in general agreed to it. This is certainly because the Holy Spirit, who *breatheth where he will* animated them to undertake eagerly such great labours and inspired in them one single concord.[92]

It goes without saying that this picture was unreal. In fact the crusaders and those associated with them naturally felt the need for a commander-in-chief and at least three attempts were made to find one. The first took place in Constantinople in the spring of 1097. The leaders already in the city, Bohemond of Taranto, Godfrey of Bouillon and Robert of Flanders, discussed with the Emperor

Alexius his assumption of the cross and leadership of the crusade as *dux et imperator.* It is not clear who took the initiative in these discussions and any response to the plan on the emperor's part may have been simply politic; certainly when Raymond of St Gilles arrived and made the taking of overall command by the emperor a precondition for his acknowledgement of his subordination to him, Alexius excused himself on the grounds that his presence was required at home.[93] The second attempt was made before 29 March 1098, when Stephen of Blois wrote to his wife that he had been elected commander-in-chief. Since he seems to have been given control of the common fund and there is no reference to him in the record of the discussions earlier in March over the custody of the fort of La Mahomerie, originally to be paid for out of the fund, he must have been elected just before he wrote. He defined his office as that of *dominus, provisor, gubernator;* to other eyewitnesses of the crusade he was *ductor nostrorum, caput nostrum* and *dictator.*[94] These words suggest that he had fairly wide powers, but the sources provide us with no examples of them being exercised: in the eyewitness accounts Stephen himself, let alone his leadership, was of no great force, although they were written in the light of his defection, for he ended his office by withdrawing from Antioch on 2 June 1098 and not returning.[95] The third attempt was made at a conference held in the Ruj on *c.*4 January 1099, when Raymond of St Gilles was prepared to offer Godfrey of Bouillon and Robert of Normandy 10,000 *solidi* each, Robert of Flanders 6,000 *solidi,* Tancred 5,000 *solidi* and two horses, and other leaders proportionate sums. His idea clearly was that they and their followers should enter into his service for the final push to Jerusalem. He was responding to pressure from below – his men were impatient to press on – but only Tancred accepted. Although they must have been tempted by sums that would have helped them to provide for their followers, the other leaders were not ready and must have been reluctant to become Raymond's subordinates.[96]

So it is obvious that a need was felt for a commander-in-chief. Why then was there such a commander for only a very short period? This question can only be answered in the light of a study of the composition of the crusading host. The crusaders can be divided into three classes, the *principes* or *maiores,* the *minores* or *mediocres* and the *plebs* or *populus.* It is fairly easy to establish who the *principes* were, since they were often listed and there is one surviving letter from them.[97] They were the papal legate Adhémar of Le Puy until his death, Bohemond of Taranto, Godfrey of Bouillon, Hugh of Vermandois until his departure, Raymond of St Gilles, Robert of Flanders, Robert of Normandy and Stephen of Blois until his flight. Nor is it difficult to see why they held the positions they did. They were great magnates in western Europe; indeed at Clermont Pope Urban expected 'princes' to be the leaders. As such they naturally exercised authority over other contingents during the first few months' march to the Bosphorus: Geoffrey Malaterra, Roger of Sicily's biographer, who implied that Bohemond of Taranto only joined the crusade to further his ambitions in Greece, made it clear that his assumption of the cross automatically gave him leadership of the south Italian crusaders, who had been 'without a prince'.[98] The dominance of the *principes* was reinforced by the Emperor Alexius's treatment of them, particularly by the way they were the first who had to pay him homage and were presented with large sums of money by him. Although their resources varied, they were richer than most of the other crusaders. They also had at their disposal the common fund.[99] And they had more chance of supplementing their incomes. During the siege of Antioch, acting perhaps with the authority over conquests posited by Urban at Clermont in his ruling on conquered churches, which was to be confirmed by a council held at Antioch under the presidency of Adhémar of Le Puy,[100] they had established a loose control over nearby regions, from which they hoped to gather supplies: Bohemond near the sea to the west of Antioch and northwards towards Cilicia; Godfrey of Bouillon and Robert of Flanders near one another around the River 'Afrin, controlling the main road to Edessa, which came to be ruled by Godfrey's brother, to Godfrey's profit in the later stages of the campaign; Tancred, south of Robert of Flanders and east of Antioch, around 'Imm and Harim; and, further to the south, Raymond of St Gilles in the Ruj and Robert of Normandy at Latakia.[101] It must have been in accordance with Urban's ruling that Raymond established the first Latin bishopric at al-Barah on the frontier of his region, as we shall see. The princes were accompanied, moreover, by small and close-knit households of vassals and retainers from home: this is especially clear in the cases of Godfrey, Bohemond and Raymond.[102] They therefore had some intrinsic strength, which is why it was said later that the crusaders besieging Jerusalem were weakened by the absence of Bohemond, Stephen of Blois and Hugh of Vermandois.[103]

But although eyewitnesses made reference to the 'armies' of the princes,[104] it would be wrong to see them as the permanent commanders of large bodies of men. In fact all they could rely on were their households and, to a lesser extent, the knights they came to employ for wages.

To understand this we must turn to the large and varied class of *minores*, comprising great lords, castellans and petty knights and containing some of the most important elements on the crusade. For instance, a lord like Anselm of Ribemont did not regard himself as a *princeps* even though he led a force of his own.[105] Tancred, who commanded a substantial body of men on the march to Jerusalem, was another in this category, as was Farald of Thouars, who probably led the Poitevin contingent,[106] Galdemar Carpenel, who was extremely rich,[107] and Roger of Barneville, a Norman knight who led a company semi-independently of the duke of Normandy and was exceptional in that he was summoned to take part in the council of the princes because of his experience as a military commander and negotiator. On 4 June 1098 Roger was killed in a sortie, in which he led fifteen of his most experienced companions, and was buried in great style by Adhémar of Le Puy in the porch of the cathedral of Antioch.[108] *Minores* could carry their own banners: certainly Tancred and Gaston of Béarn[109] and probably Baldwin of Hainault[110] did so. These banners were already of great significance. In Peter the Hermit's army the Germans marched under one and it is possible that the footsoldiers were grouped in companies under standards.[111] They were prominent in the forces of the second wave of the crusade. At one stage at Antioch the Turks 'saw' that Raymond of St Gilles and Bohemond were not present; they must have noticed the absence of their flags.[112] The loss of a banner, like Adhémar of Le Puy's *vexillum Beate Marie* in battle on 29 December 1097, was regarded as shameful;[113] six months later during the Battle of Antioch his new standard-bearer, Heraclius of Polignac, took care to pass the flag into the custody of another before seeking the engagement in which he was mortally wounded.[114] In the same battle Hugh of Vermandois's banner was saved by William of Beauvais when Odo of Beaugency, his standard-bearer, was wounded.[115] Banners were also used as signs of protection – for instance for Muslims who had made peace or had surrendered and wanted security from attack[116] – and as marks of conquest and therefore of ownership, although in this respect the flying of them could lead to disputes.[117] So their possession by *minores* is worth noting and signified a following and an independent command. Lists of crusaders in siege lines or battle formation,[118] moreover, made little distinction between the princes with their forces and the *minores*, perhaps with a few followers, perhaps alone, whose independence stemmed from their position in society, their status as knights and in some cases their wealth. They had started out technically as free agents, because the crusade was undertaken not as feudal service, but in consequence of vows freely entered into. Raymond of St Gilles was stating a legal fact when, in reaction to the Emperor Alexius's request for homage, he said that 'he had not come to make another man lord or to fight for another, except for him [God] on whose behalf he had left his homeland and its goods'.[119]

As free agents the *minores* could make up their own parties – one was perhaps the company of 200 persons of which Adjutor of Vernon (St Adjutor of Tiron) was a member [120] – or they could join whatever contingent they wished. Ties of blood and feudal service found expression throughout the crusade, as we shall see, and it was normal and practical for individuals to join relatives – Stephen of Albemarle went with his uncle Robert of Normandy[121] – and for groups to attach themselves to the nearest great lord who was departing – the Bretons also accompanied Robert of Normandy.[122] But there were also knights who joined other leaders. Baldwin Calderun from Indre was probably in Robert of Flanders' company,[123] whereas Winrich of Flanders may have travelled with Godfrey of Bouillon.[124] A group of French knights – Bartholomew Boel of Chartres,[125] Ilger Bigod[126] and Ralph the Red of Pont-Échanfray[127] – joined Bohemond of Taranto's south Italian Normans. On the march or in particular engagements *minores* appear to have served in whichever contingent needed them: Everard of Le Puiset, who came from Eure-et-Loire, served with Robert of Normandy as might be expected,[128] but also with Bohemond and perhaps with Hugh of Vermandois.[129] Knights would naturally transfer their loyalties if the force in which they served met with disaster or the leader left. Clarembold of Vendeuil, Drogo of Nesle, Hartmann of Dillingen-Kybourg, Thomas of Marle and William the Carpenter had, as we have seen, originally been in Emich of Leiningen's army. After this broke up on the Hungarian border, Clarembold, Drogo, Thomas and William went to Italy where they joined Hugh of Vermandois.[130] Hartmann seems to have remained

independent until he was forced by poverty to enter Godfrey of
Bouillon's service.[131] After Hugh of Vermandois's departure from
the crusade, Drogo appears to have joined Baldwin of Boulogne in
Edessa and William later held a fief under Bohemond in Antioch.[132]
Frederick of Zimmern[133] and the knight Fulcher of Chartres,
Bartholomew Boel's brother,[134] travelled to Asia Minor with Peter
the Hermit. Frederick later joined Godfrey of Bouillon.[135] Fulcher
went with Baldwin of Boulogne to Edessa.[136] Achard of Montmerle[137] and Anselm of Ribemont,[138] who had at times served with
Hugh of Vermandois, joined Raymond of St Gilles after Hugh left
the crusade. After the withdrawal of Stephen of Blois, Hugh of
Chaumont and Ralph of Beaugency served for a period with
Bohemond.[139] On Adhémar of Le Puy's death his knights transferred
their loyalties to Raymond of St Gilles, with whom they had always
been associated. Adhémar's brother William Hugh of Monteil
became a particularly close adherent of Raymond.[140]

We have seen that in the later stages of the crusade the richer
crusaders took their poorer confrères into their service for wages.
The anonymous author of the *Gesta Francorum*, perhaps a south
Italian Norman knight, who had travelled out with Bohemond,
seems to have entered Raymond Pilet's service, probably, like others,
for pay, and to have marched to Jerusalem under Raymond of St
Gilles, in whose force Raymond Pilet and his men served.[141] During
the last lap a struggle for power, using money payments as induce-
ments for the transfer of allegiances, developed between Raymond of
St Gilles and Godfrey of Bouillon, who was now enjoying the
revenues provided from Edessa by his brother. We have already seen
that on c.4 January 1099 Tancred, Bohemond's nephew and second-
in-command,[142] who was to lead the south Italian Norman contingent to Jerusalem, had agreed to enter Raymond's service in
return for a large gift of cash. After an obscure dispute over this
agreement he broke with Raymond and joined Godfrey, with whom
he must have entered into a similar compact, since at the time of the
capture of Jerusalem he regarded himself as Godfrey's knight; this
caused such ill-feeling that it seriously divided the army.[143] Gaston of
Béarn, who led his own force,[144] must also have deserted Raymond,
in whose following he had served: it was Godfrey who sent him with
Tancred to occupy Bethlehem; he was in charge of the siege engines
of Godfrey, Robert of Flanders and Robert of Normandy during the
investment of Jerusalem; and he assisted Tancred in occupying the

Temple area.[145] Two other important magnates in Raymond's force, Galdemar Carpenel and William of Montpellier, may have taken the same road, since they remained with Godfrey in Palestine when Raymond left it in the following autumn.[146]

The shifting composition of the princes' forces is manifest. No leader's following was coherent or permanent enough to become a platform from which he could dominate the rest.

The clergy who accompanied the crusade did not, as a body, unite it. Adhémar of Le Puy, who had some authority to legislate for all, was a unifying force while he lived, but after his death his colleagues' attitudes and activities encouraged division. At least ten bishops left their dioceses in western Europe, although one of them, Odo of Bayeux, died in southern Italy, after which Gilbert of Evreux appears to have returned home.[147] The others were the bishop of Strasbourg; the bishops of Orange and Apt in Burgundy; the bishop of Le Puy in southern France; and the bishops of Ariano, Bari, Foligno, Martirano and perhaps Anagni in Italy. In addition there were at least 2 archdeacons, 5 abbots, several monks and a nun of the nunnery of St Mary at Trier, who was taken and seduced by a Turk at the time of the destruction of Peter the Hermit's army. She was freed later by the crusaders but then eloped with her Turkish lover.[148] Of what must have been a substantial number of priests thirty are known by name; and there were other clerics in lesser orders, including, of course, Peter the Hermit himself. Most of the priests were attached to the bishops, princes and *minores* as chaplains or assistants. Adhémar of Le Puy had an entourage of chaplains and canons of Le Puy.[149] An abbot called Baldwin was chaplain to Godfrey of Bouillon, who also had in his company the archdeacon of Metz and perhaps the archdeacon of Toul.[150] Stephen of Blois had a chaplain called Alexander; another in his following was the chronicler Fulcher of Chartres, who transferred his service to Baldwin of Boulogne in October 1097 and became his chaplain.[151] The chronicler Raymond of Aguilers, who was ordained in the course of the crusade,[152] became one of Raymond of St Gilles's many chaplains; Peter of Narbonne, who was to become bishop of al-Barah in Syria, was another of them. Raymond also had in his company the bishop of Apt.[153] Bohemond of Taranto was accompanied by at least two Italian bishops.[154] Robert of Normandy's chaplain was Arnulf of Chocques, but he also had at

least two other priests in his company, Philip of Montgomery and
Robert of Rouen; in the light of Pope Urban's ruling at Clermont
there may be significance in the fact that the first Latin patriarch
of Jerusalem and the first Latin bishop of Palestine were to be
Normans, since it leads one to suppose that Duke Robert was
seriously considered as a possible future ruler of the Holy Land.[155]
Turning to the *minores*, an abbot Roger was chaplain to Anselm of
Ribemont; Peter Desiderius was chaplain to Isoard of Die; Peter of
Picca was chaplain to Bernard of *Scabrica*.[156] It is worth noting that
the ecclesiastics on the crusade were not the cream of the contemporary Church, being made up, by and large, of the magnates' house
priests.

They had, nevertheless, an elevated opinion of themselves and a
meeting of bishops and secular leaders in Antioch under the presidency of Adhémar of Le Puy to discuss the establishment of the Latin
Church became known as the Council of Antioch.[157] Sharing a tent in
the Ruj were the bishop of Apt, the priest Raymond of Aguilers,
another priest called Simon and the visionary Peter Bartholomew,
who had been adopted by the Provençal clergy,[158] and it is possible
that clerics lived apart from the laity. Until his death on 1 August
1098 they were headed by Adhémar of Le Puy, the papal legate,[159]
although the pope appointed at least two of the princes' chaplains,
Arnulf of Chocques and Alexander, subsidiary legates.[160] It may be
that Bishop William of Orange and Peter of Narbonne were also
given legations: after Adhémar's death William of Orange assumed
the leadership of the clergy until his own death on *c*.20 December
1098; thereafter, with the army divided, authority seems to have
been shared between Peter of Narbonne – now bishop of al-Barah
and, according to Raymond of Aguilers, almost the only churchman
left who could stand up to the princes – who headed the priests
accompanying Raymond of St Gilles, and Arnulf of Chocques, who
led the clergy in the other forces.[161]

Those who have devoted their lives to acting as chaplains to great
laymen have not, whatever their other virtues, been noted for being
of an independent cast of mind or for being in the forefront of church
reform. The late eleventh century was an age of rapid change in
church thinking, and the crusade was an expression of changing
ideas, but the clergy on it were on the whole a backward-looking
body of men. Adhémar of Le Puy was a man of goodness as well as of
ability.[162] William of Orange was also a man of distinction, who had

been employed by the pope on the mission to Genoa concerning the crusade.[163] Raymond of Aguilers commented that the clergy were weakened by the deaths of these two bishops, who could resist the pressures brought to bear by the secular magnates.[164] The bishop of Foligno, Blessed Bonfilius, was an ardent reformer, who lived as a hermit in the Holy Land for ten years after the crusade.[165] The visionary Stephen of Valence was a man 'of good life'.[166] Peter of Narbonne was obviously independent and efficient and had some reputation for learning; he survived into the 1120s, combining his bishopric of al-Barah with the archbishopric of Apamea.[167] Arnulf of Chocques, the future patriarch of Jerusalem, was quite a well-known scholar, who had been tutor to Cecilia of England, William I's daughter, and also to Tancred's biographer, Ralph of Caen. Robert of Normandy, to whom he was chaplain and chancellor, had at his sister's prompting already promised him the first vacant bishopric in Normandy. He was articulate and his preaching was much admired on the crusade.[168] Three of the four surviving eyewitness accounts of the crusade were written in whole or in part by the priests Raymond of Aguilers, Peter Tudebode and Fulcher of Chartres. Raymond appears to have been a typical house priest; Fulcher seems to have been moderately, although not outstandingly, educated.[169]

On the other hand Arnulf of Chocques was reputed to be a loose talker and philanderer and it was said that vulgar songs about him were composed during the crusade.[170] His close friend, Bishop Arnulf of Martirano, was corrupt and almost illiterate.[171] Adelbero of Luxembourg, a young and aristocratic archdeacon of Metz, who had crept into the undergrowth near Antioch to play dice with his companions, including a beautiful woman, was ambushed by a party of Muslims and killed.[172] Bertrand of Bas, a canon of the cathedral of Le Puy and in Adhémar's entourage, had possessed the tithes of Beauzac illegally. Falling gravely ill at sea – and so presumably on the return home – he called on his companions to witness that he left them to the parish church, to which they properly belonged.[173] A number of monks had joined without the permission of their superiors;[174] one, from Cluny, who took part 'not out of devotion but from levity', was caught with a woman and whipped through the camp.[175] The crusade had naturally attracted enthusiasts and tricksters, among them the adherents of a curious sect, who had followed Emich of Leiningen and had venerated a goose they believed was filled with the Holy Spirit, and a number of persons who, either in hysteria or to deceive, had branded or tattooed crosses on their bodies.[176] The most notorious of these was Godfrey of Bouillon's chaplain, Abbot Baldwin, who had branded a cross on his forehead and financed his journey out of oblations made by the faithful in the belief that he had been marked by an angel. At Antioch he repented and later became first abbot of St Mary of the Valley of Josaphat and the first Latin archbishop of Caesarea.[177] And while there is no evidence that Adhémar of Le Puy, who certainly had troops in his following, himself ever carried arms,[178] at least one of the crusading clergy, the bellicose Provençal priest the Byzantine princess Anna Comnena remembered hearing about, who fired his crossbow from the stern of a ship and, when he had run out of bolts, hurled stones and even biscuits at the Greeks,[179] involved himself in fighting, against the injunctions of canon law, obedience to which was increasingly being demanded. One could not expect from such a body of men the authority to impose restraints on the crusaders, the leaders of whom were anyway their masters.

The churchmen maintained some authority, however, through their right and duty to preach. Adhémar of Le Puy was reputed to have seen to it that sermons were preached by himself, the bishops, abbots and 'more erudite' clergy every Sunday and feast day.[180] Among his subordinates Arnulf of Chocques gained, as we have seen, a reputation as a preacher; indeed one commentator supposed that, when on his deathbed Adhémar had passed on his 'ministry of teaching' to his fellow clergy, he had had special words for Arnulf.[181] Several sermons were beautifully composed as reported speech by later writers, but there is trustworthy evidence for the actual content only of the sermons delivered during a great penitential procession round Jerusalem on 8 July 1099, at a time when the siege was not going well and the army was divided by ill-feeling caused by Tancred's desertion of Raymond of St Gilles for Godfrey of Bouillon. The procession halted at the Mount of Olives, where it either broke up into groups or heard a sequence of sermons, given by Arnulf of Chocques, Peter the Hermit, Raymond of Aguilers and perhaps several others. The preachers dwelt on two themes: the mercy of the Lord in bringing the crusaders to the place of his Ascension and the need for mutual concord and forgiveness. The effect on the army was striking, apparently.[182]

The churchmen also played a positive role when they fulfilled their sacramental and devotional functions. Masses were said regularly and were multiplied before important engagements, as before the Battle of Antioch[183] and after the Christian army had marched out of Jerusalem to meet the Egyptians in August 1099.[184] The crusaders all seem to have made confession and taken communion after crossing the Bosphorus, 'at the gates of the land of the Turks', and before every military action.[185] There is only one surviving reference to something that must have been common: the taking of communion, presumably with extreme unction, by a mortally wounded man.[186] The occupation of great religious sites which had been in Muslim hands was marked by solemn ceremonies of purification. Unfortunately the details survive of only one of these, the restoration of the cathedral of St Peter of Antioch, which had been converted into a mosque by the Muslims. Its altars were rebuilt; the image of Christ and the figures of the saints (presumably frescoes since an icon of Christ in the vault was still in place), which, characteristically, had had their eyes gouged out and had been whitewashed, were restored. Greek and Latin clergy were introduced, and vestments were made for them out of the loot gained when the city was sacked.[187] Before important engagements the crusaders expected solemn blessings. Adhémar of Le Puy and the other bishops and priests, vested in white, blessed the troops before the battles of Dorylaeum and Antioch; the army that marched out of Jerusalem in August 1099 venerated the newly discovered relic of the True Cross.[188] During battles the main task of the churchmen was to pray. The crusaders sallied out of Antioch on 28 June 1098 accompanied by Adhémar and a section of the clergy chanting prayers; other priests, also vested and barefoot and carrying crosses, were at prayer on the walls of the city.[189] These prayers were reinforced by the lighting of huge candles in the cathedral and the church of Our Lady.[190] Priests and clerks in vestments stood praying behind a siege tower at Ma'arrat in December 1098;[191] and it was reported that when another siege tower came to a standstill during the siege of Jerusalem the prayers of vested priests got it to move again.[192] During the short campaign before the Battle of Ascalon a constant stream of prayer, organized by Peter the Hermit, went up from the clergy in Jerusalem.[193] The army, in fact, was constantly at public prayer: every procession, every major event, every departure on a new stage of the march was marked by intercessions.[194] There was deep concern with liturgy in the ranks, with an obvious interest in the detailed instructions about a responsory, which was to be chanted in the Office for five consecutive days, passed to the priest Stephen of Valence by Christ in a vision in June 1098.[195] The extraordinarily explicit regulations for an Office of the Feast of the Invention of the Holy Lance transmitted by the visionary Peter Bartholomew astonished the churchmen who heard them from this apparently uneducated man.[196]

It was in the crusade's liturgy that the features of a pilgrimage were particularly clearly delineated. The meticulous care with which a knight called Matthew, in the army of Peter the Hermit, observed the pilgrimage rites while in Constantinople was noted.[197] The crusade struck contemporaries, as we shall see, as being like a military monastery on the move, constantly at prayer: Raymond of Aguilers twice compared the army in battle order to a church procession.[198] It was typical of the age that at every moment of crisis the fears and hopes of the crusaders were canalized into penitential processions. After an earthquake struck the camp at Antioch on 30 December 1097 Adhémar of Le Puy not only ordered the clergy to say prayers and masses; he also decreed a procession. In late June 1098, during a three-day preparation before the crusaders sortied out of Antioch to fight Kerbogha's army, there were barefoot processions from church to church in the city. On 13 January 1099 Raymond of St Gilles, Peter of Narbonne and the clergy led Raymond's army from Ma'arrat on the road south barefooted. The visionary Peter Bartholomew passed on the instruction that the army was not to approach within two leagues of Jerusalem shod, and it worried Raymond of Aguilers that many crusaders ignored this, presumably because Peter's reputation was not high by then. On 8 July, however, according to one report on instructions delivered by the ghost of Adhémar, a great procession wound its way around the outside of Jerusalem, with the clergy barefooted and vested, carrying crosses and relics, blowing trumpets and singing psalms, making its way from holy place to holy place outside the city walls. On the Mount of Olives sermons were preached to it, as we have seen. After the city fell on the 15th another great procession, again barefooted and singing 'a new song to the Lord', went to the Holy Sepulchre and on to the Temple. On 10 August, after the Christian army had left to meet the Egyptian invaders of Palestine, the Greek and Latin clergy in Jerusalem, again vested and barefooted, processed with crosses from the Holy Sepulchre to the Temple.[199] From the time the crusade reached Jerusalem, parties of crusaders made solemn visits to the

Jordan, where they underwent a ritual re-baptism.[200] The penitential nature of the crusade, stressed in these constant processions and rituals, was also expressed in alms-giving and fasting. The crusaders fasted in late June 1097 before their departure from Nicaea, in mid-April 1099 before they raised the siege of 'Arqah, and before proceeding to the election of a ruler for the new kingdom of Jerusalem on the following 22 July. Solemn three-day fasts, which were instituted by Adhémar of Le Puy, were decreed after an earthquake which took place on 30 December 1097, before the battle of Antioch on 28 June 1098, before an ordeal undergone by Peter Bartholomew on 8 April 1099 and before the procession round Jerusalem on 8 July 1099.[201] These fasts certainly made an impression on the crusaders; they could hardly have failed to have done so, since they can only have made their hunger worse. It was reported that during their fast at Antioch Turks came up to walls with loaves of white bread, with which they tempted and mocked the starving men within.[202] The achievement of the crusaders becomes even more remarkable – in fact it is quite incredible – when one considers that soldiers already weakened by starvation, who certainly appreciated the importance of taking food before battle since they took care to give their horses extra rations, deliberately fasted before their more important engagements. One wonders how they managed to fight at all.

It may also have been the clergy who were behind a series of solemn oath-takings, which should have had the effect of binding the army together. These were possibly seen in some way as renewals of the original vows, which had made the force the product of a kind of *conjuratio* or oath of association.[203] Perhaps at the start of the siege of Nicaea and certainly at the start of the siege of Antioch the crusaders swore to maintain their investment until the city fell, however long that might take. While shut inside Antioch in June 1098, inspired, it seems, by Stephen of Valence's vision and faced by the prospect of mass flight, Bohemond, Raymond of St Gilles, Robert of Normandy, Godfrey of Bouillon and Robert of Flanders swore never to desert. Tancred apparently added, perhaps because he had been associated with Baldwin of Boulogne who had now gone off to Edessa, perhaps to insure that he got the money to pay his knights' wages, that he would not turn aside from the march to Jerusalem as long as he had a following of forty knights. At Ramle there may have been a solemn renewal of vows and appeals for St

George's intercession at the time of the establishment of a Latin bishopric centred on his tomb at Lydda nearby.[204]

But the unifying force of religion and the conviction that they shared a holy cause could not make up for divided and weak leadership. The crusade was riven by national differences and distinctions. Although it was, and was regarded as, largely a French enterprise there were enough members of other nationalities to give those taking part the impression that they were in a polyglot army.[205] The inhabitants of France itself, moreover, did not see themselves as belonging to one nation: although the term 'Franks' included men from western Germany, Provençals were treated as another race and there was certainly tension between them and the French proper; it is notable that they abandoned the battle-cry *Deus hoc vult* (God wills this) used by the northern French and south Italian Normans and, following an instruction transmitted by a visionary, adopted the cry *Deus adjuva* (God aid us).[206] Tensions between groups who regarded themselves as being of different races were aggravated by disputes over spoil.[207]

With a divided host and with no leader enjoying enough power to dominate the rest, it was natural for business to be conducted through committees. At the top there was a council of the princes, occasionally enlarged. Bishops sometimes joined the legate at its meetings; Tancred was present on at least one occasion, although he may have taken part often; the experienced Roger of Barneville was once summoned to its deliberations.[208] This council, which in Antioch held at least some of its meetings in the cathedral,[209] decided whom to send as ambassadors to represent the whole army[210] and discussed military tactics and strategy: in the winter of 1098–9 there were anguished debates about the date on which to take up again the march to Jerusalem.[211] It met to consider the state of provisions when the shortage was becoming acute[212] and it elected a Latin bishop for Ramle–Lydda.[213] It gathered at a moment of real crisis in Antioch in a solemn meeting at which the princes promised each other never to desert.[214] It met to discuss who should rule Antioch[215] and probably Jerusalem, although the formal decisions were made at a much larger gathering. For it was not the only kind of meeting in which the princes were engaged. They themselves sought the advice of at least their leading followers in petty councils;[216] and occasionally the whole host was involved in a general assembly. Stephen of Blois was elected commander-in-chief by the princes, but at a meeting at which the whole army was present: he reported that he had been chosen by 'all our princes with the common counsel of the whole army'.[217] The debates on the government of Antioch and Jersualem seem to have been conducted in the same forum, and the procedure can be clearly seen at one of the assemblies in the cathedral of Antioch at which the princes and bishops withdrew apart from the rest and, gathering round what they believed had been St Peter's episcopal throne, made a judgement – as it turned out far too weak and ambiguous – which they then communicated to the people.[218] The ordinary crusaders insisted on a more radical procedure in October 1098 when it was decided to establish a Latin bishop at al-Barah. Raymond of St Gilles wanted to act in accordance with Urban's ruling at Clermont, and anyway in the manner to which he had been accustomed in France, by discussing the appointment only with his chaplains and leading followers before making a personal decision. But the people demanded an election and so the count's candidate was nominated and elected by acclamation.[219] It is noteworthy that this method of election, obviously demanded under the influence of reform ideas, was not followed when the bishop of Ramle–Lydda was installed; by that time all the princes were present in the army. In February, April and again in June 1099 there were also general assemblies to debate the advisability of marching on Jerusalem; and another one decided on the great penitential procession of 8 July.[220]

So for most of the time the crusade was managed by a committee of great lords. There was nothing particularly unusual in that, but not one of these magnates was certain of his strength, not one of them sure of his own following, which could be easily alienated.[221] Apart from Stephen of Blois's short period of command, perhaps during it also, this committee was dominated by Adhémar of Le Puy: when on the night of 10 June 1098 Stephen of Valence had a vision of Christ he was reported informing the apparition: 'There is no single lord here, but people believe the bishop [Adhémar] more than the others.'[222] It is not surprising that Adhémar's death on the following 1 August had a debilitating effect. At first the leaders scattered to their foraging centres and beyond, fearful of the epidemic that had killed him[223] but even after they had returned they could not agree on the next move and for six months they remained divided, before shambling after Raymond of St Gilles, who had been driven by his followers to march for Jerusalem. Nothing illustrates better the weaknesses inherent in a force with a fragmented leadership. The quality of the leadership, or rather the lack of it, was reflected in morale and discipline. There was bound to be an unruly element in so large and heterogeneous a collection of people and, even allowing for the puritanical attitude of many commentators, it is clear that crime and immorality were problems. In western Europe some circles, at least, believed that discipline had been good during the siege of Nicaea,[224] and while Adhémar of Le Puy lived the disorder seems to have been kept under some kind of control, even during the appalling winter of 1097–8. During this period the princes, bishops and clergy legislated for the whole army, decreeing that the use of false weights and measures, fraud, theft, fornication and adultery were to be punished with imprisonment, beatings and brandings. Adulterers, for instance, were to be stripped of their clothing and beaten through the camp.[225] It was the relatively large numbers of women, both pilgrims and the inhabitants of the localities in which the crusaders were encamped, that were seen to be creating par-ticular problems, perhaps – although this is by no means certain – because the laws of pilgrimage demanded abstinence from the sexual act. Adhémar of Le Puy's response was simple. With the first onset of real famine in December 1097 he decreed that all women, married as well as unmarried, were to be expelled from the camp; in practice this meant that they were segregated in an encampment of their own. After the fall of Antioch segregation ended with predictable results, but, with the crusaders bottled up in the city by the Muslims, Adhémar instituted segregation again.[226]

In July 1098, with Adhémar dying and the princes quarrelling over the possession of Antioch, discipline broke down completely. Leaders, accompanied by their retainers, took to robbery and they were imitated by the people. It was said that each took what he wanted because there were no judges before whom to bring criminals for trial.[227] The situation was worsened by Adhémar's death and the continuing divisions among the princes. The clergy no longer took any initiatives in maintaining discipline, although the bishops joined the princes in trying to arbitrate in the dispute over the possession of Antioch and the Provençal clergy organized the elaborate ordeal of the visionary Peter Bartholomew, which will be described later. In two of Peter Bartholomew's visions reference was made to the lack of justice in the army. In one of them, during the night of 5 April 1099,

Christ ordered a new delegated system of justice in the camp, with petty judges having the right to confiscate the goods of offenders.[228] If nothing else, these visions demonstrate the anxiety caused to ordinary crusaders by the lawlessness. The anarchy bore particularly hard on the poor, who mostly followed no great leader. Their independence is revealed in the way heralds went round before the Battle of Antioch, apparently summoning them to attach themselves to any contingent they wished.[229] But independence was actually a weakness, since it meant that they were deprived of the protection of the great, and a solution for some of them was to organize themselves into groups. It was rumoured in Europe that orphaned boys had formed their own regiment at Antioch. A particularly well-known body of very poor and hungry men was called the Tafurs and was led, as we have seen, by a Norman knight who had lost everything and had become a footsoldier. After the crusade stories about this 'king' proliferated and he passed into legend as a major personality, treating with the princes almost on equal terms.[230] It may have been in response to the emergence of this and similar movements among the poor that in February or March 1099 Raymond of St Gilles and his advisers appointed Peter the Hermit official leader of the poor and gave him responsibility for the distribution of one-twentieth of all spoil. Peter was more respectable and presumably more acceptable to them than the poor's own leaders.[231]

It was, in fact, in the winter of 1098–9 that the voice of the people began to be heard, and it was the ordinary crusaders who, fearing starvation, got the crusade moving again. In the middle of November 1098, when the princes could not decide what to do, they became fiercely critical and threatened to elect a knight as their own commander. On 23 November a large party of them forced Raymond of St Gilles and Robert of Flanders to lead them to Ma'arrat. After the fall of Ma'arrat on 11–12 December there was again a delay while the princes dithered. It was in response to popular pressure and to demands that he lead the crusade south that Raymond of St Gilles summoned the other princes to the conference in the Ruj at which he offered to take them into his service for pay, but on *c*.5 January 1099 his followers, hearing that the conference was deadlocked, pulled the walls of Ma'arrat down. Raymond was furious but, deprived of a base, had no option but to recommence the march to Jerusalem on the 13th. Meanwhile the ordinary crusaders left in Antioch were becoming more and more dissatisfied. Godfrey of Bouillon, Robert of Flanders and Bohemond bowed to public pressure and convened a general assembly on 2 February which decided to muster their forces at Latakia on 1 March and to press on from there.[232]

So allied to stress, fear, starvation, disease and death there was ineffective leadership, especially after Adhémar of Le Puy had died. Eventually it was the ordinary people who forced the leaders to march for Jerusalem.

Chapter 4

The ideas of the crusaders

Anyone who reads the letters written during the crusade and the eyewitness accounts will be struck by the crusaders' sense of wonder. Feelings of amazement at the magnitude of their achievement came over them as they left Asia Minor and neared Antioch. In a despatch of 18 October 1097 Adhémar of Le Puy and the Greek patriarch of Jerusalem summarized the successes so far and went on: 'We are few in comparison with the pagans. Truly God fights for us.'[1] This was taken up in the following January in a letter from the bishops in the army.

> How one against a thousand? Where we have a count the enemy has forty kings; where we have a regiment the enemy has a legion; where we have a knight they have a duke; where we have a footsoldier they have a count; where we have a castle they have a kingdom. We do not trust in any multitude nor in power nor in any presumption, but in the shield of Christ and justice, under the protection of George and Theodore and Demetrius and St Blaise, soldiers of Christ truly accompanying us.[2]

The success of an army so badly supplied and led could only be ascribed by them to God, and with the capture of Antioch and Jerusalem and the defeats of threatening Muslim relief forces the chorus swelled: 'We had the most victorious hand of the Father with us'; 'the earth fought for us'.[3] Astonishment persisted after the crusade, when the participants came to look back on it. 'Who could not marvel at the way we, a small people among such kingdoms of our enemies, were able not just to resist them but to survive.'[4] It was natural for them to recall the exploits of the Israelites in the Old Testament and to compare them with their own. In their sufferings they were inspired by the patience of Job; in their march, their hardships and the blessings showered upon them they were like the Israelites journeying from Egypt to the Promised Land, with Adhémar of Le Puy as their Moses; like the Maccabees they fought for Jerusalem, they faced martyrdom, and God's favour was revealed in miracles; only the crusade was even more miraculous than the enterprises of the Israelites and Maccabees, while the crusaders' sufferings were not surpassed by those of their ancient exemplars.[5]

Their growing conviction that they were operating in a supernatural context was heightened by the fact that, after a period of calm, the skies again became troubled, just as they began to move from Asia Minor into Syria. In early October 1097 a comet – one, incidentally, well-documented in Chinese and Korean records – was seen with a tail shaped like a sword. As the ground shook in the earthquake of 30 December the heavens glowed red and there appeared a great light in the form of a cross; this is possibly an early reference to 'earthquake lights'. On the night of 13 June 1098 a meteor fell from the West on to the Muslim camp outside Antioch. The night of 27 September seems to have been extraordinary, with an aurora so great that it was seen in Europe as well as in Antioch: it must have been visible over a large part of the northern hemisphere. On 5 June 1099 there was an eclipse of the moon as the crusade approached Jerusalem.[6] These were interpreted as portents of a Christian victory; indeed it was said that had a solar, rather than a lunar, eclipse taken place on 5 June 1099 it would have forecast defeat. It was, of course, an age in which the views of astrologers were sought and recorded. It was said that in the West Bishop Gilbert of Lisieux had already foretold the migration of peoples before Pope Urban preached at Clermont; so had a Muslim astrologer with whom Count Robert le Frison of Flanders had had discussions while on a pilgrimage to Jerusalem in the late 1080s.[7] During the crusade Arnulf of Chocques had been given a prediction of the victory of Antioch by one of his pupils, who was an astrologer.[8] An odd example of the crusaders' interest in astrology comes in a story that may have been circulating among them within weeks of that battle. In the *Gesta Francorum* and the *History* of Peter Tudebode there was reproduced a dialogue between the Turkish general Kerbogha, who was made out to be not only arrogant but also ignorant and naive, and his mother, who was portrayed as trying to dissuade him from engaging the crusaders in battle on the grounds that resistance to them was useless because they did not fight alone, being sons of God, while their conquest of Syria was prophesied in the Koran as well as in the Bible and was confirmed by her own astrological calculations.[9]

The discovery of relics, for which the crusaders naturally had a profound respect, helped to reinforce in their minds the message they thought they were receiving from signs in the sky. They had, of course, left Europe carrying relics with them. Raymond of St Gilles had taken with him a chalice that had belonged to St Robert of Chaise-Dieu.[10] Beside Godfrey of Bouillon as he rode into the Battle of Antioch there seems to have been carried a reliquary containing relics of a St Simeon. The compiler of the Provençal version of the *Chanson d'Antioche* thought this was the Simeon who in the *Nunc Dimittis* had rejoiced at the appearance of the child Jesus in the Temple, but, assuming the report in the *Chanson* is true, they were much more likely to have been those of St Simeon of Trier, a Sicilian Greek hermit who after living in Palestine had settled in Trier in the early eleventh century and had died there: it would have been very appropriate for his relics to have been carried in the army.[11] Adhémar of Le Puy had a relic of the True Cross, which he either brought from western Europe or acquired in the course of the journey, perhaps in Constantinople. It was carried with the other relics into the Battle of Antioch. After Adhémar's death and the departure of the crusaders from Antioch it, together with the other contents of Adhémar's chapel, seems to have been taken by Godfrey of Bouillon and Robert of Flanders to Latakia, something which worried a visionary with Raymond of St Gilles, since he reported a message from Adhémar's ghost concerning it. Raymond sent Adhémar's brother William Hugh of Monteil to fetch it and his return with it to the camp at 'Arqah was a signal for another revolt among Raymond's followers, who burnt their tents, thus paving the way for the abandonment of the siege and the continuation of the march; this was at a time of disillusionment following the visionary Peter Bartholomew's failure of the ordeal.[12] The crusaders' relics were carried in the great procession round Jerusalem on 8 July 1099.[13] Their devotion to them must have been heightened by their passage through Constantinople, where there was an astonishingly large collection of them, and by the opportunity they had to venerate prodigious images, like that of Christ in Antioch, which had been left in the vault of the cathedral even after it had been converted by the Muslims into a mosque. The story was that it was irremovable, for a Turk ordered to take it down had fallen to his death when he had tried to do so.[14] In these unfamiliar surroundings those relics that were the vestiges of familiar saints must have helped to bridge the gap between home and the alien environment in which the crusaders found themselves. And, as I have already pointed out, the Holy Land was itself a relic, glowing with the power imparted to it by physical contact with the prophets and apostles and particularly with Christ. It is not hard to imagine the growing sense of excitement as the army passed on its way to Jerusalem landmarks of such religious significance that they would have been major cult centres in western Europe: Tyre, which had been visited by Christ; Caesarea, where St Peter had preached at the house of the centurion Cornelius; and Emmaus – or rather the village the crusaders thought was Emmaus – where Christ had appeared after his resurrection. It was believed that the Egyptian caliph had threatened to pulverize all objects in Palestine associated with Christ so that the French would not come to claim them.[15] But the land was also a source of relics, because its ground continually brought forth newly discovered ones.[16]

The crusaders, in fact, had begun to pick up relics as soon as they had left home. Robert of Flanders was given some in Apulia by Duke Roger.[17] In the Byzantine empire one of his priests, Gerbault of Lille, stole an arm of St George from a Greek monastery. On Gerbault's death this relic passed to another man from Lille, Gerard of Buc, who also died – it was believed because neither he nor Gerbault had been fit custodians – whereupon the guardianship of the relic was assumed by Robert of Flanders himself. He kept it in his tent. Because of his devotion to the saint he became known as 'the son of St George'.[18] Now, as the crusaders passed into Syria others began to be discovered. A reliquary was found in the church of St Andrew in Antioch containing two of the apostle's fingers.[19] The visionary Peter Desiderius was instructed to collect four reliquaries, of SS Cyprian, Epimachus, Leontios and John Chrysostom, from the church of St Leontios in Antioch. He, Raymond of St Gilles, William of Orange and Raymond of Aguilers found the reliquaries together with a fifth, which had no inscription on it, although some of the local residents held it to be of St Mercury. On the theologically sound grounds that unknown bones could not be honoured, they left it in the church, but Peter Desiderius was visited twice by an irate St George, who claimed that the relic was another one of his and ordered Peter to pick it up together with reliquaries containing the blood of Our Lady and a relic of St Thecla.[20] As we shall see, many crusaders returned home with relics acquired in the East, among them the Norman knight Ilger Bigod, who had been a sub-commander of Tancred's force in Jerusalem and had revealed to him the hiding place of a ball of Our Lady's hair, torn out by her as she mourned Christ's death.[21]

The strangest of the discoveries was the Holy Lance which had pierced Christ's side during the crucifixion. Between 30 December 1097 and 10 June 1098 a southern French serving-man called Peter Bartholomew claimed to have had five visions of St Andrew, who transported him miraculously into Muslim Antioch and into the cathedral church of St Peter and momentarily produced the Lance from a spot in the floor, not far from where the High Altar had stood. The apostle promised that whoever carried the Lance would never be overcome in battle and instructed that it should be given to Raymond of St Gilles, to whom God had conceded it. At the moment of the crusade's greatest crisis, with the Christians enclosed in Antioch, Peter informed the princes of his visions. He was immediately taken into the protection of Count Raymond, who entrusted him to the care of Raymond of Aguilers. We have, therefore, a priceless and circumstantial, if very partisan, account of the events that followed. On 14 June twelve men from Raymond of St Gilles's following, including the count himself, Raymond of Aguilers, William of Orange and Farald of Thouars, went with Peter to the cathedral. They dug all day without finding anything, but in the evening, after Count Raymond had left to take up military duties, Peter jumped down into the trench and showed his companions the tip of the Lance sticking out of the soil. Raymond of Aguilers reported kissing it while it was still in the ground. Peter Bartholomew claimed another visit from St Andrew that night, during which the apostle repeated that Raymond of St Gilles had been given the Lance by God and issued detailed instructions for the Office of the Feast of its Invention.

The discovery of the Lance, which was believed to have been prophesied in an apocryphal Gospel of St Peter, transformed Christian morale and was an important element in the decision to sortie out of Antioch and engage Kerbogha's force. Most of the crusaders held it in great veneration.[22] Raymond of St Gilles showed particular devotion to it and was careful to follow St Andrew's instructions for its custody. It was clearly profitable for him, for oblations were showered on it – even Adhémar of Le Puy made a small donation – and Raymond, whose treasury benefited, was later accused of being greedy.[23] There was, on the other hand, open scepticism, even hostility, shown by other leaders: there was, after all, a well-known Holy Lance already in Constantinople. Adhémar of Le Puy's reaction was that of any good catholic bishop to extraordinary claims and fervour; he openly expressed his doubts. So did Arnulf of Chocques and the bishop of Apt. Robert of Normandy, Robert of Flanders, Tancred and Bohemond were all very sceptical, believing that Peter had simply brought a piece of iron with him into the cathedral.[24] But the army was in a state of euphoria and the doubters were temporarily silenced, while several events played into the hands of the believers. Raymond of St Gilles was very ill at the time of the Battle of Antioch and his men, among whom was Raymond of Aguilers carrying the Lance, accompanied Adhémar of Le Puy.[25] It therefore looked as though Adhémar himself had had the Lance borne into battle; the story even got about that he had carried it himself.[26] The most extraordinary tales circulated, such as one in which a heavenly army of saints and dead crusaders, which was supposed to have come to the aid of the Christians in the battle, lowered its standards to the Lance as it passed, and another in which before the sortie Adhémar offered the Lance to each of the magnates in turn, who all refused to carry it on the grounds that they wished to fight; so he agreed to bear it himself and persuaded Raymond of St Gilles to lend it to him.[27] A result was that even in sophisticated circles in Europe the Lance came to be regarded as genuine because it was thought, wrongly, that Adhémar had accepted its authenticity; by the thirteenth century the legend had grown up that one of Christ's shrouds, by then in the abbey of Cadouin, had been found in the same place as the Lance and kept by Adhémar.[28] The Christian victory at Antioch was, of course, attributed to the Lance's power: Raymond of Aguilers himself reported that no one fighting near it was wounded. Such was the enthusiasm that even the leaders, including Bohemond, Robert of Normandy and Robert of Flanders, referred to the relic when they informed the pope of their success.[29] It was arranged, moreover, for Adhémar's body to be buried in the trench in which it had been found,[30] while Peter Bartholomew and other visionaries reported a series of visits from the dead legate in which he confessed to them that he now knew that the Lance was genuine and that he had been punished by God for his disbelief.[31]

For a time feeling in the army seems to have been very strong. Raymond of St Gilles was regarded by the ordinary people as the natural leader of the crusade because he had been entrusted with the Lance; as we have seen, he was given specific instructions by Peter Bartholomew on where it was to be housed in southern France once the crusade was over. Even Arnulf of Chocques, the doubters' leader, faced by an assembly at which all the visionaries reported what they had seen, especially Adhémar's ghostly visitations, had to promise to make public reparation, although he never did so.[32] In fact support in the army for him may have been growing by April 1099 as Peter Bartholomew's visions became more eccentric: Bohemond and his knights had already made fun of one of them in the previous December.[33] Peter, angered by Arnulf's attitude, now suggested himself that he undergo an ordeal, and this played straight into the hands of the senior clergy, who at once agreed to it. On 8 April Peter, dressed in a tunic and carrying the relic, crossed a bed of fiercely burning olive-wood logs. He seemed to have got across safely and it was asserted later that he was only injured when he was mobbed by the crowd, who rushed on him after he had crossed and scrambled to collect the cinders as relics. It was also said that a bird was seen flying above him and that a man vested as a priest preceded him into the fire; in fact he claimed to have met Christ in the midst of the ordeal. But at any rate he was seriously injured and died twelve days later.[34] The ordinary crusaders naturally became disillusioned and Arnulf of Chocques and Bishop Arnulf of Martirano, with the intention, it seems, of creating an alternative focus for devotions, had a gold image of Christ made and encouraged oblations to it. This seems to have been placed on top of one of Godfrey of Bouillon's siege engines during the siege of Jerusalem.[35] But Raymond of St Gilles obstinately held to the Lance's authenticity. He was furious with Arnulf of Chocques and sent armed men to hunt him out: Robert of Normandy and Robert of Flanders had to give Arnulf protection. After the fall of Jerusalem Raymond solemnly and in ignorance of their significance carried out some absurd and incomprehensible instructions passed on to him on St Andrew's behalf by Peter Bartholomew: he crossed the Jordan on a raft, had himself rebaptized in a shirt and breeches and kept these underclothes with the Lance. His chaplain carried the Lance in the Battle of Ascalon.[36] He later took it with him to Constantinople and it was apparently lost in Asia Minor in the débacle of 1101, although it is possible that metal parings had been chipped off it before this; a piece was perhaps still being venerated in Jerusalem in the 1120s and a century later the church at Ardres claimed that Arnold of Ardres had brought a fragment back with him.[37]

If the Holy Lance was the most strange of the relics discovered, the most famous was the True Cross. The fragment of the cross once housed in the Church of the Holy Sepulchre had disappeared before the First Crusade. It was rediscovered on 5 August 1099 by the new Latin patriarch of Jerusalem, Arnulf of Chocques himself, who had made enquiries and found it buried in the atrium of a church, probably the 'garden' area of the Holy Sepulchre compound, after a dig which was not too dissimilar to that which had led to the Lance's discovery. Arnulf carried it in the Battle of Ascalon. Thereafter it was kept in the Church of the Holy Sepulchre and was regularly carried to war, being held in the greatest veneration throughout the Latin Christian world until it was lost during the Battle of Hattin in 1187.[38]

The signs in the heavens, the discoveries of relics, the apparitions, about which I will have more to say later, and their extraordinary success induced in the participants a state of mind in which miraculous multiplications of the Christian armies, like those of the loaves and fishes, were witnessed[39] and in which dates and times had supernatural significance: Jerusalem was taken on the Feast of the Dispersion of the Apostles, commemorating in triumph a reversal suffered by the early Church; the break into the city occurred at the hour when Christ had died on the cross.[40] With their expectations and their dawning realization that the enterprise was as miraculous as any Old Testament epic, coincidences came to be treated by them as miracles, as when the lucky shedding of his hauberk saved Raimbold Creton from drowning, or when Bohemond, demonstrating the quality of his knife in a wager with Robert of Flanders, sliced a candle in half only to see the bottom part light, or when a man badly wounded at Ma'arrat survived for a week without food, or when a Muslim carrier pigeon was shot down – 'the birds could not even fly through the air to harm us' – or when the movements of herds of stray animals confused the enemy and assisted the advance of the Christian army during the Battle of Ascalon.[41] On the other hand entirely natural occurrences were regarded as being sent providentially by God. It was reported that the noise made by the Christians as they entered the city of Antioch was muffled by a strong wind; a light shower refreshed the Christian army as it sortied before the Battle of Antioch; rain filled a Christian moat with water before Antioch and frustrated the enemy's attempts to deprive the crusade of water before Ma'arrat; and an overcast day aided the Christians at the Battle of Ascalon.[42]

The astonishment of the crusaders translated itself into a realization of the power of God's favour which helped to fuse the elements proposed by Pope Urban and taken up by the knights who had responded to his call into the idea of the crusade. The crusaders were not fools. Although they seem to have exaggerated their own numbers,[43] they knew how comparatively weak, badly led and under-provisioned they were. They had experienced great privation. Their success could have been put down to the inefficiency and inadequacy of their foes, but it was impossible for them to believe that their enemies were not powerful. For them the only explanation of their astounding achievement was the fact that they really were fulfilling the intentions of God. They had set out, of course, convinced that they were involved in God's work. That was how the crusade had been preached and its battle-cry from the first had been *Deus hoc vult* (God wills this). In a muted but clearly discernible way this conviction comes across in the first surviving letter of the campaign, sent by Stephen of Blois on 24 June 1097, after the fall of Nicaea. He or his amanuensis referred to the crusade as the 'army of God', a term which, with its variant 'knighthood of Christ', was to recur in the letters. The surrender of Nicaea was portrayed as God's triumph and the evil intentions of the Turks were described as being frustrated by divine mercy.[44] Up to now the idea of war for God had been fairly conventional, as we have seen, and could be compared to the expostulations uttered at any time in history by any ruler justifying war and any soldiers fighting on his behalf. It was now transformed because the crusaders came to recognize that in the magnitude of their achievement the rhetoric proved to have been truthful in their case. They *were* fighting a holy war on behalf of a God whose physical aid they *had* experienced. As the crusade progressed their language became more extravagant. They claimed to be taking part in a 'blessed' or 'most holy' expedition, fought for the Lord, on whose behalf the conquests were made. It followed that the Muslims' resistance to it was useless, since they fought against the wishes of God. 'Why did Kerbogha flee, who had so many men and was so well provided with horses? Since he tried to make war on God, the Lord, seeing his pomp from afar, shattered it and his power altogether.'[45] It was Christ, their only Lord, who gave them the cities they took and the victories they won. When they fought they were under divine leadership; they were aided by God's strong right arm, by his might against which nothing could prevail; indeed his miraculous power worked through them.[46] He confused or terrified their enemies. He strengthened and protected them. He personally fought in battle with and for them. 'God, strong and powerful in battle, protected his sons and cut down the enemies'.[47] Many crusaders seem to have experienced the feeling of being constantly under his watchful protection. He was their helper, their defender, their leader, their general and their co-traveller and co-worker.[48] 'As we advanced we had the most generous and merciful and most victorious hand of the almighty Father with us.'[49] The author of the *Gesta Francorum* had Kerbogha's mother saying to her son: 'Their God fights for them every day and defends them day and night and watches over them as a shepherd watches over his flock and allows no people to hurt or trouble them.'[50] Nothing was believed to happen outside the control of divine providence. God wanted a Christian army to march through the Slav regions of Greece to be an example of power and forbearance. He wanted to shut the crusaders in at Antioch to prevent the cowards fleeing. He would not let a siege tower burn at Ma'arrat.[51] It was not the crusaders who were victorious: as a letter of January 1098 put it, 'God has triumphed'.[52]

He had, moreover, clearly foretold what would happen on the campaign; by September 1099 it was occurring to the participants that their success fulfilled the prophecies of scripture, although there was no agreement on which prophetic sentences were applicable.[53] 'God has magnified his mercy by fulfilling in us what he promised in ancient times.'[54] In April 1100 this was taken up by the new pope, Paschal II.

> We see fulfilled in you what the Lord promised his people through the prophet. 'I will live,' he said, 'with them and I will walk with them.' He has lived through the faith in your hearts and he has walked with you in your works, as is clearly to be seen in your defeat of his enemies. The Lord has certainly renewed his miracles of old.[55]

God's miraculous power was also demonstrated in the visions experienced by some crusaders. In them God or Christ rebuked and advised them, either in person or through his intermediaries,[56] saints or dead crusaders, who were also believed to be fighting for them at times. It will be remembered that early in August 1097 St Giles appeared to assure a Saxon count that Raymond of St Gilles would recover from the illness he was suffering. Shortly before 18 October the Greek patriarch of Jerusalem experienced a vision in which Christ himself promised a crown of martyrdom for the dead. Peter Bartholomew did not tell the leaders of his visions until June 1098, but they had begun on the previous 30 December, at the time of the earthquake in Antioch.[57] So, as with the signs in the sky, it was with the crossing of Asia Minor that the supernatural began to assert itself.

Although visionaries were to be found among eastern Christians as well as Latins and were drawn from a wide range of classes, no less than six were from southern France and Provence and were followers of Raymond of St Gilles and Adhémar of Le Puy. Of these the bishop of Apt and the two priests Simon and Bertrand of Bas each had one vision; a priest from Lower Burgundy called Stephen of Valence had two; another priest called Peter Desiderius, who was chaplain to Isoard of Die, had six; and the poor but not illiterate servant Peter Bartholomew had thirteen. It is possible that there was something in the attitudes of the south French and Provençal crusaders that encouraged visions. It is clear that they did have a particular reputation in this respect, probably associated with Raymond of St Gilles's firm belief in the messages the visionaries delivered, although it is notable that, while St Giles made one appearance, the other objects of Raymond's own veneration, SS Robert and Faith, did not appear. Peter Bartholomew's messages were certainly treated seriously by the south French army. As we have seen, it changed its battle-cry and there was anxiety expressed because the crusaders approaching Jerusalem were not marching barefooted, as Peter had enjoined them to do. Most of the evidence for these experiences and for the reactions to them comes from the account of the crusade written by Raymond of St Gilles's chaplain Raymond of Aguilers. There has been a tendency recently to dismiss the details given by him on the grounds that his language and imagery were biblical and liturgical and therefore not strictly descriptive, but so was the language of most contemporary accounts, and Raymond's evidence is corroborated at times, particularly with regard to the visions of Stephen of Valence and Peter Bartholomew.

He included, moreover, a wealth of circumstantial detail which suggests that he was reporting what he and others in his circle believed to be the truth. On the other hand, Adhémar of Le Puy, who accepted the veracity of the reports of the Greek patriarch and Stephen of Valence, although Stephen had to swear to the truth of what he had told,[58] was doubtful about Peter Bartholomew's visions, as we have seen, and his doubts were shared by many of the senior churchmen present. They were, of course, showing a proper pastoral concern to play down manifestations of hysteria, although it cannot be said that they were any more successful in this regard than churchmen usually are.

Christ was reported to have made several visitations.[59] I have already referred to the Greek patriarch's vision. There was a remarkable appearance on the night of 10 June 1098. At this moment of real crisis in Antioch, Stephen of Valence had gone with others to pray in the church of St Mary. His companions fell asleep, but while Stephen was at prayer a beautiful figure appeared and asked Stephen if he knew him. Seeing a cross behind his head, Stephen suggested that he was Christ. The figure acknowledged that he was, ordered Stephen to make a profession of faith and questioned him about the command structure in the army, reminding him of the benefits he had already granted the crusaders. He complained bitterly about their sinful behaviour in Antioch. At this point Our Lady and St Peter appeared to intercede for them, whereupon Christ relented and ordered Stephen to tell the princes to return to the path of righteousness. Then, within five days, he would send them powerful aid: that, of course, was to be the discovery of the Lance. He ordered them in the meantime to sing in the daily Office the responsory *Congregati sunt*.[60]

Nine months later, on 5 April 1099, he appeared to Peter Bartholomew. At that time the crusade was before 'Arqah and was divided whether to continue the investment of the town or to press on with the march to Jerusalem. Raymond of St Gilles was reluctant to give up the siege and it is not surprising that Peter should have had a vision that gave divine sanction to his protector's point of view. Christ, St Andrew, St Peter and a dark stranger came to Peter when he was meditating in the count's chapel and was thinking, rather jealously, about Stephen of Valence's experience. Christ announced himself and then the image of him changed: he reappeared hanging on a wooden cross, naked except for a purple loin cloth edged in white, red and green bands, with the apostles supporting him. He told Peter how the crusaders could be distinguished according to their commitment to the enterprise and how traitors could be identified; these should be executed without delay. He issued regulations for good order in the army and apparently gave Peter the power to excommunicate the judges whom he wished to be appointed should they do wrong. But he refused to cure the illiteracy that Peter claimed to have come upon him for lying to William of Orange and Raymond of Aguilers after one of his earlier visions. The story of this remarkable apparition aroused controversy in the army and led directly to Peter's ordeal by fire.[61] Before he died Peter told Raymond of Aguilers that Christ had met him in the flames, had held his hand and had said that because he doubted his own early visions he would be injured, although he would not go to hell.[62]

In his other appearances Christ was inactive. Between 30 December 1097 and 22 September 1098 he appeared seven times to Peter Bartholomew, but always as a young man standing silently by while St Andrew or the recently dead Adhémar of Le Puy did the talking. It was not until the fifth of these apparitions, on 15 June 1098, that his identity was revealed by a wound in his foot.[63] When he did speak to the visionaries he showed himself to be angered by sin, but pacified by intercession, the proper performance of liturgical rites and righteous living. He was a legislator. He expressed hatred of nonbelievers. But in his supporting role in many visions – a role that puzzled Peter Bartholomew[64] – he seems merely to have been reinforcing by his presence the messages delivered by his intermediaries.

These were most often saints. Some were not named: an old man dressed in white who appeared to the bishop of Apt; a tall, dark, big-eyed, almost bald stranger who appeared to Peter Bartholomew (was this St John Chrysostom remembered from some Greek icon?); a virgin carrying two candles who accompanied St Agatha in a vision of Stephen of Valence; and a divine messenger who instructed Peter Desiderius to pick up some relics.[65] Two saints, Agatha and Nicholas, had walk-on parts, but Our Lady and SS Andrew, Demetrius, George, Giles, Mark, Mercury and Peter had substantial roles.[66]

It is not surprising that devotion to Our Lady was a feature of the crusade. It was originally planned to depart on the Feast of the Assumption 1096.[67] A banner depicting her was carried in Adhémar of Le Puy's company as it crossed Asia Minor.[68] She appeared three times, twice as an intercessor. The most interesting vision of her was experienced by Stephen of Valence in mid-April 1099, when she came as a silent figure accompanied by St Agatha and the ghost of Adhémar of Le Puy. Orders on her behalf were relayed by Adhémar. Stephen was to give his ring to Raymond of St Gilles with the message that this was a gift from her. If Raymond were to invoke her he would receive aid from God. The Holy Lance was to be carried only by a vested priest and Adhémar's relic of the True Cross was to precede it. Adhémar ended the session by beginning to sing the responsory *Gaude Maria virgo, cunctas haereses sola interemisti,* which was taken up by a heavenly choir.[69] Our Lady was beginning her association with crusades and with violence, which was to be a particular characteristic of devotion to her in the central Middle Ages.

Nor is it surprising to find St Peter making appearances. What is surprising is the comparatively small role he played, given that the crusade was preached by the pope, was waged under papal authority in an aura of Carolingian romance and was regarded as a French enterprise: the French prided themselves on their tradition of devotion to St Peter and the Holy See. Peter made relatively few appearances, Petrine theory, so dominant in the papal curia, was low-key, and, in the most curious development of all, the crusaders associated Peter mostly with his first see, Antioch, rather than with his second, Rome. The princes even went as far as to invite Pope Urban to journey out to Antioch, 'the original and first city of the Christian Name', where, after Peter had been enthroned, the Galileans were first called Christians.

> Afterwards St Peter will be enthroned on his episcopal throne. . . .
> We ask you, who are father and head, to come to the place of your fatherhood and you, who are St Peter's vicar, to sit on his episcopal throne.[70]

The almost total absence of the Petrine theme in what was above all a papal exercise may have worried the papacy, if one or two emphatic references to Peter emanating from Rome later are anything to go by. It is to be explained partly by the fact that the crusade was not a continuation of the war for St Peter of the Investiture Contest but really was a war for Christ, and partly by a natural consequence of the way saints were associated with localities in the minds of contemporaries. It is notable that while the personal predilections of the crusaders, as far as we know them, were for western cults, there was on the march a slight shift towards the veneration of eastern saints or the association of western saints with eastern localities. As the crusaders moved out of the confines of Latin Christendom they passed into an area in which familiar saints had different personae and where saints who had played comparatively minor parts in western devotions were now prominent. It was the most natural thing in the world for the Antiochene Peter to be in the forefront of their minds at Antioch and, as we shall see, for Greek soldier saints to be bringing aid to a Christian army fighting in their territory.[71]

Peter was, in fact, overshadowed by two saints who, although venerated in the West, had special associations with the East. One was St George. The first of these interventions seems to have followed the theft of his relic, for it was reported by Turkish deserters after the Battle of Dorylaeum on 1 July 1097 that the crusaders had been led by two horsemen with marvellous faces and glittering armour; these were later identified as SS George and Demetrius.[72] In January 1098 the Greek and Latin bishops in the army wrote of it being under the protection of SS George, Theodore, Demetrius and Blaise.[73] The crusaders, therefore, were predisposed to accept the miraculous appearance some claimed to have seen during the Battle of Antioch on 28 June 1098, when an army of angels, saints and dead crusaders, carrying white banners and riding white horses and led by SS George, Demetrius and Mercury, came to lend them assistance. This extraordinary event made a great impression: it must have been behind the appearance of the figure of St George on coins of the Latin principality of Antioch; and in Europe St George's aid to the crusade was to be the subject of paintings and sculptures for decades.[74] Some months later the visionary Peter Desiderius had, as we have seen, been addressed by an irate St George on the subject of another reliquary of his relics in Antioch which he wanted carried in the army. By this time there was a growing devotion to him and he was regarded as the army's standard-bearer; when the crusaders reached Ramle, near Lydda where he was supposed to have been buried, they chose a Latin bishop, endowed his church well and held a service of intercession to him.[75]

The other saint was Andrew, who appeared, it was claimed, at least nine times to Peter Bartholomew and once to Peter Desiderius. The fact that this ecclesiastical rival to St Peter, the apostle claimed as a patron by Constantinople in its resistance to Petrine ecclesiology, outshone Peter in the course of the crusade is further evidence of the crusaders' recognition that they had moved into a foreign region. Andrew was described as being an elderly man with red hair sprinkled with white, a bushy white beard and black eyes. The first five visitations were all concerned with the Holy Lance, but Peter Bartholomew reported that in the course of them Andrew also told him that God loved the crusaders and had chosen them out of all mankind and that the saints would return to fight at their side. After the Lance had been found Peter transmitted Andrew's command to the crusaders to offer five alms in preparation for the Battle of Antioch or, if they could not afford this, to say five paternosters in remembrance of Christ's wounds. Andrew, Peter reported, had exhorted them to hold to their faith in the Resurrection and wanted to assure them that their dead would fight at their side in the battle. He had issued instructions on their battle-cry and had forbidden them to turn aside to loot. On 3 August 1098 he intervened through Peter in the dispute over the possession of Antioch and showed himself clearly to be on the side of Raymond of St Gilles. He ordered the crusaders to appoint a Latin patriarch, to help the poor and to pray for guidance on how to proceed to Jerusalem. Crusaders who had apostasized while in Muslim captivity were to be treated as though they were Muslims and some of them should be imprisoned as an example to the others. In the second half of September another appearance was reported in which he was said to have been angry because the reliquary containing his fingers, which had been found in Antioch, was not being kept in a suitable place; to emphasize the point he had raised his hand, from which several fingers were missing. He had promised Raymond of St Gilles that as a sign from God a great candle he intended to light for the Feast of St Faith would not last, although a little candle alongside it would remain lit for more than three days. He had enjoined penitence on Raymond, to whose counsellors he objected. He had forbidden Raymond to ride a horse within two leagues of Jerusalem. On c.1 December, with the army before Ma'arrat, he was reported coming again, this time with St Peter, who did the talking; the two apostles appeared as ugly and filthy men in tattered clothes. Peter Desiderius reported an appearance in early May 1099 in which Andrew offered words of comfort to Raymond of St Gilles, but also warned him to distribute booty fairly; if he did so, God would give him not only Jerusalem but Egypt also.[76]

It is clear that the visionaries' reports of Andrew's messages – on the Lance, on the role of Raymond of St Gilles, on disputes within the army – were directly concerned either with their own status as *illuminati* or with the internal politics of the crusade. But however trivial these messages may seem to have been to us they certainly reflected the concerns of Peter Bartholomew, Peter Desiderius and their confrères. The instructions of the saints appealed to those who heard reports of them precisely because they provided them with answers to problems which, however peripheral to the crusade they may seem today, were very much on their minds; and they were intermixed with exhortations on the faith and on devotions which must have had the effect of reinforcing the crusaders' commitment to the task they had undertaken.

All this contributed to the conviction that the crusade was God's own war. There is no doubt that the crusaders believed they fought it justly,[77] and the capture of Jerusalem prompted one of them to launch into a paean of praise, containing significant liturgical information, which demonstrated how they linked their success with the Resurrection and with the renewal of the Church.

A new day. . . . This day of the enfeeblement of all paynim, of the strengthening of Christianity and of the renewal of our faith. *This is the day which the Lord hath made: Let us be glad and rejoice.* And rightly. Because on this day God has illumined and blessed his people. . . . This day is celebrated . . . the gift, in answer to the Church's prayers, of the city and fatherland which God promised to the fathers and restored in faith and blessing to the sons. On this day we sang the Office of Easter, because on this day he who rose through his might from the dead revived [his Church] through his grace.[78]

It will be remembered that Pope Urban had preached the crusade with two aims: the release of fellow-Christians from injuries suffered at the hands of the Muslims and the liberation of Jerusalem. The first of these causes is not much in evidence in the writings of the partici-pants, although Fulcher of Chartres, whose account of the sermon at Clermont contained, for the obvious reason that he himself went with Baldwin of Boulogne to Edessa, no reference to Jerusalem, made great play of the sufferings of the crusaders' co-religionists and Raymond of Aguilers referred to the poor conditions Christians had to endure under Muslim rule.[79] An echo of it may also be heard in the crusaders' generally mild attitude to eastern Christians, although there was certainly hostility felt towards eastern heretics. It is true that in one letter 'Greeks' were listed among these heretics, but this is unique and the reference may have been not to the orthodox but to Greek heretics in Syria, for the orders of the Greek clergy were respected. In fact there is no evidence of any great animosity, or even envy, shown towards the Greek people, although they were thought to be militarily incompetent and the Byzantine government and its officials were roundly abused and were accused of treachery.[80] The eastern Christians were described as brothers in the faith, who had suffered from the pagans and needed help and avenging. It is not surprising that the crusaders were portrayed as being reluctant to fight them or take plunder from them.[81]

The cause of aid to brothers was far outweighed, as in the charters of departing crusaders, by the cause of Jerusalem. The crusaders seem to have believed, in accordance with canon law, that land once Christian belonged thereafter to Christendom by right: in a letter the leaders in Antioch wrote to the ruler of Damascus they pointed out that they planned to conquer only the lands which had once belonged to the Greeks. The Muslims were suspicious, but in its stress on a standard criterion for reoccupation by force this letter expressed good canon law.[82] Jerusalem, moreover, the scene of Christ's Passion and Resurrection and the focal point of God's operations in this world, was much more than simply a piece of real estate, as we have seen, being a holy relic itself and Christ's patrimony. The purpose of the crusade was its liberation, or more specifically the liberation of the Holy Sepulchre, which involved cleansing it of the contamination of pagan presence. This accounts for the many references to the *via sancti Sepulchri* (the road to the Holy Sepulchre) and for actions taken 'on behalf of God and the Holy Sepulchre'. For instance, the first lordship established by the crusaders in Asia Minor was given to Peter of Aups to hold 'in fealty to God and the Holy Sepulchre and the princes and the [Byzantine] emperor'.[83] It was this, of course, that made the crusade a pilgrimage, as we have seen, and the crusaders referred to themselves as 'pilgrims of the Holy Sepulchre', where they went to fulfil their vows.[84]

There was also a sense in which they believed they were fighting for the expansion of Christianity, drawing on the parallel perhaps made by Urban at Clermont between the crusade and the Carolingian wars of conquest. In September 1099 Daimbert of Pisa and Raymond of St Gilles wrote how 'the power of the Muslims and the devil has been broken and the kingdom of Christ and the Church now stretches all the way from sea to sea'.[85] In the later stages of the crusade some had the ambition of conquering Egypt as a prelude to the taking of Jerusalem, and soon afterwards there was talk of mastering Asia.[86] This raises the question whether the crusade was also in their minds a war of conversion. One cannot ignore the terrible scenes in Europe in the spring and early summer of 1096, although I have tried to explain them, and there is little doubt that when combined with a contempt for the validity of pagan rule the idea of a war for the expansion of Christendom manifested itself in attitudes not far removed from those in favour of forcible conversion, even if they could be technically distinguished from them, being concerned with the nature of government rather than with proselytism. From Nicaea in the summer of 1097 the leaders sent an embassy to the Fatimid caliph in Egypt offering him Christianity or battle, and much the same choice seems to have been put by Peter the Hermit in his embassy to Kerbogha. Raymond of St Gilles refused to make a treaty with the emir of Tripoli unless he was baptized.[87] But apart from the early pogroms in Europe, there is little evidence that the crusaders misconceived their role to the extent that they thought they were fighting a war of conversion. Although they suffered badly enough, the Jewish communities in Palestine do not seem to have been subjected to the treatment meted out to the Rhinelanders. It has recently been argued that the traditional picture of the persecution of the Jews in Palestine by the crusaders should be modified. Caught up in the sack of cities, the communities suffered loss of life and in Jerusalem the synagogue and Torah scrolls were destroyed and a Karaite library taken. Many Jews were sold into slavery, but most seem to have been ransomed and at least part of the Karaite library was sold back. While conversion to Christianity was offered at times, there is no evidence that refusal meant death. Although the Jewish community in Jerusalem was wiped out, it has been pointed out that 'the crusaders liquidated a Jewish community already in a state of liquidation'.[88] In fact, if we leave aside a slightly different case of the involuntary reception of the faith, the practice of Christian priests of baptizing dying Turks as they lay on the battlefield,[89] there are only two examples outside Europe of forcible mass conversion in the sources, and one of them almost certainly did not occur.

The doubtful reference is to be found in Robert the Monk's account of the taking of al-Barah by Raymond of St Gilles in late September 1098.

> The count ordered that all should be enchained and that those who would not believe in Christ as saviour should be beheaded. . . . No one from such a great multitude was saved unless he willingly confessed Christ and was baptized. And so that city was cleansed and recalled to the worship of our faith.

But in fact it is unlikely that there was any attempt to convert by force at al-Barah. Robert was not on the crusade and his assertion is to be found nowhere else, although all contemporary accounts agree that there was great slaughter, a display of deliberate ferocity in a region with an already strong indigenous Christian presence before the establishment of the first Latin bishopric. Raymond of Aguilers, who was present at al-Barah, reported that many of the inhabitants were killed or sold into slavery in Antioch, but that those who surrendered in the course of the fighting were set free. This looks like a case in which resistance was punished by the razing of the town and the destruction of the inhabitants. It is noteworthy that some manuscripts of Raymond's *History* have the word *crediderant*, which does not really make sense in the context, substituted for *reddiderant*, and it may have been some such textual variant that persuaded Robert to write as his did.[90]

The other case is, however, well-documented. In the middle of July 1098, as we have already seen, Raymond Pilet personally financed a large expedition which he led into the countryside south of Antioch. On 17 July he reached a fortified place east of Ma'arrat called Tall Mannas, which was held by Syrian Christians, and on the 25th he took a nearby fortress which he had been informed was full of Muslims. All those in it who refused to be baptized were killed. Two days later his force, supplemented by local Christians, was bloodily repulsed from Ma'arrat. Robert the Monk commented that Raymond Pilet had an especial hatred of Turks, but it is much more likely that by allying himself to indigenous Christians he had become involved in the complex inter-religious conflicts of the region.[91] At any rate this was untypical of the crusaders' behaviour after they had

left Europe; against it should be set Bohemond's action on 28 June
1098, when he promised the soldiers of the garrison of the citadel of
Antioch who did not wish to convert safe-conducts into Muslim
territory.[92]

The fact that there are so few cases of forcible mass conversions in
Asia and therefore no consistent evidence for a missionary war
should not lead us to suppose that the crusaders were tolerant of
infidels. I have already shown how strong was their desire for vengeance on them. Their language was filled with hate. It is true that
admiration was expressed for the fighting qualities of the Turks, who
apparently believed that they and the French stemmed from a
common stock, an assertion with which the Christians did not
disagree. 'No man, unless born French or Turkish, is naturally a
knight'; if only the Turks had adhered to the Christian faith, 'it
would not have been possible to find stronger or braver or more
skilful warriors'.[93] But this was exceptional. The norm was invective.
The Muslims were said to be barbarians depraved in their morals
and deficient in their faith.[94] Instances of their blasphemy were
recorded[95] and it was believed that death sent them straight to hell.[96]
They were enemies of God, Christ and Christianity;[97] and so they
were servants of the devil and their places of worship were devilish.[98]
It was easy to regard some of them as sorcerers: two women seen
with their children on the walls of Jerusalem were believed to be
witches casting evil eyes on one of the Christian petraries.[99]

The crusaders, on the other hand, were the people, servants,
champions or warriors of God or Christ,[100] engaged in the service of
God.[101] Above all, they were 'knights of Christ', although there is no
evidence for the explicit use of that term until March 1098.[102] As one
would expect in describing an army containing men and women of
many nationalities, the West, in a general sense, was seen to be going
to the aid of the East,[103] but, echoing the message of Pope Urban, the
special contribution of the French was stressed. The crusade was,
above all, a French enterprise, fought for the honour of the Roman
Church and the French. It was the pilgrim church of the French on
the move.[104] Its story was 'the most glorious tale of the French, who
at God's orders went as armed pilgrims to Jerusalem'.[105] In it the
ancient tradition of the Franks as God's chosen people can be seen
surfacing again: 'Blessed is the nation whose God is the Lord'.[106] It

was this that bathed it in a glow of Carolingian romance; indeed at the time of its preaching a rumour had gone round Germany that Charlemagne had risen from the dead. Most of the leaders could trace their ancestry back to Charlemagne and three of them, Robert of Flanders, Godfrey of Bouillon and his brother Baldwin, seem to have been particularly conscious of this. The biographer of Tancred, Ralph of Caen, stressed the fact that in 1100 Baldwin, a descendant of Charlemagne, came to sit, as king of Jerusalem, on the throne of David. Describing the Battle of Dorylaeum he exclaimed that one could say that Roland and Oliver, the heroes of the Song of Roland, were reborn. The crusaders marching through Hungary believed that they were following a road built by Charlemagne.[107]

In fact, they were convinced that they were God's elect, chosen from all mankind, pre-elected for the task they had undertaken.

> It is manifest that God himself chose you and delivered you from all troubles and gave you this city and many others, not in the might of your strength, but to punish the impious in his rage, and he has opened up most powerfully fortified cities and has won terrible battles for you as your leader and lord.[108]

That is not to say, of course, that they could not sin and temporarily anger God themselves. For instance, God did not want 'Arqah to fall to them.[109] His approval and protection did not mean that he would not sometimes permit failure. Occasionally some of the crusaders experienced despair, as during the night of panic in Antioch on 10 or 11 June 1098, or when the false news of the destruction of the crusade at Antioch reached the emperor Alexius and his army of Greeks and crusaders advancing across Asia Minor. This report occasioned a bitter speech from Bohemond's brother Guy, in which he threatened what amounted to a form of diffidation from God. It was said that no one, not even the priests, dared to pray for many days.[110] But these were unusual cases, as far as we can tell. The normal response to reverses is to be found in Anselm of Ribemont's letter of July 1098. 'God, who "punishes all the sons he loves, trained" us in this way.'[111] The idea of God's discipline, which was of course as old as the Old Testament, was strikingly expressed in the letter Daimbert of Pisa and Raymond of St Gilles wrote in September 1099.

For nine months God held us back . . . and humbled us outside Antioch, until all our puffed-up pride had turned back to
humility. And when such was our degradation that scarcely 100
good horses could be found in the whole army, God opened for us
the treasury of his blessing and mercy and led us into the city.[112]

Sufferings, privation and misfortunes were the salutary penalties, the
rods of God, imposed to purify the crusaders and to punish them
when they disobeyed his wishes or lapsed into sin.[113] They were also
integral to the penance they had voluntarily undertaken. Fulcher of
Chartres, commenting on the catastrophic winter of 1097–8, wrote
that 'it is my belief that, pre-elected by God long before and tested in
such a great disaster, they were cleansed of their sins, just as gold is
proved three times and is purged by fire seven times'.[114] The crusade
was, in a sense, a material commentary on the penultimate phrase of
the paternoster, a divine test of the faithfulness and intentions of the
participants. When the army arrived at Jerusalem, Raymond of St
Gilles made a tour of those holy places that lay outside the walls. On
seeing the church on Mount Zion he was reported to have said to his
companions:

If we leave these holy places which God has given us and the
Muslims then occupy them, what will become of us?. . . Who
knows whether God will have given them to us in 'temptation', to
prove how much we love him? Certainly I know this; that if we do
not hold these holy places carefully, he will not give us those that
are within the city.[115]

Believing that they had taken the cross under the inspiration of the
Holy Spirit[116] and convinced by their achievements that they really
were carrying out God's intentions, the crusaders also saw themselves fulfilling the demands of Christian charity: although drawn
from many lands and speaking many tongues, they were, as one of
them put it, united in their love of God and their neighbour. Pope
Urban had told them to take the cross out of love for Christ and they
were convinced that they had done so: in fact they saw themselves
literally fulfilling those precepts of Christ quoted by the pope, 'If any
man will come after me, let him deny himself and take up his cross
and follow me' and 'Every one that hath left house or brethren or
sisters or father or mother or wife or children or lands, for my name's

sake, shall receive an hundredfold and shall possess life everlasting'.[117] The cross was of particular importance and the adoption of its imagery, even the hysterical brandings of it on their flesh, underlined how the way of the cross, the summons to take up which had in the past been one that had led inevitably to the adoption of the monastic habit and to the acceptance of a life of mortification in which one died to the world, was now being presented as a path to salvation open to laymen. Fortified and sanctified by it, the crusaders fought for its victory.[118] The strength of the image was demonstrated not only by the fact that they all wore crosses sewn to their clothes, but also in the way it almost came to be synonymous with crusading: the term *cruce signati* (those marked with the cross) came almost at once to mean those who had taken the crusade vow; and northern Europeans arriving in France on their way to the East and unable to make themselves understood would make the sign of the cross with their hands to signify that they were crusaders.[119] The crusaders believed they expressed love for their neighbours in literally carrying out Christ's maxim 'Greater love than this no man hath, that a man lay down his life for his friends' (John 15:3) or, as they put it more often, for his brothers. At times of crisis they would be reminded of their obligation to be united in Christian love.[120]

The crusader's love of God and his neighbour tended, as we have seen, to be distorted by its association with contemporary expressions of love for father and family, so that it became a justification in his mind for vengeance, for the waging of a vendetta against the infidels who had injured Christ by taking his land and oppressing his children. But the emphasis on Christian charity had another consequence too, for, in the light of the dawning realization that God was actively helping the crusade, it led to the conviction that the dead were martyrs, expressing in their martyrdom their love for God and in the process justifying themselves. The monastic writer Guibert of Nogent was later to express this clearly. 'If there was any need to suffer penalties for their sins, the spilling of their blood alone was a more powerful way of expiating all offences.'[121] These martyrs can be divided into three classes. The first consisted of those who died of disease and the ranks of martyrs therefore included all those who died good deaths, for whatever reason, on the crusade. Among them were the knight Enguerrand of St Pol, who was later seen in a vision, and Adhémar of Le Puy. The narrators of accounts of the crusade, whether eyewitnesses or not, all believed that Adhémar had gone

to heaven, although Raymond of Aguilers had him suffering temporarily in the afterlife for his scepticism about the Holy Lance. They
tended to stress the sanctity of his life rather than his martyrdom, but
in a letter written late in 1099 the archbishop of Rheims included
him and William of Orange, who had fallen ill and died on *c*.20
December 1098, among those 'who have died in peace, crowned
with glorious martyrdom'.[122] In the second category were priests and
laymen who were conventional martyrs in that they died passively,
being killed when they were non-combatants or were unarmed or
because they refused to renounce the Christian faith after being
captured by the Muslims. A good example was Raynald Porchet, a
Norman knight from southern Italy, who was captured by the
Muslims on 6 March 1098. Paraded on *c*.3 April by his captors on
the city walls of Antioch to plead for ransom, he defiantly refused to
do so and encouraged the Christian leaders to persist in the siege of
the city, informing them that the Muslim garrison was weakened. He
was taken down from the walls and brought before the Muslim
commander, who offered him whatever he wanted in return for his
apostasy. Raynald asked for time to consider the offer, but he spent it
praying that God might receive him into heaven. When told by an
interpreter that Raynald was in fact denying Islam, the enraged
commander ordered him to be beheaded and had all the other
captured crusaders brought before him and burnt in a great pyre.
Raynald's cult seems to have become quite widespread: an elabo-
rated and to some extent altered account was included in the
Chanson d'Antioche and in *c*.1130 he was referred to as a saint.[123]

The third category of martyrs consisted of those who were killed in
battle, among them Roger of Barneville, whose death has already
been described.[124] To appreciate how startling it is to find these
martyrs one should remember that martyrdom, involving the voluntary acceptance of death for the sake of the faith and reflecting the
death of Christ, is the supreme act of love of which a Christian is
capable and is the perfect example of a Christian death. It is the
martyr's gift to God of his own life and is so great an act of merit that
it justifies him at once in God's sight. The idea that a man could
achieve martyrdom when he himself was perpetrating violence was
not new. The first clear evidence for it in western Christian history
dates from 799. This was followed by a few references, growing
significantly more numerous in the eleventh century, but the evidence for a belief in warrior martyrs before 1095 is still not plentiful

and, even supposing that a few more references remain to be discovered, it is only with the sources for the First Crusade that a mass of material on the subject appears. And although after the crusade the idea of martyrdom in war was spreading fairly quickly – perhaps to the compilers of the Song of Roland; certainly to the writers of works like the Millstätter Exodus and to Geoffrey of Monmouth in his treatment of Arthur's defence of Britain – even a century later the author of a dialogue on the religious life could write: 'Read all the lives and passions of the holy martyrs and you will not find any martyr who wished to kill his persecutor. It is a new kind of martyr who wishes to kill another.'[125] It is hard to avoid concluding that in 1095 the classification of warriors in the same category as those gentle souls who passively accepted violence perpetrated against themselves was not yet universally acceptable.

It is, moreover, far from clear that death on the crusade was preached as martyrdom from the first. Of the near contemporary accounts of Pope Urban's sermon at Clermont only two, one written by a man who had heard the pope, the other by a man who had not, suggested that he had spoken of martyrdom.[126] There were no clear and unambiguous references to martyrdom in the letters written by the crusaders until March 1098, although statements that their confrères were dying that they might live and dying for Christ who had died for them began to appear in the previous January. It is significant that a letter of November 1097 asked for prayers for the dead, which suggests that they were not thought by the writer to be in heaven.[127] In other words, the conviction that dead crusaders had achieved martyrdom once again seems to have dawned gradually on the participants with the crossing of Asia Minor, as they became certain that they were engaged in a divine enterprise.

A manifestation of it was the appearance of the ghosts of dead crusaders, who from that moment on visited members of the army to admonish and counsel and even help them physically: the heavenly army which was believed to have come to their aid during the Battle of Antioch was supposed to have been made up partly of the recently dead.[128] In June 1098 a crusader who had decided to desert the army and was descending the walls of Antioch by rope was confronted by his dead brother, who exhorted him to stay, since 'the Lord is with you'.[129] Adhémar of Le Puy, who was, of course, not a warrior martyr, was reported to have made appearances immediately after his death. In all he was believed to have made seven visitations to four persons, all of them in the service of Raymond of St Gilles. The only record of these visions is in Raymond of Aguilers's *History* and it is not surprising that in five of his appearances, some of them to Peter Bartholomew, Adhémar was concerned to show that he had suffered for his doubts about the authenticity of the Holy Lance: he had been sent to hell for a time, he had been whipped, his face had been burnt and his beard singed, although a candle offered for his soul by his friends and a small oblation he had made to the Lance had saved him. He also delivered other messages. The dead would help the crusaders and he himself would appear to offer counsel. One of his cloaks should be given to the church of St Andrew in Antioch, presumably as a peace-offering for having disbelieved the messages of the saint. He reproved the crusaders for having ignored his orders and those of Our Lady. His cross, which, as we have seen, was probably a relic of the True Cross, must be carried in the vanguard of the army. In early July 1099, when the crusade was running into difficulties during the siege of Jerusalem, he again appeared with instructions on how to propitiate God which included fasting and processing barefooted round the city, and he prophesied that Jerusalem would fall in nine days. When the city was taken he was seen by many scrambling over the walls at the head of the assault.[130] In one of these appearances he was accompanied by his standard-bearer Heraclius of Polignac, who had been mortally wounded in the Battle of Antioch. Heraclius still bore on his face his injuries and told the visionary who saw him that Christ had granted him the privilege of bearing for eternity the open wounds from which he had died.[131]

Probably the best-known vision of this kind – two separate but closely related versions of it survive – was experienced by Anselm of Ribemont either the night or the siesta time before he was killed on *c.*25 February 1099. In the first version, recounted by Raymond of Aguilers, he saw the young knight Enguerrand of St Pol, who had died about two months before. Enguerrand appeared to be exceptionally handsome and, assuring Anselm that 'of course those who end their lives in the service of Christ are not dead', took him to heaven and showed him his house there, beautiful beyond compare. He told Anselm that a far more beautiful mansion was being prepared for him on the morrow. In the second, transmitted by Arnulf of Chocques who claimed to have been told it by Anselm himself, Anselm found himself standing on a pile of filth, from whence he looked up towards a splendid palace. He saw innumerable fine-looking persons, barely recognizable to him so changed were they, passing through the door. One of them, a man recently lost and presumably Enguerrand of St Pol, turned to him and told him that these were crusaders who were now crowned as martyrs. He informed Anselm that he would be the next to join them.[132]

In the main, therefore, the ghosts delivered two messages: the Lance was genuine; and the crusaders' confrères who had died – of disease or at the hands of their captors or in battle – went straight to paradise as martyrs.

So, in extreme conditions, the separate elements in Pope Urban's message were developed and fused into what was to be the body of crusading ideas. As the crusaders became aware of the greatness of their achievement, they acknowledged that the only explanation for their success was that a divine hand was intervening physically to help them. The reappearance of signs in the skies, the discoveries of relics and the apparitions to visionaries confirmed this for them. The crusade was obviously a providential activity. It really was a holy war fought by soldiers of Christ to further the intentions of God; and God desired above all that Jerusalem be liberated. God's messengers, even God himself in the person of Christ, winged to and fro between heaven and the crusade, bringing messages of comfort and admonition.

This was, of course, enough to make the crusade a righteous activity, for the crusaders were proving themselves to be loving and obedient to God's commands; and they also expressed in their actions love of their neighbours. Their activity was meritorious; indeed it was on the way to being compared to religious profession, the entry into the monastic life, which until then had been considered the most meritorious course that a man could take. The crusade was, in fact, the most startling among several expressions of a new and positive role for lay men and women for which the church reformers were seeking. One of the most remarkable features of the writings we have been considering is the transfer in them to war and to a lay activity of phrases and concepts which had previously been applied solely to monasticism. The best known of these, the literal use of the phrase 'knighthood of Christ', had already occurred a decade or two before 1095, although it was only with the First Crusade that it was systematically applied to warriors.[133] The others appear with extraordinary suddenness. The way of the cross became a description of this war, as we have seen. In contemporary monastic writings one finds the image of the heavenly Jerusalem as the true goal of the religious life, more important, as St Anselm of Canterbury stressed, than the earthly Jerusalem: to reach the heavenly Jerusalem required an internal journey, a true conversion. But while they were still on the march the crusaders also associated the goal of the heavenly Jerusalem with the crusade: in September 1098 the leaders called on the pope to come out and 'open for us the gates of both Jerusalems', which suggests that they believed they were making an internal as well as an external pilgrimage.[134] It is not surprising that, although Urban had written that he did not want 'those vowed to spiritual warfare', that is to say monks, to join the crusade, the author of the *Gesta Francorum* could put the following words in Bohemond's mouth: 'You know truly that this is not a carnal war, but a spiritual one.'[135] In the light of this application to a lay enterprise of imagery – knighthood of Christ, way of the cross, heavenly Jerusalem, spiritual warfare – previously associated with the monastic life, the idea of warrior martyrs is not eccentric.

The startling images, however, and the ideas on which they rested were very crudely expressed in the letters and eyewitness accounts and were not justified in terms that would have made them acceptable to theologians. Questions were bound to be asked of them. Could the success of the crusade only be explained as a manifestation of divine interventionary power? Why should its cause have been so dear to God? Could the earthly Jerusalem really be equated with the heavenly city; and could such a terrestrial conflict really be regarded as spiritual? Were the crusaders in fact contributing to their salvation; and, if they were, how were they doing so? Convincing answers to these questions could only be provided by commentators better trained in theology than the men who had taken part in the campaign.

Chapter 5

The crusade of 1101

From the winter of 1096–7 onwards crusaders were drifting back to western Europe. Obloquy was heaped on the heads of the early homecomers, like Emich of Leiningen, who had been turned back in the Balkans, Stephen of Blois, who had deserted the crusade at Antioch, and Hugh of Vermandois, who had never returned to the army after having been sent on an embassy to Constantinople at the beginning of July 1098.[1] Stephen of Blois was not only publicly humiliated; he also had to endure the private nagging of his formidable wife Adela of England.[2] Guy Trousseau, who had escaped over the walls of Antioch during the night of panic in June 1098, returned to France a broken man, exhausted by his journey and still unable to understand why he had given way to fear.[3] In the winter of 1099–1100 these disgraced figures were followed by the triumphant conquerors of Jerusalem. The return of the great magnates must have been welcome when one considers the disorder that often followed the prolonged absence of a lord: Flanders was in an unsettled state while Count Robert was away.[4] In fact there must always have been the risk that a crusader would return to find his family or financial affairs in crisis. A good example is the experience of Hugh of Chaumont, who made the crusade soon after coming of age and in the aftermath of a violent dispute over his inheritance. During his minority his uncle Lisois had had guard of his castle of Amboise. Lisois apparently wanted the castle for his heiress, Corba of Thorigné, his grand-daughter through the marriage of his daughter Elizabeth to Foucois of Thorigné, and he tried to ensure this by arranging with Count Fulk of Anjou that she be wed to a man called Aimery of Courron. Hugh of Chaumont had naturally reacted bitterly to the prospect of being deprived of Amboise and his vassals had resorted to violence. Fulk of Anjou had managed to arrange a composition of the differences between Hugh and Aimery and it says much for the speed with which these storms passed once the issues that caused them were resolved that Hugh and Aimery had both taken the cross at Tours in the presence of the pope and had left for the East together. Aimery had died before Nicaea and news of his death had been brought back to Anjou by Stephen of Blois and his fellow-deserters. Hugh of Chaumont had a particularly good crusade. He had been so highly regarded that he had shared with Ralph of Beaugency the guard of one of the gates of Antioch on the night the princes feared a mass break-out. Arriving home at Easter 1100, with his pilgrimage completed but, like several of his confrères, a sick man, he found himself again faced with the prospect of the loss of Amboise. In his absence Count Fulk had been bribed to marry the widowed Corba of Thorigné to an elderly hanger-on called Achard of Les Saints, resurrecting the counter-claims resolved before the crusade. Hugh's return led to a resumption of violence in which Corba was kidnapped by one of his vassals.[5]

Although soon hurled back into the belligerent world of French feudalism, many crusaders seem to have returned in a religious frame of mind. Robert of Normandy made a thanksgiving pilgrimage to Mont-Saint-Michel, Guigo of *Marra* gave the monks of St Julian of Tours, with whom he stayed on his way home, a church at Bellou-sur-Huisne.[6] For some their return was the starting point for a withdrawal from the world. The knight Grimaldus became a *confrater* of Cluny. Richard fitz-Fulk became a monk of Bec. A crusader called Gilbert became a monk of St Ouen at Rouen and was able to donate to the building of the abbey church money bequeathed to him by his lady, Aubrée Grossa, who had died on the crusade.[7] For others – a professional captain like Ralph the Red of Pont-Échanfray or an adventurer like Thomas of Marle – the crusade seems merely to have been one chapter in a career of violence.[8] The future standing of crusaders varied. Robert of Flanders, known henceforward as the *Hierosolimitanus*, seems to have been held in special esteem for the rest of his days,[9] and the adoption of similar cognomens to his seems to have been quite common, carrying with them, presumably, the sort of prestige that has always been attached to Muslim hajjis.[10] A century later Lambert of Ardres, writing of Arnold of Ardres, who, according to Lambert, had a very distinguished crusade, explained the absence of his name from the lists of crusaders in the *Chanson d'Antioche* by the fact that he had refused to bribe the author, Richard the Pilgrim, who had demanded two scarlet shoes in return for inserting it. This is evidence, at least, of the importance of the information relayed in popular epics to a man's reputation and his family's pride.[11] On the other hand the disasters which afflicted Robert of Normandy were attributed to God's wrath because it was believed that he had refused the crown of Jerusalem, 'not out of reverence, but out of fear of the work involved', wrote one commentator, who added that he had 'stained his nobility with an indelible blot'.[12] And Anselm of Ardres, who had been captured by the Muslims and forced to apostasize, was so cold-shouldered when he returned home after many years that he had to leave again.[13]

How rich were they? The final stages of the crusade were portrayed by the eyewitnesses as being profitable. Much was said to have been made from the sack of Jerusalem and the ransoming of captives: 'at Jerusalem many poor men were made rich'. The victory at Ascalon a month later was reported to have brought the crusaders large quantities of spoil. One might suppose that the survivors were now fairly comfortably off, even though there is evidence that they gave away part of their winnings in alms and in benefactions to the Holy Sepulchre.[14] But presumably they had been only moderately rewarded. The riches of Jerusalem were religious rather than commercial, and the crusaders were not only reluctant to despoil the shrines of significance to them; they also gave what they looted from Muslim shrines to their new Christian occupiers. Tancred, for instance, was forced to endow the new Christian guardians of the Temple with much of the spoil he had taken there, which must have included the legandary wealth in the al-Aqsa mosque.[15] It is not beyond reason that the invading Eqyptian army carried great riches with it, but it is also possible that the poverty of the crusaders led them to exaggerate the value of the booty they took. At any rate they were now confronted with the cost of returning home. They marched north some 300 miles, retracing their steps through a countryside they had devastated earlier in the year. It was reported that already by the time they had reached Latakia – that is after a month's journey – they were exhausted and in great want; some of them gratefully accepted a Greek offer of free passage to Constantinople.[16] In fact I have found only one reference that might be construed as evidence for a crusader returning home wealthy and, curiously enough, it relates to the crusade of 1101. Count Guy of Rochefort, Guy Trousseau's uncle, came home '*famose copioseque*'. The word *copiose* might be taken as meaning that he returned rich in material goods. But it could also bear another meaning, for there is no doubt that many crusaders came home rich in relics, which they presented to local churches.[17] Count Robert of Flanders, who had already sent relics home from southern Italy on his way to the East, gave the arm of St George stolen by Gerbault of Lille to the monastery of Anchin, where a church dedicated to the saint had been built a decade earlier. Ilger Bigod divided hairs from the ball of Our Lady's hair he had found in Jerusalem among several cathedrals and monasteries in France; his relative Arnold, a monk of Chartres, displayed two hairs in the church of Maule, where many of the sick were said to have been healed through their power. Peter Fasin brought relics for the monastery of Maillezais. Payen Peverel, who had been Robert of Normandy's standard-bearer for a time, endowed Barnwell priory with relics he had acquired in the East. Simon of Ludron brought home the portion of the True Cross and the fragment of the Holy Sepulchre which Riou of Lohéac had left to his home church of St Saviour. Arnold of Ardres presented his local church with a reliquary containing a piece of the Holy Lance and relics of St George and other saints, acquired in Antioch, and a hair from Christ's beard, a piece of the True Cross and a stone from the spot of the Ascension, acquired in Jerusalem. Peter the Hermit, who returned with relics of the Holy Sepulchre and St John the Baptist, joined Conon and Lambert of Montaigu in founding the Augustinian priory of Neufmoustier, at Huy near Liége, dedicated to these patrons. In the thirteenth century it was believed that this foundation stemmed from a vow made by the returning crusaders during a storm at sea. Peter also gained a charter from the bishop of Liége, whom he had apparently persuaded that he had been granted by Patriarch Arnulf of Jerusalem the privilege of allowing crusaders who were too poor or ill to fulfil their vows to gain the full benefits of the indulgence merely by visiting his new foundation. A Venetian fleet brought home relics of St Nicholas and other saints from Myra. On the other hand the crusading knight Albert brought back to St Nicholas-de-Port a relic of St Nicholas which a relative of his, who had been a clerk at Bari, had stolen from the great reliquary there.[18]

Many crusaders must have brought wives and families bad tidings, as did Boso of La Chêze, Simon of Ludron and Stephen of Blois of the deaths of Bernard Le Baile, Riou of Lohéac and Aimery of Courron.[19] The widow Ebroalda of the crusader Berengar, who had died in Jerusalem, became a nun of Marcigny. Another crusader's widow, Estiburga, gave houses and a vineyard to the monks of St Andrew the Less in Vienne in return for a pension and the annual commemoration of her dead husband Peter. Ida of Hainault, uncertain of the fate of her husband Count Baldwin, who had actually been killed while accompanying Hugh of Vermandois from the crusade on an embassy to the Byzantine emperor, travelled all the way to the East in the forlorn hope of finding him.[20] But of course they also announced the liberation of Jerusalem. One has only to read any collection of contemporary chronicles to see how the news swept through Europe, inspiring songs in its honour,[21] and leading to the desire to transfer to other struggles and theatres of war the imagery and reflected glory of the way to Jerusalem; for instance in an attempt in 1108 to present the German war against the Wends across the Elbe in crusading terms:

> Follow the good example of the inhabitants of Gaul and emulate them in this also. . . . May he who with the strength of his arm led the men of Gaul on their march from the far West in triumph against his enemies in the farthest East give you the will and power to conquer these most inhuman gentiles (the Wends) who are near by.[22]

The enthusiasm led directly to the raising of another group of crusading armies. Crusaders, of course, had been leaving western Europe in small parties since 1097 and the despatching of additional large armies had been planned well before the news of the fall of Jerusalem reached the West. We have already seen that it was known that many of those who had taken the cross had not fulfilled their vows, that the hard-pressed crusaders in the East had been bringing this to the pope's attention and that before his death Urban had taken steps to see that these vows were enforced. In the first half of 1099, perhaps during or following the Council of Rome of 24–30 April, he had also commissioned the archbishop of Milan to summon the Lombards to crusade. There was a fervent response in northern Italy to the archbishop's preaching, with the aid of a popular song, 'Ultreia, ultreia'.[23] The movement gathered pace with the news of Jerusalem's liberation and it was taken up by the new pope, Paschal II. Caught up in the general excitement, Paschal himself was prepared to follow the fashion of extending crusading ideas to other areas of conflict. He wrote an extraordinary letter to Robert of Flanders, after Robert's return, exhorting him to aim now to reach the heavenly Jerusalem by fighting on behalf of the reformers against the German emperor.[24] But although, like his predecessor, he strictly forbade Spaniards to leave the peninsula and confirmed the extension of crusade privileges to Spain,[25] he was prepared to throw his weight behind the cause of Jerusalem. In April 1100 he wrote to those Latins still in Palestine informing them of his appointment of a new legate, and in this letter we can discern the first reaction of serious theologians to their triumph. Paschal suggested that their achievements fulfilled the prophecies and renewed the miracles of the Old Testament. He drew attention to the discoveries of the Holy Lance and the True Cross. He attributed the crusaders' success to the glory of God working through them; and he praised them for their adoption of a voluntary exile, their abandonment of their homes to defend their brothers. But he also enjoined devotion to St Peter; perhaps the curia was worried by the way St Peter had been over-shadowed by other objects of veneration on the crusade. The restrained yet elevated language of this short letter reinforces the impression gained from the eyewitness accounts but also points the way to the more theological interpretations that were to follow.[26]

In December 1099 Paschal renewed Urban's threat to excommunicate those who had still not fulfilled their vows to crusade to the East and ordered the bishops to enforce this in their dioceses. We have evidence of the papal mandate being put into effect in at least one province; and at a synod held at Anse in the following spring an impressive number of bishops, led by the archbishop of Lyons, reissued the pope's ruling. Those who had deserted in the course of the crusade were also threatened with excommunication by the pope if they did not return to the East to complete their pilgrimages.[27] They included, of course, Stephen of Blois and Hugh of Vermandois. But there were other, lesser persons. Hugh and Norgeot of Toucy, who had never reached Jerusalem, set out again.[28] So did Simon and William Sansavoir of Poissy, the brothers of Walter Sansavoir, who had commanded Peter the Hermit's forces, and the relatives of another Walter, who was also on the First Crusade. After the deaths of the two Walters, Simon and William seem to have returned home, before leaving for the East once more in 1100.[29] And thousands of men and women in France, Italy and Germany, who had not considered taking the cross before, or who had considered it and had put it out of their minds, now flocked to the banners, inspired by the victories in the East.[30] Paschal's legates, the cardinals John of St Anastasia and Benedict of St Eudoxia, held a council at Valence towards the end of September 1100 and then proceeded to Limoges, where, probably in their presence, Duke William of Aquitaine and many of his vassals took the cross,[31] and to Poitiers where on 18 November, the fifth anniversary of the opening of the Council of Clermont, another council met. The legates preached the crusade at Poitiers and probably elsewhere too. Their preaching, and that of others, was highly successful. There can be no doubt that the armies that departed from Italy, Aquitaine, northern and eastern France and Germany were at least as large as those which had left in 1096. They were led by laymen of equal or greater rank: William of Aquitaine, Stephen of Blois and Hugh of Vermandois, William of Nevers, Odo of Burgundy, Stephen of Burgundy and Welf of Bavaria. The ecclesiastical contingent was stronger. Hugh of Die, the archbishop of Lyons, was the chief papal legate, assisted, as Adhémar of Le Puy had been, by subordinate legates appointed by the pope.[32] There were three other archbishops – Anselm of Milan, Thiemo of Salzburg and Hugh of Besançon – and at least eight bishops. 'No more glittering army was ever seen by the French.'[33]

The goals set, however, were significantly different from those proposed to the first crusaders. Urban, apparently carried away by the news of the successes in the East, had suggested to the Milanese that they conquer Egypt. Presumably the idea was that they should march overland to Jerusalem and then push on into Africa.[34] Paschal was more realistic. In his letter of December 1099 he stressed the need to help the Christians now occupying the Holy Land. This messsage was certainly passed on by at least one archbishop to his suffragans and it was repeated in the following year by the papal legates in France, who called on their listeners 'to rush to help the faithful who were on God's expedition'.[35] The emphasis on aid to a land now in Christian hands rather than on its liberation meant that the pilgrimizing element in crusading became even more prominent. Reading the charters issued in 1100 by departing crusaders it is hard to find any references to holy war.

> Since the path we tread is crooked, especially for those of us who are involved in lay knighthood in secular clothing, it is meet that we should try to return to that fatherland, from which we are exiled on account of our first parent's sins and for which we sigh, by doing what good we can. . . . I, Stephen of Neublens, considering the multitude . . . of my sins . . . have decided to repay

something to God for all the mercies that he of his grace has given me, unworthy though I am. I have decided to go to Jerusalem, where God was seen as man and had dealings with men and to adore his feet in the place where they trod.[36] When after its capture by the Christians a measureless multitude of all kinds of men wished to go to the holy city of Jerusalem, burning with love and desire, a certain noble knight, Milo son of Ingelbert of Vignory, burning with divine fire to perform good works, wished to fulfil that which he had long before desired concerning that pilgrimage.[37] Bernard Veredun, going to Jerusalem moved by the example of those wishing to save their souls. . . . [38]

In the preparations for this expedition we can see the earliest evidence for the ceremonies of taking the cross and they are very clearly pilgrimage rites. The abbot of Cluny placed a cross on Stephen of Neublens's shoulder and a ring on his finger. Milo of Vignory received a pilgrim's purse. Herbert of Thouars was given 'the habit of pilgrimage' by his bishop.[39]

One can also perhaps discern for the first time motivations which were always to be associated with the crusades. Some individuals may have taken the cross because they believed that close relatives who had died on the First Crusade had not fulfilled their vows: examples may have been Viscount Bernard of Béziers,[40] Hugh Bardolf of Broyes[41] and Corba of Thorigné.[42] There is, in fact, evidence that ordinary Christians, perhaps not convinced yet of the martyrdom of crusaders, were anxious whether they would enjoy the indulgence if they died before reaching the Holy Sepulchre.[43] Others may have taken the cross to expunge from the family name the dishonour that stemmed from a relative's desertion in the course of the First Crusade. Guy Trousseau's flight has already been referred to. It cannot be coincidence that the two senior members of his family, his father Miles of Bray and his uncle Guy of Rochefort, took part in the crusade of 1101.[44] In general the crusaders' motives seem to have been just as devotional as those of their predecessors. Welf of Bavaria's decision to crusade was the climax to a period of conversion in which he had begun to make benefactions to churches and monasteries. 'Wishing to show God more painful satisfaction for his sins, he took the road to Jerusalem'.[45] Duke Odo of Burgundy, who was to die in Asia, prepared himself in just such a self-abnegatory way as had Nivelo before the First Crusade. He abandoned the 'bad customs' he and his ancestors had imposed on the estates of St Benignus of Dijon.

> Taking the road to Jerusalem in penitence for my sins, leaving to my heirs in the present charter some precaution against sin, since divine clemency has inspired me to go to the Sepulchre of Our Saviour on account of the enormity of my wickedness, so that the obedience of my devotion may be cherished more acceptably in the sight of the Lord, I have judged not unreasonably that I ought to depart at peace with all, and especially with the servants of God.[46]

In the sources there are the same references to self-imposed exile, to obedience to Christ's precept to forsake family and lands for him.[47] The same kinds of financial sacrifice were made to raise money. William of Aquitaine offered to pledge his duchy to the king of England, but William Rufus died before the deal was completed. Arpin, viscount of Bourges, sold the town of Bourges to the king of France. At a lower level, Fantin and his son Geoffrey *Incorrigiatus*, who seem to have gone with Herbert of Thouars, about whom more below, engaged in a complicated transaction to get cash: Fantin gave some land to his son, who then sold his share to his mother.[48] We find feudal lords and relatives involved in the same way, approving the mortgages and sales necessary.[49] We also find the same desire to benefit from the intercessory power of the Church. Odo of Burgundy made gifts to the abbey of Molesme, requesting the community to 'pray assiduously to the Lord for his prosperity in body and soul and for the fulfilment of his vow'. William of Nevers also asked to be allowed to benefit from the prayers of the monks of Molesme. Stephen of Neublens became a *confrater* of Cluny. He promised the abbot that should he die a servant would bring news of his death to the abbey; and the abbot assured him that his *obit* would be recorded. Bernard, viscount of Béziers, made a donation to the abbey of Gellone 'for the redemption of my soul and those of my parents and so that almighty God may make my pilgrimage prosper'.[50] Herbert, viscount of Thouars, made gifts to his family's foundation of Chaise-le-Vicomte in return for the community's prayers. He had bought a mantle of precious material from the church of St Aubin at Angers for 300 *solidi*; presumably he intended to exchange this for cash later in the journey. But on his way he was persuaded by a member of the community to return the mantle without getting his money back. He gave way because

> since we go on the way of the Lord and the 300 *solidi* would have been quickly spent, it is better to return it so that we may be helped by the prayers of the saint of the church and the monks there.[51]

But if there is every reason for supposing that the motivation of the crusaders of 1100–1101 was just as devout as had been that of their predecessors, there is, perhaps because they were journeying to an already liberated land, perhaps because they believed that their enterprise had already been proved to be so divinely inspired that it could not possibly fail, perhaps because of the attractive, bubbling nature of William of Aquitaine, who 'wished to demonstrate his power and spread his fame',[52] something light-hearted about these glittering French armies, something more akin to knight-errantry and to the attitudes of their paragons in the *chansons* than to the dogged pertinacity of the first crusaders. 'Many burned with zeal . . . to go on pilgrimage, to see the Holy Sepulchre and the holy places and to perform deeds of knightly valour against the Turks.'[53] It would be wrong, nevertheless, to suppose that they were not serious. In fact there are some indications that they had tried to learn from the mistakes of their predecessors. The size and importance of the ecclesiastical contingent with them is one. Another is the number of horses and beasts of burden with which they began to cross Asia Minor and the wealth – in cash and jewellery – they carted with them.[54]

The first crusaders to march were the Lombards, who left Milan on 13 September 1100. Their wintering in Bulgaria was marked by disorders, as was their stay outside Constantinople for two months from late February or early March 1101, as they waited for their confrères from Germany and France. When the Emperor Alexius tried to force them to cross to Asia Minor by refusing them licences to buy supplies, they attacked his palace of Blachernae, an act which so embarrassed their leaders that they agreed to be ferried across the Bosphorus. At Nicomedia they were joined by the first, and smaller, of the German armies and by the crusaders from Burgundy and from northern France under Stephen of Blois. They were also joined by Raymond of St Gilles, who had reached Constantinople in the summer of 1100 with his household and the Holy Lance and had reluctantly allowed himself to be attached to them as an adviser.[55] It was now that the decision was made, against the advice of the Greeks and of Stephen of Blois and Raymond of St Gilles, not to wait for the rest of the crusade but

> to enter the kingdom of Khorassan by force and extract or free Bohemond [who had been taken prisoner in the previous summer by the Danishmend emir Malik-Ghazi Gümüshtigin] from Turk- ish captivity or to besiege with their force and destroy the city of Baghdad, the capital of the kingdom of Khorassan, and thus to snatch their confrère [Bohemond] from his manacles.[56]

In early June they marched from Nicomedia, carrying with them relics of St Ambrose and the Holy Lance.[57] On reaching Ankara they turned north-east to Gangra and from there swung east again, towards Niksar where Bohemond was imprisoned. In the early part of August, somewhere near Merzifon, they were met by an army raised by a coalition of Turkish princes. There followed several days of fighting before they panicked and fled. The survivors indulged in mutual recrimination and later generations have held that it was their own stupidity, their decision to march north-east instead of south-east, that led to their downfall. But the armies that followed more direct routes had no greater success, and the freeing of Bohemond was not in itself a bad idea. Bohemond had been the most skilful of the captains on the First Crusade and the security of his principality of Antioch as a staging post to Jerusalem was vital to the Christian cause. The Lombard army, moreover, was the only one which had been raised to liberate new territory rather than to help the Latins in the Holy Land. If the Italians really were aiming to conquer Baghdad, as the chronicler Albert of Aachen suggested in what is admittedly a confused passage, then the adoption of a route through northern Anatolia, which would have debouched into Mesopotamia by way of Malatya and then either Diyar-Bakr or Edessa, made some sense, even if it was very rash.[58]

The army under William of Nevers reached Constantinople in June 1101 and, overtaking the force of William of Aquitaine which was already there, crossed the Bosphorus and set out on 24 June to catch up with the Lombards. At Ankara William gave up the pursuit and turned south towards Konya, which he reached in the middle of

August after a three-day running battle with the Turks. He failed to take the town and moved on to Ereghli, which had been deserted by the Muslims, who had blocked the wells. After several thirsty days the crusaders were attacked by the Turks and routed. Meanwhile the third army under William of Aquitaine, which had left western France in the middle of March, had joined the Bavarians under Welf and had marched in an unruly fashion through the Balkans, reached Constantinople at the beginning of June. It remained near Constantinople for five weeks, while the leaders purchased supplies and took advice from the emperor, although a number of the Germans, including our only eyewitness reporter, Ekkehard of Aura, elected to go to Palestine by sea.[59] William of Aquitaine and Welf of Bavaria led their forces eastward in the middle of July, helped by guides provided by Alexius. They followed the route taken by the first crusaders, but it had been devastated by the constant passage of Christian forces since 1097 and by the Turks themselves, and once they left Byzantine territory they quickly ran out of food, in spite of all their planning.[60] Near Ereghli they were ambushed and annihilated. Among those taken by the Turks were Ida, the dowager margravine of Austria, who was reputedly placed in the harem of a Muslim prince, Archbishop Thiemo of Salzburg, the story of whose subsequent martyrdom became quite popular in Europe, and poor Corba of Thorigné, whose marriages in Anjou had made Hugh of Chaumont so angry.[61] William of Aquitaine and Welf of Bavaria escaped, as had William of Nevers, Stephen of Burgundy, Stephen of Blois and Raymond of St Gilles from the earlier disasters. Hugh of Vermandois died of a wound at Tarsus. Some of the survivors joined Raymond of St Gilles in Syria and took the town of Tortosa, which was to be his base for the creation of the county of Tripoli. Then most of them gathered in Jerusalem where they fulfilled their vows. Some, delayed by adverse winds from leaving for home, joined the forces of the kingdom of Jerusalem to meet an Egyptian invasion. Unlucky to the end, they were heavily defeated on 17 May 1102. Stephen of Blois was killed. Arpin of Bourges was immured in Egypt for three years until the Byzantine emperor negotiated his release.

The crusaders suffered heavy financial losses. William of Aquitaine, who reached Antioch 'poor and beggarly with six companions', had lost everything he had brought with him, his money as well as the men of his entourage. He left Palestine for home 'impoverished and abandoned to all kinds of poverty'.[62] Herbert of

Thouars, who had left Poitou in so devout a frame of mind, arrived penniless in Jerusalem. He was helped out of his difficulties by friends and his entourage stuck by him loyally, but on 28 May 1102, near the church in Jaffa dedicated to his patron saint Nicholas, he died, it was said of sorrow at the loss of his brother Geoffrey.[63] In Palestine in 1102 Arpin of Bourges was apparently a *vir magnificus*, so he must still have had a large part of the proceeds of the sale of Bourges: either he had had it transferred directly to the Holy Land or he himself had sailed straight there, taking no part in the catastrophe in Asia Minor. But after his captivity in Cairo he returned to Europe a man transformed by his sufferings, and on Pope Paschal's advice entered the abbey of Cluny.[64]

In the course of the summer of 1101 three substantial and well-prepared crusading armies had been separately and ignominiously thrashed by the Turks. On the face of it the most surprising thing about this humiliating episode, the history of which was 'in the way of a tragedy both miserable and splendid',[65] was that it had such little effect on contemporaries. Nearly all the histories of the First Crusade, with their glowing accounts of God's interventions on behalf of his chosen army and their apotheosis of the crusaders, were written after the debacle of 1101, one of them, indeed, by Ekkehard of Aura who had taken part in it. Nor was recruitment affected: the first quarter of the twelfth century was the most intensive period of crusading before 1187, with Bohemond's crusade of 1107–8, the Norwegian crusade of 1107–10 under King Sigurd, and a crusade preached by Pope Calixtus II in *c.*1120, which seems to have been planned on a large scale and resulted in campaigns in Palestine in 1123–4 and Spain in 1125–6.[66] To these should be added crusades in Spain in 1108, 1114, 1116 and 1118. This can partly be explained by the fact that in the short run at least the crusade of 1101 harmed no one but those who took part in it. The Christian occupation of Jerusalem and hold on Palestine and Syria was not put in jeopardy; indeed the area under Christian control was to be gradually extended over the next fifty years. But it would be wrong to treat the crusade of 1101 as a non-event. It was viewed positively by contemporaries and was important for the development of their ideas.

The Turkish victories, in fact, helped to prove just how astounding a triumph the First Crusade had been, for they underlined a theme already in the propaganda, the portrayal of the Muslim powers as formidable foes. Westerners did not know that the Turkish princes had been at odds with one another in 1097–8, whereas those in Asia Minor had come together in a league against the crusaders in 1101. For them it was enough that the first crusaders, starving, without horses, without a real leader, united in their faith and poverty, had succeeded against forces which destroyed more opulent and brilliant armies only a short while later. The crusade of 1101, in other words, confirmed the miraculous character of the successes of 1097–9.

This lesson could be drawn from it because the propagandists were able to explain satisfactorily the defeats of 1101. They did this by developing a theme to be found in the Old Testament and the writings of St Augustine and his Christian successors, according to which defeat in a holy cause was a punishment, a humiliation imposed by God on man for sin. Defeats, especially those suffered in a holy enterprise, were God's judgements, the sanctions of an infinitely just judge on those frail instruments of his whom he had deputed to carry out the tasks he had allotted, but on whom he would not spare the rod. It was a conventional idea, with which Pope Urban himself had explained other reverses in the Christian cause, using the phrase *peccatis exigentibus*, which was to have a long history in crusading thought.[67] We have seen that the first crusaders themselves had interpreted their troubles and difficulties as salutary punishments, and this was taken up by later commentators, to whom failures were to be attributed above all to the crusaders' own sins. They were to be viewed as chastisements, as a means not only of punishing them – 'the judgements of God are never unjust'[68] – but also of keeping a rein on them, guiding them back on to the right path.

> God chastised them because of their insolence, lest perchance their minds should be inflamed somewhat with pride on account of their many victories.[69]
> In the same way we read in holy scripture that the children of Israel were frequently afflicted and defeated in war by the Philistines and the Edomites and Midianites and other neighbouring peoples, to force them to run back again to God and to persevere in keeping his commandments.[70]

It was natural, therefore, for the disasters of 1101 to be considered salutary punishments brought by the participants on their own heads. 'This befell them, it seemed to us,' wrote a contemporary in the East who must have met the survivors in Jerusalem, 'as much as others, because of their sin and pride.'[71] The surviving leaders were treated with the scorn that befitted those who had proved themselves unworthy of God's favour.

> Duke William of Aquitaine went with many others to Jerusalem, but nevertheless he contributed nothing to the Christian cause. He was, indeed, a fervent womanizer and for that reason he showed himself to be inconstant in what he did.[72]

And the first crusaders were bound to benefit from being favourably compared to their worthless successors.

> This was the way, this the rule of life of the pilgrims marching to Jerusalem [on the First Crusade]. While they held rigorously to this discipline and abounded in charity, it was manifest that God dwelt among them and fought his battles through them. We have spoken in this way so that by extolling them we might show to be false the way of life and the pilgrimage of those undisciplined men who haughtily followed in the wake of this glorious expedition.[73]

So the failure of the crusade of 1101 actually enhanced the achievements of 1097–9.

Chapter 6

Theological refinement

The odyssey of the first crusaders was retold for later generations in paintings and sculpture, in popular songs and poems, the greatest of which, the *Chanson d'Antioche*, was composed by a participant even though it has survived only in a version reworked in *c*.1180 by the poet Graindor of Douai, and above all in histories. No other event in the central Middle Ages inspired anything like the quantity of historical writing to be encountered here: apart from the authors of eyewitness narratives, who wrote soon after the crusade and have already been discussed, there are at least twelve western Christian historians of significance. Their message is a remarkably consistent one, the only major difference being the emphasis given to the role and importance of the French, which is natural in a corpus containing contributions from all over western Europe. But in terms of the expression of ideas three historians stand out. They were all Benedictine monks from northern France. They wrote at about the same time, within a decade of the liberation of Jerusalem; indeed their works may have pre-dated that of the eyewitness Peter Tudebode, although with them we are in another world. They had not, however, taken part in the crusade or even visited the East,[1] although two of them had been at the Council of Clermont. They all used as a basic source the same anonymous eyewitness account in the *Gesta Francorum*, although each had something to add to it from information he had gathered personally.

The first was Robert the Monk (or of St Remy or Rheims). The date of his birth is unknown. He may have been a pupil of Baldric of Bourgueil, the third of these historians. At any rate he had a reputation for scholarship and, after being a monk of St Remy and Marmoutier, he was made abbot of St Remy. In this capacity he was present at the Council of Clermont. But he seems to have been an extremely incompetent administrator, which was perhaps why, accused of various misdemeanours and excommunicated, he was deposed in 1097. His appeal against this sentence to Pope Urban II was successful to the extent that it was quashed, but he was not able to return to his abbey and was retired to the priory of Senuc, from which in turn he was deposed for bad administration by Pope Calixtus II in 1122. He died a few months later. The date at which he wrote his very popular history of the crusade has been disputed, but there are strong reasons for supposing that it was completed by 1107. It was written on the orders of an abbot B, almost certainly Bernard of Marmoutier, who died in 1107. But even if it was not, the extraordinary Magdeburger *Aufruf*, to which reference has already been made and which dates from 1108, drew on it; so it must have been completed by then.[2] The second was Guibert of Nogent, who was born into a noble family in 1053 and was professed into the abbey of St Germer of Fly. He pursued his studies diligently – for a time he was a pupil of St Anselm – and he became another well-known scholar. In 1104 he was elected abbot of Nogent-sous-Coucy, which was, incidentally, a foundation of St Remy, and he was dead by 1125. His history of the crusade, on which he seems to have worked between 1104 and 1108, making some final corrections in 1111, contains quite a lot of original material, drawn on the whole from people like Robert of Flanders whom he knew; he also made use of an early redaction of Fulcher of Chartres's *History*.[3] Guibert's work, however, does not seem to have enjoyed the popularity of the *History* of Robert the Monk or that of Baldric of Bourgueil, the last of the trio, who was born in 1046. Baldric was successively monk, prior and abbot of Bourgueil and attended the Council of Clermont. From 1107 to his death in 1130 he was the largely absentee archbishop of Dol in Britanny. Another learned and sophisticated writer, he composed his history of the crusade in 1108. There are a few fresh details in it, such as those on the Breton contingent, but it has been criticized for being merely a graceful reworking of the *Gesta Francorum*. We shall see that it was much more than that. It was another popular work. Two major historians, Orderic Vitalis, who admired Baldric very much, and Vincent of Beauvais, employed it as the basis of the sections in their *Histories* on the crusade, and it was also used by at least two other writers, one of whom turned it into verse.[4]

So three senior monks in northern France, among the best products of the last flowering of a monastic scholarship that was already giving way to the learning of the schools, chose, possibly without each other's knowledge, to write histories of the First Crusade on the basis of the narrative provided by the *Gesta Francorum*. The *Gesta*, written, it will be remembered, by a south Italian Norman, must have been already circulating in France, perhaps in connection with Bohemond of Taranto's propaganda drive to raise men for a new crusade. Bohemond had arrived in France early in 1106. After visiting the shrine of St Leonard at St-Léonard-de-Noblat, at which he fulfilled a vow he had made while he was imprisoned at Niksar, he made a triumphant tour of the country, presenting churches and monasteries with relics and precious objects he had brought from the East and relating his adventures to appreciative audiences: many French nobles wanted him to be godfather to their children. He and the papal legate, Bruno of Segni, formally proclaimed a new crusade at a council held at Poitiers, describing it as a *via sancti Sepulchri* with the aims of helping the Christians in the East and forcing the Muslims to disgorge their Christian prisoners. But Bohemond was also accompanied by a pretender to the Byzantine imperial throne and his Greek entourage and, on the occasion of his marriage to Constance of France at Chartres in April or May, he himself preached in the cathedral a crusade sermon in which he urged French knights to join him in an invasion of the Byzantine empire and promised them rich lands. He seems to have been proposing something very similar to the plan of the fourth crusaders a century later to appear in force outside Constantinople on the way to the East to engineer a change of government there, although when he wrote to the pope a few months later he mentioned the usurpation of Alexius as only one issue and also justified an attack on the Greeks as vengeance for the way they had treated the crusaders and as a means of ending schism.[5]

Robert, Guibert and Baldric each gave as his reason for writing his history the uncouth way in which the *Gesta Francorum* had been written. Robert told how Abbot (Bernard of Marmoutier)

> showed me a history . . . but it displeased him very much, partly because it contained no description of the foundation of the crusade at the Council of Clermont, partly because it neglected to adorn the sequence of such beautiful events, and the literary composition staggered in a rough manner.

He went on to add, a little sharply:

> If our edition displeases anyone brought up in scholarly studies

... we would like to inform him that it seemed to us more acceptable to throw light on what was obscure in the manner of a countryman than to becloud what was clear in the manner of a philosopher.[6]

Guibert explained:

There was, indeed, a history [of the crusade], but it was written in words more artless than correct; in it there were departures from the rules of grammar in many passages; and it often had the effect of deadening the interest of the reader with the flat insipidity of ordinary speech.

He then gave a strong justification for a properly written history.

At a time when we see an enthusiasm for the study of grammar everywhere and we know that this teaching is available to the poorest of persons on account of the great number of scholars, it would be a scandal not to write about the glory of our time as we ought, or at least to the best of our ability, and on the contrary to allow its history to remain available in the uncouth roughness of ordinary speech.[7]

Baldric wrote much the same.

I was not worthy to be among that blessed knighthood, nor have I told of things that I have seen. But I do not know which anonymous author had published a little book on this affair which was very crude. He contrived to tell the truth, but because of the uncouthness of his writing he cheapened a noble subject and the inelegant and artless language turned the more guileless away from it at once. I engaged in the study of the subject not desirous of empty glory, nor puffed up with swollen pride, but I wrote the sentences carefully in order to please future Christianity.[8]

So three monastic scholars took it upon themselves to rework in better language a popular eyewitness account of the crusade. They did so because they felt the subject merited proper literary treatment, and by that they meant, as Guibert and Baldric made clear, proper theological treatment. To men educated in the eleventh-century monastic schools theology was open only to *grammatici*, those trained not only in linguistic skills but also in philosophy.[9] What these three monks were in effect saying was that the *Gesta Francorum* was not theological enough. Given the euphoria in Europe at the crusade's success it is not surprising that the need should have been felt to discuss a series of events so clearly manifesting the workings of divine providence in more theological terms than hitherto, particularly as another crusade was now being preached. It is striking that, in spite of natural differences in style and interest, the message that flowed from these three pens was already recognizably one message. French Benedictine monastic circles must have arrived at a common interpretation of the crusade. So part of the importance of the works of Robert, Guibert and Baldric is the way they demonstrate how intelligent minds were working in the decade after the fall of Jerusalem. In them we find an intellectual expression of the semi-popular ideology forged in the traumas of the expedition and with them the crusading idea as it had developed in the course of the crusade passed back into the province of theologians.

The astonishment expressed by the crusaders at their own achievement was the starting point for the sequence of ideas they put forward. The crusade was for them a wonderful event.

> We are speaking [wrote Guibert] of the recent and imcomparable victory of the expedition to Jerusalem. Those of us who have not grown foolish glory so much in it that we rejoice that our times are enobled with a title no former ones have deserved.[10]

This was, of course, because it was fought under Christ's leadership.[11] It was 'not human work, but divine', as Robert put it,[12] and this was a subject to which he returned again and again. In two moving passages he tried to portray the bewilderment of devout Muslims, Kilij Arslan of Rum and al-Afdal, the Egyptian vizier, at their defeats at Dorylaeum and Ascalon at the hands of soldiers they were convinced in their ignorance were instruments of the devil,[13] and he made Bohemond explain the crusaders' successes in terms of divine interventionary power in a dialogue with the captain who was to betray Antioch to him.

O Pyrrhus, does it not seem to you to be a great miracle that the Lord Jesus Christ, in whom we believe, works through us? For by as many as we are fewer in numbers, so the greater is our strength; and by as many as you are the more numerous, so you are the weaker. To whom do you attribute this power, to humankind or to the divinity? Man is nothing by himself. All he is, he is by the will of his creator, from whom he has not only existence but the potential for action.[14]

And after the Battle of Dorylaeum he made the crusaders sing a marvellous hymn, based on Moses' hymn of gratitude in *Exodus* after the destruction of the Egyptians in the Red Sea.

You are glorious, Lord, in your holy works, wonderful in your majesty, *terrible and praiseworthy, doing wonders. Thy right hand, O Lord, hath slain the enemy and in the multitude of thy glory thou hast put down* our *adversaries. The enemy said: I will pursue and overtake; I will divide the spoils, my soul shall have its fill; I will draw my sword; my hand shall slay them.* But you, Lord, were with us, as a strong warrior. In your mercy you were leader and protector of *the people thou hast redeemed.* Now, Lord, we acknowledge that you are bearing us *in thy strength to thy holy habitation,* that is your Holy Sepulchre.[15]

In a staggering phrase he went further when he tried to place the crusade in its rightful place in providential history, for he argued that as an example of God's interventionary might it stood comparison with only two other events, the creation and the redemption of mankind on the cross.

But apart from the mystery of the healing cross, what more marvellous deed has there been since the creation of the world than that which was done in modern times in this journey of our men of Jerusalem?[16]

Guibert of Nogent drew much the same conclusion.

God himself, who makes miracles, not wishing to allow another to assume the honour due to his name, was their only leader. He personally regulated them. He personally corrected them. He

personally directed what had been begun to its conclusion. He
personally extended to such a degree the bounds of their rule. He
gathered the lambs, which he had fashioned from wolves, in his
arms, not theirs. He embraced them in his protective care. He
transported his brood of young, joyful in devout hope, to see what
they desired.[17]

A theme of his book, to which he returned many times, was the
argument that the crusade was a more significant manifestation of
divine approval than any exploit in history, even than the divinely
authorized wars of the Israelites described in the Old Testament.

If we consider the battles of the gentiles and think of great military
enterprises in which kingdoms have been invaded, we will think
of no army and absolutely no exploit comparable to ours. We
have heard that God was glorified in the Jewish people, but we
acknowledge that there is reliable proof that Jesus Christ lives and
thrives today among our contemporaries just as he did yesterday
among men of old.[18]
We have said not once but many times, and it bears repetition,
that such a deed has never been done in this world. If the children
of Israel oppose this by referring me to the miracles which the
Lord performed for them in the past, I will furnish them with an
opened [Red] Sea crowded with gentiles. To them I demonstrate,
for the pillar, the cloud of divine fear by day, the light of divine
hope by night. To the crusaders Christ himself, the pillar of
rectitude and strength, gave instances of inspiration; he strengthened them, without any earthly hope, only with the food of the
word of God, as it were with heavenly manna.[19]

For Guibert God was now magnified by the crusaders as once he had
been by the Jews, but the difference between the Israelites and the
crusaders – what made the crusaders' achievement worthier – lay in
the aims of the two chosen peoples. The Israelites had 'fought carnal
wars only to fill their bellies'.[20] They had fought, moreover, for
the old law, 'for rituals and the Temple' or 'for circumcision and
abstinence from pork', whereas the crusaders, 'fighting to cleanse
the churches and propagate the faith' and 'starting out only with
spiritual desire . . . marked modern times with a display of divine
power, such as has never occurred in history'.[21] So the special nature

of the crusade, the reason why it was such an astounding demonstration of God's strength, was that it witnessed a conjunction of
divine interventionary power and the good intentions of the participants. It really was, as the title of Guibert's book indicated, 'The tale
of God working through the French' *(Gesta Dei per Francos)*.

Robert, Guibert and Baldric also saw the crusade as the literal
fulfilment of certain prophecies in scripture. Like the crusaders
themselves, they associated these triumphs with those of the Israelites and identified crusaders and the crusade with the great figures
and events in Jewish history,[22] but they also took up and developed
the idea that passages in scripture foretold the crusade. Baldric[23] was
much more hesitant about this subject than Guibert and Robert, and
the approaches of the last two were different. Guibert ranged widely,
with one prophecy each from Job, the Psalms, Proverbs, Isaiah,
Zacharias and Luke; he wrote a long exposition of Zacharias 12:1–
10, in which the prophet foretold an apocalyptic siege of Jerusalem
involving Judah, with which Guibert identified the crusaders.[24]
Robert, on the other hand, referred once to Deuteronomy and once
to Proverbs, but spent most of his time on Isaiah and particularly on
the great prophecy of a future Jerusalem in Isaiah 9:9–11, 15–16, in
which references were made to the sons of Jerusalem coming from
afar, to foreigners rebuilding her walls and to her gates being open
day and night: for pilgrims, Robert suggested.[25] The novelty of the
situation in which they found themselves and the astonishment the
crusade's success had caused is demonstrated by the fact that, like the
eyewitnesses, Robert, Guibert and Baldric made use of different
prophetic passages. They had no common ground in any tradition of
exegesis that could be applied to these events. A further illustration
of this was the startling suggestion that what had been regarded in
the past as allegorical should now be treated as literal. Guibert,
commenting on the passage in Zacharias (12:3), 'and all the kingdoms of the earth shall be gathered together against her', wrote that
'this is not to be understood as allegory, but with the eyes of the
soul it is to be looked on as recent history reported'.[26] Robert moved
towards the same conclusions when he wrote of the passage in Isaiah
(55:12), 'The mountains and the hills shall sing praise before you',
that 'then was fulfilled in reality what was expressed spiritually',[27]
and in his use of the phrases: 'We now see in that event the promise
which God made through the mouth of Isaiah the prophet' and 'in
that place there occurred that which is said in Proverbs'.[28] 'These and

many other things we find in the prophetic books, which correspond to this liberation done in our days.'[29] It is not hard to imagine the shock caused by a realization that passages in scripture which had always been thought to have been susceptible only to allegorical interpretation were suddenly being literally fulfilled.

Another aspect was prophecy of what was yet to come to pass, especially the Last Days. In his version of Urban II's sermon at Clermont, Guibert made the pope point out that it was clear from scripture that Antichrist would reside in Jerusalem. Being certain to attack Christians, he could hardly appear until Jerusalem was occupied by them. A traditional interpretation of a prophecy in Daniel 7:24, moreover, was that Antichrist would kill kings of Egypt, Africa and Ethiopia for their Christian faith, something, again, that could not come to pass until North Africa was converted. The crusade, therefore, might well be a prelude to mass conversion and to Doomsday, particularly since the liberation of Jerusalem from the gentiles was associated in St Luke's Gospel (21:24) with the Last Days. It has been suggested recently that eschatological writing of this kind is so rare that millenarianism cannot have been a major element in the crusade, but the ideas were certainly in the air, as we have seen.[30]

Divine approval and support were, of course, enough to have made the crusade the Lord's and sacred.[31] Fought, as in the eyewitness accounts, against 'a race absolutely alien to God', indeed against the devil's agents,[32] it was an expression of God's anger and vengeance on them. 'God is angry with our people [the Muslims], because we do not heed his voice or do his will; and therefore he has aroused his people from the distant West against us and has given this land into their possession.'[33] The crusaders were also carrying out the judgement of God. 'Jerusalem will be ours, not through the gift of men, but through the justice of heavenly judgement. For this judgement proceeds from the severity of God; that Jerusalem will be ours.'[34] In this respect the crusade was believed to have stemmed from an arbitrary decision of God, just as had the Israelites' original occupation of the Promised Land. 'The children of Israel, who were led out of Egypt and, after crossing the Red Sea, prefigured you [the crusaders], appropriated this land for themselves by force, with Jesus as their leader.'[35]

But the conviction that God was the authorizer did not absolve the propagandists from justifying the crusade in terms of moral theology. Robert, Guibert and Baldric referred to the propagation of the faith as an attraction of crusading, but it is clear that they saw this as a bonus, not a justification,[36] although Robert may have been slightly less committed to the canon law criteria for a just war than Guibert and Baldric.[37] Guibert's treatment of the subject, with its references to the Christian Republic and to war being most justly fought in defence of the Church, was typical of the views of advanced reformers.

> If they [the knights] were to take up the cause of safeguarding liberty and defending the commonwealth [*pro publica re*], they might at least be able to put forward an honest excuse. When, moreover, an invasion of barbarians or of gentiles is feared, no soldier ought to absent himself from the discipline of arms. Even if these conditions do not exist, wars traditionally have been fought absolutely legitimately only for the protection of Holy Church. But because nobody has had this right intention and the lust for possessions has pervaded the hearts of all, God has instituted in our time holy wars. . . . [38]
>
> If the Maccabees in days of old were renowned for their piety because they fought for rituals and the Temple, then you too, Christian soldiers, may justly defend the freedom of the father-land [*patria*] by the exercise of arms. . . . Until now you have fought unjust wars: you have often savagely brandished your spears at each other in mutual carnage only out of greed and pride, for which you deserve eternal destruction and the certain ruin of damnation! Now we are proposing that you should fight wars which contain the glorious reward of martyrdom, in which you can gain the title of present and eternal glory.[39]

Baldric echoed these arguments when he put into Urban's mouth at Clermont the statement that 'the Holy Church keeps for herself an army to come to the aid of her own people', and when he had Bohemond call on the crusaders before the Battle of Dorylaeum to 'run to defend yourselves and your commonwealth [*respublica*]'.[40]

The treatment of cause, in fact, strictly followed the twin lines of liberation of people and place laid down by Urban. Guibert defined it as 'aid to all Christianity, to redeem Jerusalem for God and to liberate his Sepulchre'.[41] With regard to the first of these causes, all three writers expatiated on the abuses suffered by pilgrims and the oppression endured by eastern Christians.[42] One rather surprising feature, considering that they were writing at a time when Bohemond was travelling through France fulminating against the Greeks, is that, as in the eyewitness accounts, there is no evidence of feelings of animosity towards the Greek people in general. Alexius's government came in for abuse and his subjects were despised as effeminate,[43] but in no sense were they regarded as heretics. Describing the capture of Nicaea and its return to the Greeks, Robert reminded his readers of the first great general council of the Church held there and commented that it was, therefore,

> worthy that Nicaea should be taken from the enemies of the holy faith and reconciled to God and reintegrated as a limb into our holy mother the Church. And so God provided and disposed that this new reintegration was consecrated by the martyrdom of many who were killed there.[44]

The Greek capital, Constantinople, was, to Robert and Guibert, owed reverence as a royal city and as an apostolic see. It was equal with Rome, except that Rome was the seat of the popes and therefore the capital of Christendom. It was the greatest storehouse of relics in the Christian world and so was an important place of pilgrimage.[45] Baldric showed himself to be intensely concerned to stress the brotherhood of all Christians. The Greeks were, in fact, the full uterine brothers of the Latins, calling for their help.

> Our brothers, members of Christ's body.... Your blood-brothers, your comrades-in-arms, those born from the same womb as you, for you are sons of the same Christ and the same Church.... Christian blood, which has been redeemed by Christ's blood, is spilled and Christian flesh, flesh of Christ's flesh, is delivered up to execrable abuses and appalling servitude.[46]

With respect to the liberation of territory, moreover, Robert, Guibert and Baldric all knew of the formal criterion for just violence of recovery of property. The region belonged rightfully to Christendom because before it had been seized by the Muslims it had been part of the Christian Roman empire.

The land . . . is not theirs, although they have possessed it for a long time, for from the earliest times it was ours and your people attacked it and took it . . . and so it ought not to be yours just because you have held it for a long time; for by heavenly judgement it is now decreed that that which was unjustly taken from the fathers should be mercifully returned to the sons.[47]

But of course Jerusalem and the land around it was also the scene of Christ's redemptive act and the source of Christian doctrine, being

the city from which we have received the grace of redemption and the source of all Christianity. . . . If it is true that we derive the whole of our Christian teaching from the fountain of Jerusalem, the hearts of all catholics should be moved by the streams which spread through the whole world to remember wisely the debt they owe to a spring so bounteous.[48]

It was, therefore, 'the mother church of all the churches'.[49] It was also a royal city[50] and Christ's personal possession, his inheritance referred to in the Psalms: 'O God, the heathens are come into thy inheritance'.[51] It was also a relic, its ground and stones sanctified by the physical presence of God himself.

If . . . this land was the inheritance and the holy temple of God before the Lord walked and appeared there, how much more holy and worthy of reverence must we consider it became when the God of Majesty was incarnate there, was nurtured, grew up and in his physical nature walked and travelled from place to place?. . . What veneration do we consider to be fitting for the place where the blood of the son of God, holier than heaven or earth, poured out and where his body, dead to the fearful elements, rested in the grave? If when Our Lord himself had recently been killed and the city was still in the hands of the Jews it was called holy by the evangelist . . . no subsequent evil can remove that same holiness, since it has been imparted to the city by God himself, the sanctifier, by his own action. . . . If you consider that you ought to take great pains to make a pilgrimage to the graves of the apostles [in Rome] or to the shrines of other saints, what expense of spirit can you refuse in order to rescue, and make pilgrimage to, the cross, the blood, the Sepulchre?[52]

As in the eyewitness accounts, it was the sanctity of the place that made its usurpation so unacceptable, for the domination of the infidels over it polluted it.

> May you be especially moved by the ιoly Sepulchre of Our Lord and Saviour, which is in the hands of unclean races, and by the Holy Places, which are now treated dishonourably and are polluted irreverently by their unclean practices.[53]

We have already seen that in the minds of the crusaders themselves their battle for the terrestrial Jerusalem had become in some way a progress towards the heavenly Jerusalem. This was unacceptable, since in no sense could the liberation of an earthly city, however sacred, be equated with conversion. Baldric and Robert refined the idea by treating the liberation of the earthly Jerusalem as a preliminary to the gaining of the heavenly city. Jerusalem

> both prefigures and simulates the heavenly city. You can see that visible enemies oppose us here. Invisible enemies, moreover, hem in the roads coming to her, against whom a spiritual conflict remains. And it is more important for us to struggle *against the spirits of wickedness in the high places* than *against flesh and blood* which we see. . . . We will be altogether unfitted and ineffectual in the spiritual struggle if we do not take a stand against these weak dogs [the Muslims].[54]

And to Guibert the crusade was spiritual in so far as the intentions of the participants were spiritual.[55]

In their treatment of these participants Robert, Guibert and Baldric were at their most striking. The crusaders were, like the Jews in the Old Testament, God's elect; and it was no accident that they were French.[56] The traditional national pride in Frankishness, already expressed in the eyewitness accounts, comes across very strongly indeed. Robert made Bohemond declare, on learning that the crusade was being preached: 'Are we not of Frankish stock? Did not our ancestors come from France and liberate this land [south Italy] with arms? What disgrace! Will our blood-relatives and brothers go to martyrdom and indeed to paradise without us?'[57] The French, indeed, were that 'blessed nation whose God is the Lord'.[58] France was the region of the world to be extolled above all others: like Israel, 'how beautiful' were its 'tabernacles' when its tents were pitched in Asia Minor.[59] God was especially the God of the French, whom he loved and had reserved for this particular deed: their history, their special faith in him and their traditional devotion to the Holy See revealed this.

> If they were injured by neighbouring peoples, it was customary from of old for the popes always to seek aid from the French. Popes Stephen and Zacharias fled to Kings Pippin and Charles, the first of whom . . . having campaigned as far as the Ticino to recover the Church's Patrimony restored the pope to his own see. . . . I acknowledge, and it is worthy of everyone's belief, that God has reserved that people for such a great matter as this [crusade]; especially since we know for certain that from the time they received the sign of faith at the hands of St Remigius they have never caught the contagion of perfidy.[60]

These French crusaders were lay knights, not religious or secular clergy. Over and over again in these writings, composed, it should be remembered, for monastic audiences, one finds evocations of knighthood as romantic and coruscating as any in the *chansons*. Robert the Monk, for instance, made the despondent Kilij Arslan ascribe his defeat at Dorylaeum to men

> who do not fear death or the enemy. . . . Who could bear the sight of the splendour of their terrifying arms? Their lances flashed like sparkling stars; their helmets and mailcoats like the glimmering light of a spring dawn. The clashing of their arms was more terrible than the sound of thunder. When they prepare themselves for battle they raise their lances high and then advance in ranks, as silently as though they are dumb. When they draw close to their adversaries then, loosing their reins, they charge with great force like lions which, spurred on by hunger, thirst for blood. Then they shout and grind their teeth and fill the air with their cries. And they spare no one.[61]

The monastic writers were able to give rein to imaginative eulogies of this sort, perhaps restrained since their childhoods when they must

themselves for a brief time have shared the ideas of the martial world
into which they had been born, because in their minds they could,
following Urban II, divorce the image of the old barbaric knight from
his new Christian successor.

> Listen and understand. You have strapped on the belt of knight-
> hood and strut around with pride in your eye. You butcher your
> brothers and create factions among yourselves. This, which scat-
> ters the sheepfold of the Redeemer, is not the knighthood of
> Christ. The Holy Church keeps for herself an army to come to the
> aid of her own people, buy you pervert it with knavery. To speak
> the truth, the preachers of which it is our duty to be, you are not
> following the path that leads you to life. You oppressors of
> orphans, you robbers of widows, you homicides, you blas-
> phemers, you plunderers of others' rights; you hope for the
> rewards of brigands for the shedding of Christian blood and just
> as vultures nose corpses you watch and follow wars from afar.
> Certainly this is the worst course to follow because it is utterly
> removed from God. And if you want to take counsel for your
> souls you must either cast off as quickly as possible the belt of this
> sort of knighthood or go forward boldly as knights of Christ,
> hurrying swiftly to defend the eastern Church.[62]

The realization that the laity was coming into its own and was being
given a role which laymen could profitably fulfil without adopting
the monastic habit was stressed by Guibert of Nogent.

> God has instituted in our time holy wars, so that the order of
> knights and the crowd running in their wake, who, following the
> example of the ancient pagans, have been engaged in slaughtering
> one another, might find a new way of gaining salvation. And so
> they are not forced to abandon secular affairs completely by
> choosing the monastic life or any religious profession, as used to
> be the custom, but can attain in some measure God's grace while
> pursuing their own careers, with the liberty and in the dress to
> which they are accustomed.[63]

Guibert pointed out that what was important was not only that such
a proposal had been put to laymen, but also that they had responded
to it.

Foremost in the minds of all was only the ambition for a holy death for the love of God. . . . No one could have hoped in our time – he would have been ridiculed had he said it – that God would place such a contempt for material things in the hearts of savage and greedy men.[64]

It was natural for monks, under the influence of a reform movement which was anyway seeking to impose their values on the world, to see the crusaders as lay pilgrims adopting a kind of monastic life, albeit temporary, while at the same time fighting for Christ and the Church. I have already pointed out that the army had in some sense the appearance of a great monastic community on the move, its path marked by regular and solemn intercessory liturgies. Robert, Guibert and Baldric seized on this and built their picture of the crusade round it. Guibert went so far as to state that the crusaders could be seen leading 'not a military but a monkish life, as far as frugality and chastity are concerned'.[65] It was obviously this that led Baldric and Robert to use terms to describe the army – *sanctum collegium, Christianorum congregatio, sacra fidelium Dei societas* – which would have reminded their readers of the early Church, the model for monasticism. Baldric was quite explicit.

In that expedition dukes themselves fought and took their turns at the watch, so that one could not tell duke from knight or knight from duke. Beyond this, so many goods were held by the commonalty that scarcely anyone could say that anything was his own, but, just as in the primitive Church, nearly all things were shared in common.[66]

The picture of the crusade painted by Robert, Guibert and Baldric comes into focus once one realizes that they were portraying it as a monastery in motion. Almost every point they made was in tacit comparison to monasticism. The crusaders made vows – and therefore a kind of profession and conversion – under the inspiration of the Holy Spirit.

We see nations moved by the inspiration of God. . . . The highest offices of government, the lordships of castles or cities were despised; the most beautiful wives became as loathsome as something putrid; the lure of every jewel, welcome once to both sexes as security, was spurned. These men were driven by the sudden determination of totally changed minds to do what no mortal had ever been able to urge by command or achieve by persuasion. . . . What can this universal response be except an expression of that plain goodness which moves the hearts of the most numerous peoples to seek one and the same thing?[67]

Renouncing wives, children and earthly possessions they sought voluntary exile for the love of God,[68] adopting temporary poverty and chastity, although Baldric pointed out that wives who went with their husbands lived with them 'but in marriage or in lawful ministry'.[69] What, of course, was very unlike a monastery was the lack of a single leader or clear chain of command for most of the time, but Robert, Guibert and Baldric made the most of this, for it enabled them to stress the unity and brotherhood that they believed had animated the participants. 'Without a king, without a prince, devotion alone showed them the path to their salvation.'[70] Moved not only by their love of God, but also by their love of their brothers, their fellow-Christians, literally carrying out Christ's maxim to lay down their lives for their friends,[71] the crusaders had, in fact, adopted the way of the cross: Baldric compared their liberation of Jerusalem to Joseph of Arimathea taking Christ down from the cross.[72]

Nowhere is the picture of a secular but semi-monastic way of the cross clearer than in these writers' treatment of martyrdom. I have already described how the conviction that their dead were martyrs grew among the crusaders as their triumph became apparent. In the eyewitness accounts, however, the notion was unformed and crude and it was Robert, Guibert and Baldric who put it on firm theological foundations by relating it to Christian love. Martyrdom was for them an expression of the crusaders' love for God and their brothers.[73] It was a voluntary act by which they exchanged temporal for eternal life.[74] They died for Christ, who had died for them, and for the faith, of which they were witnesses.[75] Guibert laid particular stress on the fact that it was laymen who were being martyred. He devoted a passage in his book to a knight called Matthew, who had crusaded in the army of Peter the Hermit, had been captured by the Muslims in Asia Minor and had been beheaded by them because he would not renounce his faith. Guibert and Matthew had, in fact, grown up together: Matthew's parents and then Matthew himself had held a fief in Guibert's family lordship. In his account Guibert went out of his way to stress Matthew's goodness. He was nobly born and a good knight, but Guibert considered that he was entirely immune from the vice of wantonness, which he clearly associated with knighthood. In the imperial palace at Constantinople Matthew was well-known for the care with which he followed the religious observances of the pilgrimage. He was so prayerful that his life appeared to be more that of a bishop than a knight. Devout and generous in alms-giving, he was saintly in intention and deserved nothing better than his martyrdom. Guibert used his life and death to illustrate what to him was an important point: that the crusading martyrs were 'not only priests nor simply lettered men, but military men, some of them common people. There had been no previous hope that these would bear witness to their faith.'[76] His biography of Matthew demonstrated how a layman could achieve salvation in his own way.

The story told by Robert, Guibert and Baldric – of a miraculous demonstration of divine power in a war fought for Christian brothers and for Christ's inheritance by a chosen people, the French lay knights, who adopted a kind of temporary monastic life in an army that was similar to a great abbey in all respects save in its ephemeral nature and democracy – was obviously an idealized one. They did not completely gloss over the bad aspects of the crusade, but they certainly did not dwell on them. Nevertheless the picture they painted was still recognizably the crusade, even if it was the crusade theologized. No idea put forward by them was entirely new, since all echoed notions that can be found somewhere in the letters and narrative accounts of eyewitnesses; but they gave the often crude and inchoate ideas they found a sophisticated and coherent expression, making them acceptable to an audience of churchmen. The Church had proclaimed and publicized the crusade, but it had not yet explained what had become a truly popular devotion in its own terms. Robert, Guibert and Baldric gave the corpus of ideas a form which made it capable of theological, as well as popular, development.

Conclusion

Pope Urban II's appeal to lay knights in 1095–6 was the culmination of the movement of the Church towards lay people which had begun earlier in the eleventh century. As a scion of the petty nobility of Champagne and a Cluniac monk, he revived an alliance between the Holy See and the French which had not flourished for 200 years by calling on French knights to take part in an enterprise that was to be a pilgrimage, unusual in that it was explicitly for the young and healthy, and at the same time a war with the twin aims of freeing their Christian brothers, whose needs were associated with those of all Christendom, and liberating the holy city of Jerusalem. He followed a conventional practice among the reformers by referring to this war as Christ's own, to be fought in accordance with God's will and intentions. He equated service in it with love of God and neighbour and he applied to the actions of the participants Christ's injunctions to take up their crosses and follow him and to abandon for his sake their families and properties. Potential crusaders were to confirm their commitment by taking vows similar to those already made by pilgrims. Realizing that the campaign would be long and arduous, Urban recognized it as a penitential exercise so severe that it would be 'satisfactory', outweighing any punishment that would have been imposed by God on the crusaders for their previous sins. Nothing he said was particularly novel, at least in terms of the ideas current in reforming circles in Italy, and had it not been for its striking success we might now consider his summons merely to have been another example of the hyperbolic utterances favoured by reforming churchmen of his time.

But his preaching had two remarkable consequences. The first was that the faithful responded enthusiastically to it. There can be little doubt that those who took the cross, and the families who helped to finance them, were moved on the whole by idealism. The only explanation for their enthusiasm seems to be that Urban's message encountered the laity's growing aspirations and the hand stretched out by the Church to lay people was suddenly grasped. That is not to say, of course, that laymen thought in quite the same way as did the pope, even though he came from the same background, and an early example of the disjunction of ideas was the pogrom against the Jews, caused above all by the conviction of many crusaders that they were engaged in a vendetta. Summoned to help their oppressed brothers and to liberate the patrimony of their father and lord, they thought, as there always was the danger that they would, in family and feudal terms and embarked upon a blood feud in which they found it hard to distinguish between peoples they identified as 'enemies of Christ'.

The second was the crusade itself and the traumatic experiences of the crusaders: their suffering, fear and homesickness; the humiliation of the knights who lost their horses and were reduced to poverty; the intensification of feelings in an army enveloped in the supernatural penumbra of signs and apparitions and in the devotional and liturgical atmosphere of the pilgrimage; the incompetence and inadequacy of the leadership; military weakness; and astounding success. It is not surprising that the crusaders were astonished or that they became convinced that the enterprise in which they were engaged really was God's own, that they were experiencing his omnipotent interventionary power, that they really were his chosen people and that their dead were martyrs. It was natural for them to relate all of this to scripture, above all to the trials and triumphs of the Israelites. But most of the clergy with them were not of a high intellectual calibre and the resulting ideas, as they appeared in the eyewitness accounts, were awkward and unsophisticated.

Urban's message had been distorted and popularized, and also greatly developed, in the traumas of the crusade, but the result was too rough to be of much use to the Church without some theological restatement, especially when one remembers that most churchmen were probably more conservative in their views on Christian violence than the extreme reformers. It was later writers, especially Robert the Monk, Guibert of Nogent and Baldric of Bourgueil, who provided a *modus vivendi* for both theologians and the general public, even if they could never hope to bridge the yawning gulf that lay between them. Robert, Guibert and Baldric put the miraculous nature of the crusade into the framework of providential history and they treated the crusading army as though it were a great nomadic monastery and the crusaders as though they were temporarily professed religious who had adopted voluntary exile for the love of God and their neighbours, were united in brotherhood and followed a way of the cross that could lead to martyrdom. To their readers the goal of the reformers for a century, the infusing of the outside world with monastic values, must have seemed to be attainable at last.

But if so they were mistaken. Robert, Guibert and Baldric provided a pattern of thought that could be of immediate utility, but it does not seem to have survived long. It is my impression that, although the preaching of and the devotional practices on the Second Crusade were monastic – which is not surprising when one considers the leading role of Cistercians like Pope Eugenius III and St Bernard – crusading was becoming markedly less monastic by 1200, perhaps because a clear and individual function for the laity was coming to be emphasized more as the twelfth century progressed, perhaps because the establishment of the military orders, the brothers of which were both professed religious and warriors, channelled the monastic impulses away from ordinary crusading. This, I repeat, is merely an impression. There can be no certainty until the question has been properly researched. But whatever the results of such research, nothing can detract from the intellectual achievement of these three representatives of almost the last generation of monastic cultural dominance.

Chronological table
List of abbreviations
Notes
Index

Chronological table

6–7 August	Peter the Hermit and Walter Sansavoir crossed Bosphorus
c.11 August	Crusaders reached Kibotos
c.15 August	Flight of Emich of Leiningen's forces from Wieselberg
	Godfrey of Bouillon left for East
September	Bohemond of Taranto and Tancred took cross
September–October	Robert of Normany, Robert of Flanders and Stephen of Blois left for East
c.24 September	Italian and German crusaders established base close to Nicaea
29 September	Defeat and destruction of Italian and German crusaders
October	Hugh of Vermandois crossed Adriatic
21 October	Remaining crusaders in Asia Minor defeated
c.26 October	Bohemond of Taranto left Italy
November	Hugh of Vermandois reached Constantinople
23 December	Godfrey of Bouillon reached Constantinople
December–January 1097	Raymond of St Gilles and Adhémar of Le Puy crossed Dalmatia
c.20 February	Godfrey of Bouillon's force crossed Bosphorus
c.10 April	Bohemond of Taranto reached Constantinople
26 April	Bohemond's force crossed Bosphorus
c.27 April	Raymond of St Gilles reached Constantinople
6 May	Godfrey of Bouillon, Tancred, Robert of Flanders and Hugh of Vermandois came before Nicaea
14–28 May	Robert of Normandy and Stephen of Blois at Constantinople
16 May	Raymond of St Gilles reached Nicaea
3 June	Robert of Normandy and Stephen of Blois reached Nicaea
19 June	Surrender of Nicaea to the Greeks
26–29 June	Departure of crusaders
1 July	Battle of Dorylaeum
c.15 August	Crusaders reached Konya
c.10 September	Crusaders reached Ereghli and defeated a Turkish army
c.14 September	Tancred and Baldwin of Boulogne left for Cilicia
c.21 September	Tancred and Baldwin took Tarsus
c.27 September	Main body of crusade reached Kayseri
September–October	Tancred took Adana and Misis
5–6 October	Main body of crusade reached Göksun
c.13 October	Main body of crusade reached Marash
c.15 October	Baldwin of Boulogne rejoined main army
c.17 October	Baldwin left main army
20–22 October	Crusaders arrived before Antioch
c.17 November	Genoese fleet reached Suwaidiyah

30 December	Earthquake at Antioch
c.20 January 1098	Attempted flight of Peter the Hermit and William the Carpenter
20 February	Arrival of Baldwin of Boulogne at Edessa
5 March	Decision to construct siege castle of La Mahomerie before Antioch
10 March	Baldwin of Boulogne took over government of Edessa
before 29 March	Stephen of Blois elected commander-in-chief
2 June	Stephen of Blois left Antioch
3 June	Antioch taken by the crusaders
4–5 June	Kerbogha's army began to arrive before Antioch
10–11 June	Night of panic among the crusaders and flight
11 June	Visions of Stephen of Valence and Peter Bartholomew reported
14 June	Discovery of the Holy Lance
c.20 June	Emperor Alexius heard erroneous reports of the situation in Antioch and decided to withdraw from Akshehir
27 June	Embassy of Peter the Hermit to Kerbogha
28 June	Battle of Antioch
14 July– after 15 August	Raymond Pilet's expedition
1 August	Death of Adhémar of Le Puy
c.25 September	Raymond of St Gilles established Latin bishopric at al-Barah
27 November	Investment of Ma'arrat
11–12 December	Fall and sack of Ma'arrat
c.4 January 1099	Conference in the Ruj at which Raymond of St Gilles proposed to take the other leaders into his service for pay
c.5 January	Raymond of St Gilles's followers dismantled the walls of Ma'arrat
13 January	Raymond of St Gilles departed for the south
14 January	Robert of Normandy joined Raymond of St Gilles
2 February	Remaining crusaders in Antioch decided to assemble at Latakia
c.14 February	Raymond of St Gilles reached 'Arqah
c.25 February	Death of Anselm of Ribemont
c.14 March	Godfrey of Bouillon and Robert of Flanders joined siege of 'Arqah
8 April	Peter Bartholomew underwent ordeal
20 April	Death of Peter Bartholomew
24–30 April	Council of Rome. Pope Urban appealed to Lombardy for crusaders
13 May	Siege of 'Arqah raised
19 May	Crusade reached Beirut
23 May	Crusade passed Tyre

3–6 June	Crusaders at Ramle. Latin bishopric of Ramle–Lydda established
6 June	Tancred took Bethlehem
7 June	Crusaders arrived before Jerusalem
8 July	Procession round Jerusalem
15 July	Jerusalem taken
22 July	Election of Godfrey of Bouillon as ruler of Jerusalem
29 July	Death of Pope Urban II
1 August	Election of Arnulf of Chocques as Latin patriarch of Jerusalem
5 August	Discovery of the True Cross
12 August	Battle of Ascalon
end of August	Bulk of crusaders left for home
c.1 December	Pope Paschal II threatened to excommunicate crusaders who had not yet fulfilled their vows and called for aid for the Christians in Palestine
spring 1100	Synod of Anse ordered crusaders to fulfil their vows
c.15 August	Bohemond captured by Gümüshtigin ibn-Danishmend
13 September	Lombard crusaders left for East
October	William of Aquitaine took cross at Limoges
18 November	Cross preached by papal legates at Council of Poitiers
early February 1101	William of Nevers left for East
February – March	Lombard crusaders reached Constantinople
12–19 March	William of Aquitaine left for East
1 April	Welf of Bavaria left for East
21 April	Lombards crossed Bosphorus
early June	Lombards with some Germans and French and Raymond of St Gilles and Stephen of Blois departed from Nicomedia
	William of Aquitaine and Welf of Bavaria reached Constantinople
c.14 June	William of Nevers reached Constantinople
23 June	Lombard crusaders reached Ankara
mid-July	William of Aquitaine and Welf of Bavaria crossed Bosphorus
early August	Lombards defeated near Merzifon
mid-August	William of Nevers reached Konya; marched on to Ereghli, where defeated
early September	William of Aquitaine defeated at Ereghli
31 March 1102	Surviving crusaders gathered in Jerusalem
17 May	Battle of Ramle. Death of Stephen of Blois
before 1104	The *Gesta Francorum* written
1104–8	Guibert of Nogent composed his *Gesta* (with final corrections in 1111)
before 1105	Fulcher of Chartres wrote first redaction of his *Historia* (writing a second redaction in 1124, which he continued to 1127)

	Raymond of Aguilers completed his *Historia*
1107	Robert the Monk wrote his *Historia*
1108	Baldric of Bourgueil wrote his *Historia*
before 1111	Peter Tudebode wrote his *Historia*

List of abbreviations

AOL   *Archives de l'Orient latin*

MGH   *Monumenta Germaniae historica inde ab anno Christi quing-*
        entesimo usque ad annum millesimum et quingentesimum
        auspiciis societatis aperiendis fontibus rerum Germanicarum
        medii aevi, ed. G.H. Pertz *et al.* (1826 ff.)

MGHS   *MGH Scriptores in Folio et Quarto*, 32 vols (1826–1934)

PL   *Patrologiae cursus completus. Series Latina*, comp. J.P. Migne,
        217 vols and 4 vols of indexes (1844–64)

RHC   *Recueil des historiens des croisades*, ed. Académie des Inscrip-
        tions et Belles-Lettres (1841–1906)

RHC arm.   *RHC Documents arméniens*, 2 vols (1869–1906)

RHC Oc.   *RHC Historiens occidentaux*, 5 vols (1844–95)

RHC Or.   *RHC Historiens orientaux*, 5 vols (1872–1906)

RHGF   *Recueil des historiens des Gaules et de la France*, ed. M.
            Bouquet *et al.*, 24 vols (1737–1904)

Notes
Introduction

1 C. Erdmann, *The Origin of the Idea of Crusade* (1977), especially pp. 306–54.

2 See especially E. Delaruelle, 'Essai sur la formation de l'idée de croisade', *Bulletin de literature ecclésiastique*, 42 (1941), pp. 24–45, 86–103; 45 (1944), pp. 13–46, 73–90; 54 (1953), pp. 226–39; 55 (1954), pp. 50–63; M. Villey, *La Croisade: Essai sur la formation d'une théorie juridique* (1942), *passim*; P. Rousset, *Les Origines et les caractères de la première croisade* (1945), pp. 13–198.

3 E.-D. Hehl, *Kirche und Krieg im 12. Jahrhundert* (1980), pp. 1–142.

4 H.E.J. Cowdrey, 'Pope Urban II's Preaching of the First Crusade', *History*, 55 (1970), pp. 177–88.

5 E.O. Blake, 'The Formation of the "Crusade Idea" ', *Journal of Ecclesiastical History*, 21 (1970), pp. 11–31, esp. pp. 20–6.

6 J.T. Gilchrist, 'The Erdmann Thesis and the Canon Law, 1083–1141', *Crusade and Settlement*, ed. P.W. Edbury (1985), pp. 37–45.

7 G. Duby, *The Three Orders. Feudal Society Imagined* (1980), p. 151.

8 Duby, *The Three Orders*, pp. 125–8, 134–9, 149–57; H.E.J. Cowdrey, 'The Peace and the Truce of God in the Eleventh Century', *Past and Present*, 46 (1970), pp. 42–67; Erdmann, *The Origin*, pp. 70–2.

9 Erdmann, *The Origin*, pp. 57–94; Duby, *The Three Orders*, pp. 192–8. See M.-D. Chenu, *Nature, Man and Society in the Twelfth Century* (1968), pp. 219–30.

10 Erdmann, *The Origin*, pp. 118–47, 182–5.

11 Erdmann, *The Origin*, pp. 241–56; I.S. Robinson, 'Gregory VII and the Soldiers of Christ', *History*, 58 (1973), pp. 184–90; A. Stickler, 'Il potere coattivo materiale della Chiesa nella Riforma Gregoriana secondo Anselmo di Lucca', *Studi gregoriani*, 2 (1947), pp, 235–85. For summaries of aspects of Augustine's thought, see J. Riley-Smith, 'Crusading as an Act of Love', *History*, 65 (1980), pp. 185–9; L. and J. Riley-Smith, *The Crusades. Idea and Reality, 1095–1274* (1981), pp. 4–6.

12 Robinson, 'Gregory VII', pp. 178–80.

13 Orderic Vitalis, *Historia aecclesiastica*, ed. M. Chibnall (1969–79), 3, p. 216; I.S. Robinson, *Authority and Resistance in the Investiture Contest* (1978), pp. 100–3.

14 Erdmann, *The Origin*, pp. 256–68. *Cf.* Urban II's moderate treatment of fighters for the reform movement in one of his letters. Urban II, 'Epistolae et Privilegia', *PL* 151, col. 394.

15 For example see Erdmann, *The Origin*, pp. 202–3, 250.

16 H.E.J. Cowdrey, 'Pope Gregory VII's "Crusading" Plans of 1074', *Outremer*, ed. B.Z. Kedar, H.E. Mayer and R.C. Smail (1982), pp. 27–40. Perhaps linked to this is the odd charter in Auch (C. Lacave la Plagne Barris, *Cartulaires du chapitre de l'église métropolitaine Sainte-Marie d'Auch* (1899)), pp. 44–5.

17 G. Duby, *La Société aux XIe et XIIe siècles dans la région mâconnaise* (1971), pp. 217–27, 322–5; G. Duby, *The Chivalrous Society* (1977), *passim*, esp. pp. 59–80; M. Bloch, *Feudal Society* (1961), pp. 123–44, 224–5; K.F. Werner, 'Liens de parenté et noms de personne. Un problème historique et méthodologique', *Famille et parenté dans l'occident médiéval*, ed. G. Duby and J. Le Goff (1977), p. 27. For conditions generally, see N.J.G. Pounds, *An Historical Geography of Europe 450 BC–AD 1330* (1973), pp. 227–312.

18 M. Keen, *Chivalry* (1984), pp. 31, 51–4; Rousset, *Les Origines*, pp. 110–33.

19 H. Hagenmeyer, *Die Kreuzzugsbriefe aus den Jahren 1088–1100* (1901), pp. 63–6; J. Riley-Smith, 'Death on the First Crusade', *The End of Strife*, ed. D.M. Loades (1984), p. 27.

20 Lambert of Ardres, 'Historia comitum Ghisnensium', *MGHS* 24, pp. 625–6. See also A. Murray, *Reason and Society in the Middle Ages* (1978), pp. 346–9.

21 See H.E.J. Cowdrey, *The Cluniacs and the Gregorian Reform* (1970), pp. 121–8.

22 Bloch, *Feudal Society*, pp. 81–7; B. Ward, *Miracles and the Medieval Mind* (1982), *passim*; P.J. Geary, *Furta Sacra* (1978), *passim*; J. Sumption, *Pilgrimage* (1975), pp. 11–167.

23 A. Becker, *Papst Urban II (1088–1099)*, 1 (1964), pp. 24–78.

Chapter 1   Pope Urban's message

1 Becker, *Papst Urban*, 1, pp. 213–26; R. Somerville, 'The Council of Clermont (1095) and Latin Christian Society', *Archivum historiae pontificiae*, 12 (1974), pp. 62–82; H. Hagenmeyer, *Chronologie de la première croisade (1094–1100)* (1902), pp. 11–13, 15, 30; Orderic Vitalis, 5, pp. 228, 230 note 1; 'Gesta Ambaziensium dominorum', ed. L. Halphen and R. Poupardin, *Chroniques des comtes d'Anjou et des seigneurs d'Amboise* (1913), pp. 100–1.

2 Bernold of St Blasien, 'Chronicon', *MGHS* 5, p. 462.

3 'Historia monasterii novi Pictavensis', ed. I.M. Watterich, *Pontificum Romanorum vitae* (1862), 1, p. 598.

4 Erdmann, *The Origin*, pp. 319–28.

5 Fulcher of Chartres, *Historia Hierosolymitana*, ed. H. Hagenmeyer (1913), pp. 132–8; Robert the Monk, 'Historia Iherosolimitana', *RHC Oc.* 3, pp. 727–30; Baldric of Bourgueil, 'Historia Jerosolimitana', *RHC Oc.* 4, pp. 12–16; Geoffrey of Vendôme, 'Epistolae', *PL* 157, col. 162.

6 R. Somerville, *The Councils of Urban II. 1: Decreta Claromontensia*

(1972), pp. 74, 124; J. Vaissete, C. Devic and A. Molinier, *Histoire générale de Languedoc* (1872–1904), 5, col. 748.

7   J. von Pflugk-Harttung, *Acta pontificum Romanorum inedita* (1881–6), 2, p. 205; Fulcher of Chartres, pp. 740–1. See R. Somerville, 'The Council of Clermont and the First Crusade', *Studia gratiana*, 20 (1976), pp. 335–7.

8   See Cowdrey, 'Pope Urban II's Preaching', p. 181; also 'Notitiae duae Lemovicenses de praedicatione crucis in Aquitania', *RHC Oc.* 5, pp. 350, 352.

9   Hagenmeyer, *Kreuzzugsbriefe*, pp. 136–7, 141, 164–5. See also F. Vercauteren, *Actes des comtes de Flandre 1071–1128* (1938), p. 63; Sauxillanges (H. Doniol, 'Cartulaire de Sauxillanges', *Mémoires de l'académie des sciences, belles-lettres et arts de Clermont-Ferrand*, NS 3 (1861)), pp. 966–7.

10 Urban II, col. 288.

11 Urban II, col. 345.

12 Urban II, cols 370–1 (and see col. 510); Pflugk-Harttung, *Acta pont. Rom. inedita*, 2, p. 142.

13 Fulcher of Chartres, pp. 132–8; Robert the Monk, pp. 728–30; Baldric of Bourgueil, pp. 12–16.

14 Hagenmeyer, *Kreuzzugsbriefe*, pp. 137, 164; Urban II, col. 504; Pflugk-Harttung, *Acta pont. Rom. inedita*, 2, p. 168.

15 Hagenmeyer, *Kreuzzugsbriefe*, pp. 138, 144, 146, 148, 150.

16 Cluny (A. Bernard and A. Bruel, *Recueil des chartes de l'abbaye de Cluny* (1876–1903)) 5, p. 51; Vercauteren, *Actes*, pp. 62–3, 66; St Victor of Marseilles (B.E.C. Guérard, *Cartulaire de l'abbaye de Saint-Victor de Marseille* (1857)) 1, p. 167.

17 Guibert of Nogent, 'Gesta Dei per Francos', *RHC OC.* 4, p. 140; Trinity of Vendôme (C. Metais, *Cartulaire de l'abbaye cardinale de la Trinité de Vendôme* (1893–4)), 2, pp. 104–7. See St Vincent of Le Mans (R. Charles and S.M. d'Elbenne, *Cartulaire de l'abbaye de Saint-Vincent du Mans* (1886–1913)) 1, col. 190.

18 See, for example, Cowdrey, *The Cluniacs*, pp. 36–7.

19 Gregory VII, *Register*, ed. E. Caspar (1955), 1, p. 75.

20 Somerville, *Decreta Claromontensia*, pp. 74, 124; Hagenmeyer, *Kreuzzugsbriefe*, pp. 136, 137; W. Wiederhold, 'Papsturkunden in Florenz', *Nachrichten von der Gesellschaft der Wissenschaften zu Göttingen. Phil. -hist. Kl.* (1901), p. 313; P.F. Kehr, *Papsturkunden in Spanien. I. Katalanien*, 2 (1926), p. 287; Fulcher of Chartres, pp. 132–6; Robert the Monk, pp. 727–8; Baldric of Bourgueil, pp. 12–15.

21 Hagenmeyer, *Kreuzzugsbriefe*, p. 136; Wiederhold, 'Papsturkunden', p. 313; Urban II, col. 478; Robert the Monk, pp. 728–9; Baldric of Bourgueil, pp. 13–15. There are no references to Jerusalem in Fulcher of Chartres's account of Urban's sermon at Clermont, but this may be explained by the fact that Fulcher himself accompanied Baldwin of Boulogne to Edessa and did not take part in the liberation of Jerusalem.

22 See Fulcher of Chartres, pp. 132–6; Robert the Monk, pp. 727–8; Baldric of Bourgueil, pp. 12–14.

168 *The First Crusade*

23 Hagenmeyer, *Kreuzzugsbriefe*, p. 137.
24 Urban II, col. 506; Kehr, *Papsturkunden in Katalanien*, 2, p. 298.
25 Robert the Monk, p. 728.
26 See Guibert of Nogent, 'Gesta', p. 135.
27 Pflugk-Harttung, *Acta pont. Rom. inedita*, 2, pp. 142–3; Urban II, cols. 302–3, 332–3; Kehr, *Papsturkunden in Katalanien*, 2, pp. 286–7. See Becker, *Papst Urban*, 1, p. 246.
28 Kehr, *Papsturkunden in Katalanien*, 2, pp. 287–8.
29 P. Riant, 'Inventaire critique des lettres historiques des croisades', *AOL* 1 (1881), pp. 127–30. Date corrected in Erdmann, *The Origin*, p. 318 note 38.
30 Guibert of Nogent, 'Gesta', p. 135; Urban II, col. 504; Pflugk-Harttung, *Acta pont. Rom. inedita*, 2, p. 168.
31 Urban II, cols 289, 370–1, 504.
32 Sumption, *Pilgrimage*, pp. 114–38; P. Alphandéry and A. Dupront, *La Chrétienté et l'idée de croisade* (1954–9), 1, pp. 9–42.
33 Vaissete, *Hist. gén. de Languedoc*, 5, cols 737–8; Jumièges (J.J. Vernier, *Chartes de l'abbaye de Jumièges* (1916)) 1, pp. 121–3. So the assertion in the *Chronicon sancti Petri Vivi Senonensis* (ed. R.H. Bautier and M. Gilles (1979), p. 140) that just before the crusade no Christian was daring to go to Jerusalem was nonsense.
34 Erdmann, *The Origin*, pp. 298–9; Cowdrey, 'Pope Gregory VII's "Crusading" Plans', pp. 38–9; B. McGinn, *Visions of the End* (1979), pp. 43–5, 82–93.
35 Erdmann, *The Origin*, pp. 355–71.
36 Cowdrey, 'Pope Urban II's Preaching', pp. 177–88:
37 Hagenmeyer, *Kreuzzugsbriefe*, p. 167; W. Holtzmann, 'Zur Geschichte des Investiturstreites (Englische Analekten II)', *Neues Archiv*, 50 (1935), pp. 280–1. See Erdmann, *The Origin*, p. 326 note 68.
38 See Landulf the Younger of Milan, 'Historia Mediolanensis', *MGHS* 20, p. 22.
39 Cluny 5, pp. 51–3, 59, 108; St Vincent of Le Mans 1, cols 69, 190–1, 222–3, 266–7, 301, 384, 423; K.F. Stumpf-Brentano, *Die Reichskanzler* (1865–83), 3, p. 88; Trinity of Vendôme 2, pp. 104–7; Aureil (G. de Senneville, 'Cartulaire du prieuré d'Aureil', *Bulletin de la société archéologique et historique du Limousin*, 48 (1900)), pp. 21, 29; Vaissete, *Hist. gén. de Languedoc*, 5, cols 745, 748, 757; St Victor of Marseilles 1, p. 167, 2, p. 568; Molesme (J. Laurent, *Cartulaires de l'abbaye de Molesme* (1907–11)) 2, p. 229; St Père of Chartres (B.E.C. Guérard, *Cartulaire de l'abbaye de Saint-Père de Chartres* (1840)) 2, p. 428; Paray-le-Monial (C.U.J. Chevalier, 'Cartulaire du prieuré de Paray-le-Monial', *Collection de cartulaires dauphinois*, 8, 2 (1890)), p. 108; St Chaffre of Le Monastier (C.U.J. Chevalier, 'Cartulaire de l'abbaye de St.-Chaffre du Monastier', *Collection de cartulaires dauphinois*, 8, 1 (1884)), p. 140; J. Malbrancq, *De Morinis* (1639–54), 3, p. 27; H. and P. d'Outreman, *Histoire de la ville et comté de Valentiennes. Preuves* (1639), p. 7, Vercauteren, *Actes*, pp. 63, 66; A. Van Hasselt, 'Document inédit pour servir à l'histoire des croisades',

Annales de l'académie d'archéologie de Belgique, 6 (1849), p. 99; L.V. Delisle, *Littérature latine et histoire du moyen âge* (1890), p. 28; St George of Rennes (P. de la Bigne Villeneuve, *Cartulaire de l'abbaye de Saint-Georges de Rennes* (1875)), pp. 269–70; Forez (G. Guichard, Comte de Neufbourg, E. Perroy, and J.-E. Dufour, *Chartes de Forez* (1933–70) 1, no. 1, p. 1; Aniane (L. Cassan and E. Meynial, *Cartulaire d'Aniane* (1900)), pp. 358–9; Auch, p. 57; Grenoble (J. Marion, *Cartulaires de l'église cathédrale de Grenoble* (1869)), p. 165; St Philibert of Tournous (R. Juënin, *Nouvelle histoire de l'abbaïe royale et collegiale et Saint Filibert* (1733)) 2, p. 135; St Vincent of Mâcon (M.-C. Ragut, *Cartulaire de Saint-Vincent de Mâcon* (1864)), p. 315; Apt (N. Didier, H. Dubled and J. Barruol, *Cartulaire de l'église d'Apt* (1967)), pp. 248–9; Marmoutier (C. Chantelou, *Marmoutier. Cartulaire Tourangeau* (1879)), pp. 40–1; St Lambert of Liége (S. Bormans and E. Schoolmeesters, *Cartulaire de l'église Saint-Lambert de Liége* (1893–1933)), 1, p. 47. See also Angers (C. Urseau, *Cartulaire noir de la cathédrale d'Angers* (1908)), pp. 130, 133.

40 Vaissete, *Hist. gén. de Languedoc 5*, col. 748; Vercauteren, *Actes*, p. 63.

41 St Victor of Marseilles 1, p. 167.

42 Geoffrey of Vendôme, col. 162.

43 Somerville, *Decreta Claromontensia*, pp. 124, 150; Pflugk-Harttung, *Acta pont. Rom. inedita*, 2, pp. 161, 168; Hagenmeyer, *Kreuzzugsbriefe*, p. 175; *Conc. Lateran I*, canon 10 (J. Alberigo, P.-P Joannou, C. Leonardi and P. Prodi, *Conciliorum Oecumenicorum Decreta* (1962), pp. 167–8); Guibert of Nogent, 'Gesta', p. 140; J.A. Brundage, *Medieval Canon Law and the Crusader* (1969), pp. 12–15, 159–61, 165; Villey, *La Croisade*, pp. 151–2.

44 Hagenmeyer, *Kreuzzugsbriefe*, p. 138; Robert the Monk, p. 729.

45 Hagenmeyer, *Kreuzzugsbriefe*, p. 137. See Kehr, *Papsturkunden in Katalanien*, 2, p. 288; J.A. Brundage, 'The Army of the First Crusade and the Crusade Vow: some reflections on a recent book', *Mediaeval Studies*, 33 (1971), pp. 334–43.

46 Bernold of St Blasien, p. 462.

47 Hagenmeyer, *Kreuzzugsbriefe*, pp. 175, 176; Fulcher of Chartres, pp. 322–34; Baldric of Bourgueil, pp. 25, 103. See Raymond of Aguilers, *Liber*, ed. J.H. and L.L. Hill (1969), p. 41.

48 'Annales Altahenses maiores', *MGHS* 20, pp. 815–17; Brundage, *Medieval Canon Law*, p. 17 note 64.

49 Brundage, *Medieval Canon Law*, pp. 30–9; J. Riley-Smith, *What were the crusades?* (1977), pp. 39–40.

50 Hagenmeyer, *Kreuzzugsbriefe*, pp. 142, 148–9, 160, 165, 175, 176; Orderic Vitalis 5, pp. 268, 322–4. See Hagenmeyer, *Kreuzzugsbriefe*, p. 155; Guibert of Nogent, 'Gesta', p. 140.

51 St Vincent of Le Mans 1, col. 69 (a charter that is almost certainly to be dated to 1096). See also Cluny 5, pp. 51–3, 59; St Père of Chartres 2, p. 428; Auch, p. 57.

52 St Victor of Marseilles 1, p. 167. Cf. Guibert of Nogent, 'Gesta', p. 153.

53 Hagenmeyer, *Kreuzzugsbriefe*, pp. 141, 154, 160; and see below pp.

83–5. But cf. A. Dupront, 'La spiritualité des croisés et des pélerins d'après les sources de la première croisade', *Convegni del Centro di Studi sulla spiritualità medievale*, 4 (1963), pp. 451–83.

54 For perhaps a hint of contemporary criticism, see Robert the Monk, p. 791. A new study of criticism of crusading by E. Siberry is expected shortly.

55 Hagenmeyer, *Kreuzzugsbriefe*, pp. 137–8; Wiederhold, 'Papsturkunden', pp. 313–14; Robert the Monk, p. 729. Cf. W. Porges, 'The Clergy, the Poor and the Non-Combatants on the First Crusade', *Speculum*, 21 (1946), p. 2.

56 Ward, *Miracles*, pp. 110–26.

57 Fulcher of Chartres, pp. 140–3; Robert the Monk, pp. 729–30; Baldric of Bourgueil, p. 16; Riley-Smith, 'Death on the First Crusade', pp. 28–9.

58 Kehr, *Papsturkunden in Katalanien*, 2, p. 292.

59 Hagenmeyer, *Kreuzzugsbriefe*, p. 164; Robert the Monk, pp. 728, 730; Baldric of Bourgueil, p. 16; 'Gesta Ambaziensium dominorum', p. 100. See also the preamble to the crusader Wolfker of Kuffern's mortgage. Göttweig (A.F. Fuchs, *Die Traditionsbücher des Benediktinerstiftes Göttweig* (1931)), p. 194.

60 Hagenmeyer, *Kreuzzugsbriefe*, pp. 137–8.

61 P.F. Kehr, *Regesta pontificum Romanorum. Italia pontificia* (1906–75), 6, 2, p. 323; Riant, 'Inventaire', pp. 119–20.

62 Kehr, *Italia pontificia*, 3, p. 359, 6, 1, p. 54.

63 There is still force in the arguments, drawn from a study of the pope's itinerary, of A. Fliche, 'Urbain II et la croisade', *Revue d'histoire de l'église de France*, 13 (1927), pp. 289–306.

64 Hagenmeyer, *Kreuzzugsbriefe*, p. 136. See also Robert the Monk, pp. 727–8.

65 'Fragmentum historiae Andegavensis', ed. Halphen and Poupardin, *Chroniques des comtes d'Anjou*, pp. 237–8. A fragment from Limoges, which cannot be dated, tells the same story. 'He had come to Gaul to summon the people of Gaul, disciplined in arms and war.' Riant, 'Inventaire', pp. 109–10 note.

66 Robert the Monk, p. 728.

67 Urban II, col. 481.

68 Wiederhold, 'Papsturkunden', pp. 313–14; Geoffrey of Vendôme, col. 162; Anselm of Canterbury, *Opera omnia*, ed. F.S. Schmitt (1938–61), 4, pp. 85–6; Somerville, *Decreta Claromontensia*, p. 124; Hagenmeyer, *Kreuzzugsbriefe*, pp. 137–8; Robert the Monk, p. 729. See also Kehr *Italia pontificia*, 5, p. 156.

69 Hagenmeyer, *Kreuzzugsbriefe*, p. 136.

70 Fulcher of Chartres, pp. 136–7; Robert the Monk, pp. 728, 748; Baldric of Bourgueil, pp. 14–15.

71 Somerville, *Decreta Claromontensia*, p. 143; Rousset, *Les Origines*, pp. 55, 60–1; Cowdrey, 'The Peace and the Truce of God', pp. 56–8.

72 Wiederhold, 'Papsturkunden', p. 313; Somerville, *Decreta Claromontensia*, p. 74; Hagenmeyer, *Kreuzzugsbriefe*, p. 137.

73 Hagenmeyer, *Kreuzzugsbriefe*, pp. 137, 164; Robert the Monk, pp.

728, 730; Baldric of Bourgueil, pp. 15, 16; 'Gesta Ambaziensium dominorum', p. 100. In his use of the verb *expono* Urban echoed John 15:13: '*ut animam suam ponat quis pro amicis suis*', See also Kehr, *Papsturkunden in Katalanien*, 2, pp. 287, 288.

74 See Riley-Smith, 'Death on the First Crusade', pp. 21–2.

75 Riley-Smith, 'Crusading as an Act of Love', pp. 185–7.

76 Cluny 5, pp. 59, 108; St Vincent of Le Mans 1, col. 69; St Père of Chartres 2, pp. 428–9; St Victor of Marseilles 2, pp. 568–9. See also Fulcher of Chartres, pp. 135, 136; Robert the Monk, p. 729; Baldric of Bourgueil, p. 15.

77 Peter of Blois, 'De Hierosolymitano peregrinatione acceleranda', *PL* 207, col. 1061.

78 Orderic Vitalis 5, pp. 16–18. See also 'Chronica monasterii Casinensis', *MGHS* 34, p. 475; Hagenmeyer, *Kreuzzugsbriefe*, p. 137.

79 Kehr, *Papsturkunden in Katalanien*, 2, pp. 287–8.

80 Somerville, *Decreta Claromontensia*, p. 74.

81 Hagenmeyer, *Kreuzzugsbriefe*, p. 137.

82 Hagenmayer, *Kreuzzugsbriefe*, p. 136.

83 S. Löwenfeld, *Epistolae pontificum Romanorum ineditae* (1885), p. 43. See A. Ferreiro, 'The Siege of Barbastro, 1064–5: a reassessment', *Journal of Medieval History*, 9 (1983), pp. 133–5.

Chapter 2   The response of lay people

1 Hagenmeyer, *Kreuzzugsbriefe*, pp. 136–7.

2 Hagenmeyer, *Kreuzzugsbriefe*, p. 167.

3 Hagenmeyer, *Chronologie*, p. 225.

4 Fulcher of Chartres, pp. 134–5; Baldric of Bourgueil, p. 15; 'Narratio Floriacensis de captis Antiochia et Hierosolyma', *RHC Oc.* 5, p. 356.

5 Raymond of Aguilers, var. ms. in *RHC Oc.* 3, p. 307; Baldric of Bourgueil, p. 16.

6 Somerville, *Decreta Claromontensia*, pp. 46, 58–9; Lambert of Arras, 'De Atrebatensi episcopatu ab Urbano II restituto', *RHGF* 14, p. 755, Somerville, 'The Council of Clermont and the First Crusade', p. 325. For Lambert and the council, see Somerville, 'The Council of Clermont and Latin Christian Society', pp. 55–90 *passim*.

7 Orderic Vitalis 5, pp. 18–24. See Somerville, *Decreta Claromontensia*, pp. 20–41, esp. pp. 38–9 note 91.

8 Baldric of Bourgueil, pp. 5, 8.

9 Orderic Vitalis 5, p. 26.

10 Guibert of Nogent, 'Gesta', p. 124.

11 Guibert of Nogent, 'Gesta', p. 149.

12 Ekkehard of Aura, 'Hierosolymita', *RHC Oc.* 5, p. 12. I am grateful to Dr W.G. Waddington for information about solar activity in the central Middle Ages.

13 'Historia peregrinorum euntium Jerusolymam', *RHC Oc.* 3, p. 173.

14 Sigebert of Gembloux, 'Chronica', *MGHS* 6, p. 367; Baldric of Bourgueil, p. 16; Hugh of St Maria, 'Itineris Hierosolymitani com-

pendium', *RHC Oc. 5*, p. 363; 'Narratio Floriacensis', p. 356; 'Chronica monasterii Casinensis', p. 475; Orderic Vitalis 5, pp. 8–10; Lupus Protospatarius, 'Annales', *MGHS 5*, p. 62; 'Annales Seligenstadenses', *MGHS* 17, p. 31; 'Annales Sancti Dionysii Remenses', *MGHS* 13, p. 83; 'Annales Parmenses minores', *MGHS* 18, p. 662. An eclipse of the sun in 1093 was regarded later as foretelling the crusade. 'Primordia Windbergensia', *MGHS* 17, pp. 561–2.

15 Guibert of Nogent, 'Gesta', pp. 149–50, 252; Ekkehard of Aura, 'Chronicon universale', *MGHS* 6, p. 208; 'Annalista Saxo', MGHS 6, p. 728; 'Annales Rosenveldenses', *MGHS* 16, p. 101; *La Chronique de Saint-Maixent*, ed. J. Verdon (1979), p. 154. See also the references in two charters. St Maixent (A. Richard, 'Chartes et documents pour servir à l'histoire de l'abbaye de Saint-Maixent', *Archives historiques du Poitou*, 16 (1886)), pp. 222, 224.

16 Ekkehard of Aura, 'Hierosolymita', p. 18; 'Narratio Floriacensis' pp. 357–8; *Chronique de Saint-Maixent*, pp. 158, 164 (which erroneously reported an eclipse of the moon rather than the sun in December 1098); Ralph of Caen, 'Gesta Tancredi', *RHC Oc.* 3, p. 648; Bernold of St Blasien, p. 466; Lupus Protospatarius, p. 63; 'Annales Casinenses', *MGHS* 19, p. 307; Orderic Vitalis 5, pp. 192, 216; Sigebert of Gembloux, p. 368; 'Annales Seligenstadenses', p. 31; Hugh of Flavigny, 'Chronicon', *MGHS* 8, p. 481. See Hugh of Fleury, 'Historia regum Francorum', *MGHS* 9, p. 405; 'Catalogus imperatorum et pontificum Romanorum Cencianus', *MGHS* 24, p. 106. The solar eclipse in December 1098 was actually on Christmas Day.

17 Fulcher of Chartres, p. 154; Guibert of Nogent, 'Gesta', p. 141; Orderic Vitalis 5, p. 8; Ekkehard of Aura, 'Hierosolymita', p. 17. See Robert the Monk, p. 728. For earthquakes as portents, see Albert of Aachen, 'Historia Hierosolymitana', *RHC Oc.* 4, p. 274; Ekkehard of Aura, 'Hierosolymita', p. 12; *Chronique de Saint-Miaxent*, pp. 158, 164.

18 Albert of Aachen, pp. 272–4; 'Historia peregrinorum', p. 169; 'Annalista Saxo', p. ʾ28; *La Chanson d'Antioche*, ed. S. Duparc-Quioc (1977–8), 1, pp. 20–2, 30–6; William of Tyre, 'Historia rerum in partibus transmarinis gestarum', *RHC Oc.* 1, pp. 32–5; Riant, 'Inventaire', pp. 96–9, 110–11, 714. For another 'celestial' letter, see Ekkehard of Aura, 'Hierosolymita', p. 40.

19 Albert of Aachen, pp. 415–16, 481–2, 486–8; Ekkehard of Aura, 'Hierosolymita', pp. 38–9; Caffaro, 'De liberatione civitatum orientis', ed. L.T. Belgrano, *Annali Genovesi* (1890–1929), 1, pp. 100–1 (a report that is obviously spurious).

20 See below pp. 81–2.

21 (Solomon) Bar Simson, 'Chronicle', tr. S. Eidelberg, *The Jews and the Crusaders* (1977), p. 28; Alphandéry and Dupront, *La Chrétienté.*, 1, pp. 74–6. For the Hebrew sources, see A.S. Abulafia, 'The interrelationship between the Hebrew chronicles on the first crusade', *Journal of Semitic Studies*, 27 (1982), pp. 221–39.

22 Ekkehard of Aura, 'Hierosolymita', p. 20; Bar Simson, pp. 28, 70;

'Mainz Anonymous', tr. Eidelberg, *The Jews and the Crusaders*, p. 107; Ekkehard of Aura, 'Chronicon', p. 261. For Emich's death, see Ekkehard of Aura, 'Chronicon', p. 253; Otto of Freising, *Gesta Frederici I. Imperatoris*, ed. G. Waitz (1912), p. 29.

23 Ekkehard of Aura, 'Hierosolymita', p. 17. See Sumption, *Pilgrimage*, p. 75; Cowdrey, 'The Peace and the Truce of God', p. 56 note 45.

24 Hagenmeyer, *Kreuzzugsbriefe*, p. 138; Robert the Monk, p. 729.

25 Vaissete, *Hist. gén. de Languedoc*, 5, col. 757. For another attempt to control response see Hagenmeyer, *Kreuzzugsbriefe*, p. 167.

26 B. McGinn, 'Iter Sancti Sepulchri: the Piety of the First Crusaders', *The Walter Prescott Webb Lectures: Essays in Medieval Civilization*, ed. R.E. Sullivan *et al.* (1978), pp. 47–8, 66–7. See, for the Muslims as attendants of Antichrist, Robert the Monk, p. 828; Ralph of Caen, p. 695. For references to the Last Days, see Hagenmeyer, *Kreuzzugsbriefe*, p. 136; Guibert of Nogent, 'Gesta', pp. 138–9, 239; Ekkehard of Aura, 'Hierosolymita', pp. 12, 38; Bartolf of Nangis, 'Gesta Francorum Iherusalem expugnantium', *RHC Oc.* 3, p. 498; Bar Simson, p. 28; Orderic Vitalis 5, p. 8.

27 Ralph of Caen, pp. 605–6. See also 'Chronica monasterii Casinensis', p. 475.

28 Vaissete, *Hist. gén. de Languedoc*, 5, cols 747–8; St George of Rennes, pp. 269–70; St Vincent of Le Mans 1, col. 87.

29 d'Outreman, *Histoire de Valentiennes. Preuves*, pp. 6–9; Lambert of Ardres, pp. 580–1; Vaissete, *Hist. gén. de Languedoc*, 5, cols 743–6, 747. Did Geoffrey of Clairvaux's remarkable gift to St Martin of Tours of jurisdiction and patronage at Parcé also fall into this category? *Chronique de Parcé*, ed. H. de Berranger (1953), p. 10.

30 'Triumphus Sancti Lamberti de Castro Bullonio', *MGHS* 20, p. 499 (see St Hubert in Ardenne (G. Kurth, *Chartes de l'abbaye de Saint-Hubert en Ardenne* 1 (1903)), p. 85); Lawrence of Liége, 'Gesta episcoporum Virdunensium', *MGHS* 10, p. 498; Paray-le-Monial, pp. 107–8; St Vincent of Le Mans 1, cols 292–3. For Godfrey of Bouillon, see also H.E. Mayer, *Mélanges sur l'histoire du royaume latin de Jérusalem* (1984), pp. 43–8.

31 St Père of Chartres 2, pp. 428–9.

32 Trinity of Vendôme 2, pp. 104–7.

33 St Philibert of Tournous 2, p. 135.

34 St Chaffre of Le Monastier, pp. 139–41. See also Auch, p. 57; Apt, p. 248; and perhaps Chamalières (A. Chassaing, *Cartulaire de Chamalières-sur-Loire en Velay* (1895)), pp. 16–18.

35 Albert of Aachen, pp. 415–16.

36 Ekkehard of Aura, 'Hierosolymita', p. 17.

37 Somerville, *Decreta Claromontensia*, p. 74; Hagenmeyer, *Kreuzzugsbriefe*, p. 137; Fulcher of Chartres, pp. 137 (and see p. 749), 740–1; Robert the Monk, p. 728; Baldric of Bourgueil, p. 15; Pflugk-Harttung, *Acta pont. Rom. inedita*, 2, p. 205.

38 Göttweig, p. 194; Cluny 5, p. 52. For Achard's death, see *Gesta Francorum et aliorum Hierosolimitanorum*, ed. R. Hill (1962), p. 89;

Peter Tudebode, *Historia de Hierosolymitano itinere*, ed. J.H. and L.L. Hill (1977), p. 135; Raymond of Aguilers, p. 141.

39 *Gallia christiana*, 12, instrumenta, cols 107–8; J. Ramackers, *Papsturkunden in Frankreich* (1932 ff.), 6, pp. 115–16. For Norgeot and his brothers, see also Molesme 1, pp. 138–9, 2, pp. 63–5, 83–4, 105–6. One story current after the crusade was of a knight-crusader, who had made a pact with the devil, a condition of which was that he should not practise his religion. The fact that the crusade could contain a 'lapsed' crusader was not commented on. Guibert of Nogent, 'Gesta', pp. 248–50.

40 Orderic Vitalis 5, pp. 228–32.

41 'Chronica monasterii de Hida juxta Wintoniam', ed. E. Edwards, *Liber monasterii de Hyda* (1866), pp. 301–2. See Raymond of Aguilers, pp. 58, 89; Guibert of Nogent, 'Gesta', pp. 161, 193; Ralph of Caen, pp. 603–4, 622, 668; Hugh of St Maria, p. 363; Orderic Vitalis 5, pp. 6, 268.

42 Duby, *La Société*, pp. 334–5.

43 Albert of Aachen, p. 503; Fulcher of Chartres, p. 389; J. Riley-Smith, 'The motives of the earliest crusaders and the settlement of Latin Palestine, 1095–1100', *English Historical Review*, 98 (1983), pp. 723–4, 726–7, 728–9.

44 Raymond of Aguilers, pp. 104–5, 137.

45 Riley-Smith, 'The motives', pp. 721–36.

46 R.P. Grossman, 'The Financing of the Crusades' (Ph.D. Thesis, Chicago, 1965), pp. 27–9. But cf. the wild optimism of Stephen of Blois at Nicaea. Hagenmeyer, *Kreuzzugsbriefe*, p. 140. For Peter of Aups, see *Gesta Francorum*, pp. 25–6; Peter Tudebode, p. 60; and for Hugh Bunel, see Orderic Vitalis 5, pp. 156–8.

47 See Albert of Aachen, p. 281; also Guibert of Nogent, 'Gesta', p. 124.

48 See the discussion in Grossman, 'The Financing of the Crusades', pp. 5–8.

49 Ralph of Caen, pp. 606–7.

50 Van Hasselt, 'Document inédit', p. 99. But note the argument in Mayer, *Mélanges*, pp. 43–8.

51 Vaissete, *Hist. gén. de Languedoc*, 5, col. 748. For the terminology of the charters, see G. Constable, 'The Financing of the Crusades in the Twelfth Century', *Outremer*, ed. B.Z. Kedar, H.E. Mayer and R.C. Smail (1982), p. 77.

52 Fulcher of Chartres, p. 154; Guibert of Nogent, 'Gesta', p. 141. See Ekkehard of Aura, 'Hierosolymita', p. 17; Robert the Monk, p. 728; Orderic Vitalis 5, p. 8.

53 Göttweig, pp. 195–6.

54 Guibert of Nogent, 'Gesta', p. 141; Orderic Vitalis 5, p. 16.

55 'Triumphus Sancti Lamberti', p. 499; Florence of Worcester, *Chronicon*, ed. B. Thorpe (1848–9), 2, p. 40; William of Malmesbury, *Gesta regum Anglorum*, ed. W. Stubbs (1887–9), 2, pp. 371–2. See also 'Leges Edwardi Confessoris', ed. F. Liebermann, *Die Gesetze der Angelsachsen* (1903–16), 1, pp. 636–7. The stripping of reliquaries of

their jewels to finance crusaders became quite common. See Lambert of Ardres, p. 632; St Chaffre of Le Monastier, p. 42. See also Constable, 'The Financing of the Crusades', p. 74.

56 For Robert and William, see *Gesta Francorum*, pp. 21, 63–5; Peter Tudebode, pp. 38, 55, 105–7; Baldric of Bourgueil, p. 33.

57 Baldric of Bourgueil, p. 33; Orderic Vitalis 5, p. 59.

58 Albert of Aachen, p. 317.

59 Albert of Aachen, p. 315.

60 Albert of Aachen, p. 316; 'Fragment d'une Chanson d'Antioche en Provençal', ed. P. Meyer, *AOL* 2 (1884), p. 473.

61 Lambert of Ardres, pp. 580–1. For Fulk, see Riley-Smith, 'The motives', p. 735.

62 *Gesta Francorum*, p. 9; Peter Tudebode, p. 41; 'Chronica monasterii Casinensis', p. 477.

63 'Chronique de Zimmern', ed. H. Hagenmeyer, *AOL* 2 (1884), pp. 23–9.

64 Peter Tudebode, pp. 13, 97, 116.

65 Raymond of Aguilers, p. 64.

66 Albert of Aachen, pp. 472, 477.

67 Albert of Aachen, p. 413; although these may have been cousins.

68 Albert of Aachen, pp. 299, 366, 413.

69 *Gesta Francorum*, p. 56; Peter Tudebode, p. 97; Orderic Vitalis 5, p. 35. See also Orderic Vitalis 4, pp. 230, 336–40.

70 Albert of Aachen, p. 299; *La Chanson d'Antioche*, 1, pp. 129, 404, 405.

71 Peter Tudebode, p. 44; Raymond of Aguilers, p. 38.

72 Baldric of Bourgueil, pp. 17, 65 note; Robert the Monk, p. 831.

73 Orderic Vitalis 5, pp. 28, 346.

74 Molesme 1, pp. 138–9, 2, pp. 63–5, 83–4, 105–6.

75 Molesme 2, p. 229. They were accompanied by a relative called Simon.

76 Auch, p. 65.

77 Sauxillanges, p. 967; St Victor of Marseilles 1, pp. 167–8, 2, pp. 568–9; Vaissete, *Hist. gén. de Languedoc*, 5, col. 751; St Chaffre of Le Monastier, pp. 139–41.

78 'Chronique de Zimmern', p. 24.

79 See Molesme 1, pp. 63–5, 83–4, 105, 2, p. 229; Aureil, p. 29; Lawrence of Liége, p. 498; Van Hasselt, 'Document inédit', pp. 99–100; St Hubert in Ardenne, p. 86; Aniane, pp. 358–9; St Vincent of Mâcon, p. 315; Apt, pp. 248–9; St Victor of Marseilles 1, pp. 167–8; Vaissete, *Hist. gén. de Languedoc*, 5, cols 747–8.

80 G.M. Dreves, *Analecta hymnica Medii Aevi*, 45b (Leipzig, 1904), p. 78. For the date of this hymn, see H. Brinkmann, *Entstehungsgeschichte des Minnesangs* (1926), p. 71.

81 Delisle, *Littérature latine*, pp. 28–9; Auch, pp. 57–8, 65; Grenoble, pp. 165–6; d'Outreman, *Histoire de Valentiennes. Preuves*, p. 7; Reiner of St Lawrence of Liége, 'Triumphale Bulonicum', *MGHS* 20, p. 584 (see St Hubert in Ardenne, p. 85); Cluny 5, pp. 52–3; Vaissete,

Hist. gén. de Languedoc, 5, col. 751; St Vincent of Mâcon, p. 315; St Vincent of Le Mans 1, cols 190–1, 301, 384; P.H. Morice, *Mémoires pour servir de prewes à l'histoire ecclesiastique et civile de Bretagne* (1642–6), 1, col. 488; St George of Rennes, pp. 269–70; St Victor of Marseilles 1, pp. 167–8; 'Chronique de Zimmern', p. 24; Stumpf-Brentano, *Die Reichskanzler*, 3, pp. 88–9; 'Cantatorium Sancti Huberti', ed. Baron de Reiffenberg, *Monuments pour servir à l'histoire des provinces de Namur, de Hainault et de Luxembourg* (1844–74), 7, pp. 338–40; 'Gesta Ambaziensium dominorum', p. 101.

82 St Père of Chartres 2, pp. 428–9; Trinity of Vendôme 2, pp. 104–7; St Chaffre of Le Monastier, pp. 140–1; St Vincent of Le Mans 1, col. 423; St Andrew of Vienne (C.U.J. Chevalier, *Cartulaire de l'abbaye de Saint-André-Le-Bas de Vienne* (1869)), p. 281; Angers, pp. 140–1.

83 Malbrancq, *De Morinis*, 3, p. 27.

84 Hagenmeyer, *Kreuzzugsbriefe*, p. 161. See also Raymond of Aguilers, p. 134; Riley-Smith, 'Crusading as an Act of Love', pp. 190–2.

85 Baldric of Bourgueil, p. 101.

86 Hagenmayer, *Kreuzzugsbriefe*, p. 137.

87 'Mainz Anonymous', pp. 99–100 (for the date, see Riant, 'Inventaire', p. 111); Guibert of Nogent, *De vita sua*, ed. E.-R. Labande (1981), pp. 246–8; 'Annales Rotomagenses', ed. F. Liebermann, *Ungedruckte Anglo-Normannische Geschichtsquellen* (1879), p. 47; Richard of Poitiers, 'Chronicon', *RHGF* 12, pp. 411–12; Geoffrey of Breuil, 'Chronica', *RHGF* 12, p. 428. For general accounts of the persecutions, see T. Wolff, *Die Bauernkreuzzüge des Jahres 1096* (1891), *passim*; J.W. Parkes, *The Jew in the Medieval Community* (1938), pp. 58–89; J. Riley-Smith, 'The First Crusade and the Persecution of the Jews', *Studies in Church History*, 21 (1984), pp. 51–72.

88 Bar Simson, pp. 22–4, 28–67; (Eliezer) Bar Nathan, 'Chronicle', tr. Eidelberg, *The Jews and the Crusaders*, pp. 80–92; 'Mainz Anonymous', pp. 99–102, 105–15; Bernold of St Blasien, pp. 465–6; 'Annalista Saxo', p. 729; Albert of Aachen, pp. 291–3; William of Tyre, pp. 66–7; Ekkehard of Aura, 'Chronicon', p. 209; 'Annales Brunwilarenses', *MGHS* 1, p. 100; 'Annales Corbeienses', *MGHS* 3, p. 7; 'Annales Sancti Albani Moguntini (Wirziburgenses)', *MGHS* 2, p. 246; 'Annales Hildesheimenses', *MGHS* 3, p. 106; 'Gesta Treverorum', *MGHS* 8, pp. 190–1; Hagenmeyer, *Chronologie*, pp. 16–30. For the dates of the massacres and the names of the dead, see also *Das Martyrologium des Nurnberger Memorbuches*, ed. S. Salfeld (1898), pp. 97–8, 101–19, 133–4, 137–41, 143, 151; 'Le Memorbuch de Mayence', ed. A Neubacher, *Revue des études juives*, 4 (1882), pp. 10–11, 14.

89 Bar Simson, pp. 62, 67; Bar Nathan, p. 92; Ekkehard of Aura, 'Chronicon', p. 208. The events at Regensburg were dated by the Mainz necrology to 23 May, which seems to fit with the probable dates of Peter the Hermit's passage through Bavaria. See Hagenmeyer, *Chronologie*, pp. 21–2.

90 Bar Simson, pp. 62, 67–8; Bar Nathan, p. 92; Cosmas of Prague,

Chronica Boemorum, ed. B. Bretholz (1955), pp. 164–5; 'Annales Pragenses', *MGHS* 3, p. 120; Hagenmeyer, *Chronologie*, pp. 16–18. For an apparently slightly later outbreak, see Lambert Waterlos, 'Annales Cameracenses', *MGHS* 16, p. 510.

91 Guibert of Nogent, 'Gesta', pp. 142–3, 251; Ekkehard of Aura, 'Hierosolymita', p. 19; Albert of Aachen, pp. 291, 295; Bernold of St Blasien, p. 464; William of Tyre, p. 66; Bar Simson, p. 27.

92 Albert of Aachen, pp. 272, 276–89 *passim*.

93 Albert of Aachen, pp. 277, 278, 281, 283. See Riley-Smith, 'The motives', pp. 730, 736.

94 'Chronique de Zimmern', pp. 22–9. See H. Hagenmeyer, 'Étude sur la Chronique de Zimmern', *AOL* 2 (1884), pp. 69–72, 77–9.

95 Hagenmeyer, 'Étude', pp. 74–7.

96 Albert of Aachen, p. 291. See also Ekkehard of Aura, 'Hierosolymita', p. 20. The combined armies under Emich's leadership had a substantial body of knights. Albert of Aachen, p. 294.

97 Albert of Aachen, pp. 293–5, 299; William of Tyre, p. 66.

98 Albert of Aachen, pp. 304–5, 398; Hermann, 'Liber de restauratione monasterii Sancti Martini Tornacensis', *MGHS* 14, p. 283; William of Tyre, pp. 80, 218; Robert the Monk, p. 833; *La Chanson d'Antioche*, 1, pp. 69, 440, 450, 451.

99 Albert of Aachen, pp. 315, 332, 422, 464, 468; William of Tyre, pp. 46, 134, 263, 352; *La Chanson d'Antioche* 1, pp. 69, 94, 155, 156, 160, 171, 307, 441, 451, 526; Robert the Monk, p. 833. See *Dictionnaire de biographie française*, 9, cols 867–8.

100 *Gesta Francorum*, pp. 33–4; Peter Tudebode, pp. 68–9; Riley-Smith, 'The motives', pp. 730–1.

101 Duparc-Quioc in *La Chanson d'Antioche*, 2, p. 229; Riley-Smith, 'The motives', p. 736.

102 S. Runciman (*A History of the Crusades* (1951–4), 1, p. 340) estimated Peter the Hermit's army at 20,000, which may be about right: Albert of Aachen, the best-informed source, gave (p. 287) the size of this force in Asia Minor, after Peter and Walter Sansavoir had come together, as 25,000 foot and 500 knights. But Peter's was not the largest of the early armies: Emich of Leiningen's was reputedly vast. Albert of Aachen, p. 293.

103 Albert of Aachen, pp. 281, 289–90, 293.

104 Bar Simson, pp. 29, 34–5, 50, 62; 'Mainz Anonymous', pp. 100, 107, 110, 112; 'Notitiae duae Lemovicenses', p. 351; Geoffrey of Breuil, p. 428; Sigebert of Gembloux, p. 367; 'Anonymi Florinensis brevis narratio belli sacri', *RHC Oc.* 5, p. 371; Albert of Aachen, pp. 292–3; 'Annales Sancti Disibodi', *MGHS* 17, pp. 15–16. See also Riley-Smith, 'The First Crusade and the Persecution of the Jews', pp. 56–8.

105 Albert of Aachen, p. 295. See also Bernold of St Blasien, p. 466.

106 Bar Simson, pp. 22, 47; 'Mainz Anonymous', pp. 99, 102; Bar Nathan, p. 80; Ekkehard of Aura, 'Hierosolymita', p. 20. See 'Annales S. Disibodi', pp. 15–16.

107 Bar Simson, pp. 22–3, 35–44, 45–7, 50–8, 60–3, 65–8; Bar Nathan,

pp. 80–1, 83–90; 'Mainz Anonymous', pp. 102–5, 107, 109–14; Albert of Aachen, pp. 292–3; Ekkehard of Aura, 'Hierosolymita', p. 20; Ekkehard of Aura, 'Chronicon', p. 208; Bernold of St Blasien, p. 465; 'Notitiae duae Lemovicenses', p. 351; Geoffrey of Breuil, p. 428; 'Anon. Florinensis', p. 371; Cosmas of Prague, pp. 164–5; 'Gesta Treverorum', p. 190; 'Annalista Saxo', p. 729; 'Annales Augustani', *MGHS* 3, p. 139; Sigebert of Gembloux, p. 367; 'Sigeberti Semblacensis chronica auctarium Aquicineuse', *MGHS* 6, p. 394; 'Annales S. Disibodi', pp. 15–16; 'Annales S. Albani Moguntini', p. 264; 'Annales Hildesheimenses', p. 106; 'Annales Pragenses', p. 120; 'Annales Sancti Pauli Virdunensis', *MGHS* 16, p. 501.

108 Guibert of Nogent, *De vita sua*, pp. 246–50.
109 Albert of Aachen, p. 295. For a concise account of the canon law, see F. Lotter, *Die Konzeption des Wendenkreuzzugs* (1977), pp. 34–8.
110 Cosmas of Prague, p. 164.
111 Bar Simson, pp. 22–4, 28–30, 44–5, 50, 57, 63–5; Bar Nathan, pp. 83–4, 86; 'Mainz Anonymous', pp. 101–6, 107, 109, 114; Cosmas of Prague, p. 164; Albert of Aachen, p. 292; Ekkehard of Aura, 'Chronicon', p. 209; 'Annalista Saxo', p. 729; 'Gesta Treverorum', pp. 190–1. For the protection of a local civil authority, see Bar Simson, pp. 67–8.
112 See below pp. 109–11.
113 Richard of Poitiers, pp. 411–12.
114 Guibert of Nogent, *De vita sua*, pp. 246–8. See Bar Simson, p. 22; 'Mainz Anonymous', pp. 99.
115 Orderic Vitalis 5, p. 44. See Raymond of Aguilers, p. 115; Ekkehard of Aura, 'Chronicon', p. 208.
116 Bar Simson, pp. 22, 25–6, 30; Bar Nathan, p. 80; 'Mainz Anonymous', pp. 99, 102; 'Annalista Saxo', p. 729.
117 Albert of Aachen, p. 292; 'Mainz Anonymous', p. 100; Bar Simson, p. 39. See 'Annales Blandinienses', *MGHS* 5, p. 27.
118 Baldric of Bourgueil, p. 103 note.
119 'Mainz Anonymous', p. 99; also Bar Simson, p. 22; Bar Nathan, p. 80.
120 *La Chanson d'Antioche*, 1, pp. 25–9, 68, 79, 223, 363, 383; A. Gieysztor, 'The Genesis of the Crusades: the Encyclical of Sergius IV (1009–1012)', *Medievalia et Humanistica*, 5 (1948), pp. 21–2, 6 (1948), pp. 29–30, 33–4. For Graindor's interpolation, see Duparc-Quioc in *La Chanson d'Antioche*, 2, pp. 100, 125, 143. See also L.A.T. Gryting, *The Oldest Version of the Twelfth-Century Poem, La Venjance Nostre Seigneur* (1952).
121 Bar Simson, p. 25.
122 Ivo of Chartres, 'Decretum', *PL* 161, cols 824–5; Ivo of Chartres, 'Panormia', *PL* 161, col. 1311; P. Jaffé, *Regesta pontificum Romanorum* (1885–8), 1, nos 4532–3; Gratian, 'Decretum', C. XXIII, q. 8, c. 11. See Hehl, *Kirche und Krieg*, p. 239; Riley-Smith, 'The First Crusade and the Persecution of the Jews', pp. 70–72.

Chapter 3   Conditions on the march

1   See R.-J. Lilie, *Byzanz und die Kreuzfahrerstaaten* (1981), pp. 17–23.
2   For the complex issues, see Lilie, *Byzanz*, pp. 34–54.
3   Hagenmeyer, *Kreuzzugsbriefe*, pp. 138–42, 144–74.
4   See R. Hill, intr. to *Gesta Francorum*, pp. ix–xvi; J.H. and L.L. Hill, intr. to Peter Tudebode, pp. 7–24; J.H. and L.L. Hill, intr. to Raymond of Aguilers, pp. 9–12; H. Hagenmeyer, intr. to Fulcher of Chartres, pp. 1–19, 42–8, 65–7.
5   Ralph of Caen, p. 603.
6   Guibert of Nogent, 'Gesta', p. 225.
7   For instance, Fulcher of Chartres, pp. 168, 171, 246–7; Raymond of Aguilers, p. 53. For heavy losses at Antioch, see Raymond of Aguilers, p. 104.
8   St Vincent of Le Mans 1, cols 266–7; Peter Tudebode, p. 107; Baldric of Bourgueil, p. 73 note; Orderic Vitalis 5, p. 270.
9   Runciman, *Crusades*, 1, pp. 339–40; Raymond of Aguilers, p. 148 (and see also p. 136).
10   See Porges, 'The Clergy', pp. 3, 13–14. For women bringing water to the troops, see *Gesta Francorum*, p. 19; Peter Tudebode, p. 52; *La Chanson d'Antioche*, 1, pp. 408–9.
11   *Gesta Francorum*, p. 33; Peter Tudebode, p. 68; Albert of Aachen, p. 414. On the other hand, Matthew of Edessa ('Chronicle', *RHC arm.* 1, p. 33) reported that the Armenian princes and clergy did their best to supply the crusaders at Antioch.
12   *Gesta Francorum*, pp. 19–20.
13   Hagenmeyer, *Kreuzzugsbriefe*, pp. 162, 167, 172; *Gesta Francorum*, pp. 20, 28, 79–82, 85, 92, 95, 97; Peter Tudebode, pp. 54, 63, 124, 131, 141, 145, 148–9; Fulcher of Chartres, pp. 198, 301–2, 316–18; Raymond of Aguilers, pp. 58, 61, 65–7, 78, 83, 98, 105–6, 142, 150, 156; Albert of Aachen, pp. 344, 363–4, 468, 497.
14   Fulcher of Chartres, p. 154.
15   Bar Simson, pp. 24–5.
16   *Gesta Francorum*, pp. 8, 10; Albert of Aachen, p. 303.
17   *Gesta Francorum*, pp. 8, 11; Fulcher of Chartres, pp. 175–6; Raymond of Aguilers, pp. 38–40; Albert of Aachen, pp. 302–7, 310–11.
18   Fulcher of Chartres, p. 185; Albert of Aachen, pp. 312, 321; *Gesta Francorum*, pp. 7, 12–14.
19   Hagenmeyer, *Kreuzzugsbriefe*, pp. 138–9; *Gesta Francorum*, p. 7.
20   Hagenmeyer, *Kreuzzugsbriefe*, pp. 138, 140, 145; Fulcher of Chartres, pp. 179, 188–9; Albert of Aachen, pp. 311–13, 321; *Gesta Francorum*, p. 18; Peter Tudebode, p. 51; Raymond of Aguilers, p. 44.
21   Hagenmeyer, *Kreuzzugsbriefe*, p. 140; Fulcher of Chartres, p. 179; Albert of Aachen, p. 311.
22   Fulcher of Chartres, p. 198.
23   *Gesta Francorum*, p. 23; Peter Tudebode, p. 57; Fulcher of Chartres, p. 202.

24 Hagenmeyer, *Kreuzzugsbriefe*, p. 157; *Gesta Francorum*, p. 34; Peter Tudebode, p. 69; Raymond of Aguilers, pp. 50, 55. See J. Richard, 'La confrèrie de la croisade: à propos d'un épisode de la première croisade', *Mélanges E.-R. Labande* (1974), pp. 617–22. For Raymond's gifts of horses, see Raymond of Aguilers, p. 112; Albert of Aachen, pp. 427–8, 455.

25 Hagenmeyer, *Kreuzzugsbriefe*, p. 169; Albert of Aachen, p. 427; Raymond of Aguilers, p. 82; Fulcher of Chartres, p. 252; Caffaro, p. 108.

26 Hagenmeyer, *Kreuzzugsbriefe*, pp. 157, 163, 166; Raymond of Aguilers, pp. 53, 77; *Gesta Francorum*, pp. 57, 62; Peter Tudebode, pp. 98, 104; Fulcher of Chartres, p. 225; Albert of Aachen, p. 412.

27 Albert of Aachen, pp. 381, 427–8.

28 See Raymond of Aguilers, p. 65; 'Historia peregrinorum', p. 187.

29 Hagenmeyer, *Kreuzzugsbriefe*, p. 145; *Gesta Francorum*, pp. 8, 20, 28, 31, 37, 85, 89, 94; Peter Tudebode, pp. 54, 63, 72; Fulcher of Chartres, pp. 198, 256; Raymond of Aguilers, pp. 63, 83, 105. For the Byzantine general Tatikios's offer to return with horses, see *Gesta Francorum*, p. 34; Peter Tudebode, pp. 69–70.

30 Raymond of Aguilers, p. 51.

31 Raymond of Aguilers, pp. 111–12; Albert of Aachen, pp. 395, 427–8, 455. See *La Chanson d'Antioche*, 1, p. 440. Note the gifts of horses and pack-animals made by Muslim rulers in 1099. *Gesta Francorum*, pp. 82, 86; Peter Tudebode, pp. 130, 132; Raymond of Aguilers, pp. 107, 111–12, 125.

32 Raymond of Aguilers, p. 99.

33 *Gesta Francorum*, p. 23; Peter Tudebode, p. 57; Fulcher of Chartres, pp. 200–1; Albert of Aachen, p. 343.

34 Raymond of Aguilers, p. 49; Caffaro, p. 102.

35 Raymond of Aguilers, p. 59; Albert of Aachen, p. 383.

36 Fulcher of Chartres, pp. 222–4; Albert of Aachen, pp. 373–4, 379; Ibn al-Qalanisi, *The Damascus Chronicle*, extr. tr. H.A.R. Gibb (1932), p. 43. See Bartolf of Nangis, p. 500; also the enigmatic words in Raymond of Aguilers, p. 65. Cf. *Gesta Francorum*, p. 43; Peter Tudebode, p. 82; 'Anonymous Syriac Chronicle', tr. A.S. Tritton, *Journal of the Royal Asiatic Society* (1933), p. 72.

37 *Gesta Francorum*, pp. 30–3; Peter Tudebode, pp. 65–8; Raymond of Aguilers, pp. 50–3; Albert of Aachen, pp. 374–5. For another raid, organized by lesser people, see Albert of Aachen, pp. 375–6.

38 Fulcher of Chartres, pp. 222–4; Albert of Aachen, pp. 375–6; Ralph of Caen, pp. 649–50. See below p. 75.

39 Raymond of Aguilers, pp. 68–72; Hagenmeyer, *Chronologie*, pp. 116–17, 127, 140, 161, 167–8. For William Peyre of Cunhlat, see also Raymond of Aguilers, p. 105; William of Tyre, p. 295; Riley-Smith, 'The motives', p. 732.

40 *Gesta Francorum*, p. 17; Peter Tudebode, p. 50.

41 *Gesta Francorum*, pp. 33–5; Peter Tudebode, pp. 68–70; Raymond of Aguilers, pp. 53, 55; Fulcher of Chartres, pp. 225–6; Albert of

Aachen, pp. 373–4; Hagenmeyer, *Chronologie*, pp. 119–20.

42 Bartolf of Nangis, p. 500; *Gesta Francorum*, p. 62; Peter Tudebode, p. 104; Raymond of Aguilers, pp. 65, 76–7; Albert of Aachen, p. 412; Ibn al-Qalanisi, p. 46; Ibn al-Athir, 'Sum of World History', *RHC Or.* 1, pp. 194–5; 'Anonymous Syriac Chronicle', p. 72.

43 Hagenmeyer, *Kreuzzugsbriefe*, p. 167; Ibn al -Athir 1, p. 196.

44 Albert of Aachen, pp. 395–6.

45 Raymond of Aguilers, pp. 94–6, 101; Hagenmeyer, *Kreuzzugsbriefe*, p. 170; *Gesta Francorum*, p. 80; Fulcher of Chartres, pp. 266–7; Peter Tudebode, pp. 121, 124–5; Albert of Aachen, p. 450; Ekkehard of Aura, 'Chronicon', p. 209. For an interesting, but unlikely, interpretation of this and other events, see M. Rouche, 'Cannibalisme sacré chez les croisés populaires', *La Religion populaire*, ed. Y.-M. Hilaire (1981), pp. 29–41.

46 Raymond of Aguilers, pp. 101–3.

47 *Gesta Francorum*, pp. 82, 86; Peter Tudebode, pp. 130, 132–3; Raymond of Aguilers, pp. 103, 107, 111–12, 125.

48 See, for instance, Raymond of Aguilers, pp. 105, 108, 134; Peter Tudebode, p. 131; Caffaro, p. 110.

49 Fulcher of Chartres, pp. 270–1; Peter Tudebode, p. 132.

50 *Gesta Francorum*, pp. 88–9; Peter Tudebode, p. 136; Raymond of Aguilers, pp. 139–40; Fulcher of Chartres, pp. 294–5; Albert of Aachen, pp. 469–70.

51 *Acta sanctorum. September*, 7, p. 523.

52 *Gesta Francorum*, pp. 33, 62; Peter Tudebode, pp. 68, 104; Albert of Aachen, p. 412; Fulcher of Chartres, p. 246.

53 Raymond of Aguilers, pp. 46, 54–5, 62, 77, 79, 83–4, 88; Orderic Vitalis 5, p. 328. For the sick in his army, see Raymond of Aguilers, p. 111.

54 Albert of Aachen, pp. 398, 415; *Gesta Francorum*, p. 63; Peter Tudebode, p. 105; Ralph of Caen, p. 649.

55 Suger of St Denis, *Vita Ludovici Grossi regis*, ed. H. Waquet (1929), p. 36.

56 'Gesta Ambaziensium dominorum', p. 102.

57 See Albert of Aachen, p. 435; Matthew of Edessa, p. 34.

58 Hagenmeyer, *Kreuzzugsbriefe*, p. 145.

59 Fulcher of Chartres, p. 226.

60 Raymond of Aguilers, pp. 70–1.

61 Hagenmeyer, *Kreuzzugsbriefe*, p. 150; *Gesta Francorum*, p. 33; Peter Tudebode, p. 68; Fulcher of Chartres, p. 222. For the many types of coin in circulation in the army, see D.M. Metcalf, *Coinage of the Crusades and the Latin East* (1983), pp. 1–6.

62 *Gesta Francorum*, p. 51.

63 *Gesta Francorum*, p. 74; Peter Tudebode, p. 117; Raymond of Aguilers, p. 88.

64 *Gesta Francorum*, pp. 18, 67–8, 90, 92, 94; Peter Tudebode, pp. 51, 110, 142, 145; Raymond of Aguilers, pp. 54, 77, 97, 101, 127, 145; Fulcher of Chartres, pp. 188–9, 247. Note also the alms provided for

the souls of the dead. Raymond of Aguilers, p. 85; Albert of Aachen, pp. 322, 325.

65 *Gesta Francorum*, pp. 72–3; Peter Tudebode, p. 115; Orderic Vitalis 5, p. 130.

66 Raymond of Aguilers, pp. 88–9, 92–3, 101–2.

67 Raymond of Aguilers, p. 111. Perhaps this was in response to a message to the visionary Peter Bartholomew. Peter Tudebode, p. 122. See Raymond of Aguilers, p. 116.

68 Albert of Aachen, p. 427; Guibert of Nogent, 'Gesta', p. 242.

69 Albert of Aachen, p. 427; For Henry's relationship to Godfrey, see Albert of Aachen, p. 413.

70 Hagenmeyer, *Kreuzzugsbriefe*, p. 150; Peter Tudebode, pp. 78–9; 'Historia peregrinorum', p. 193; Albert of Aachen, pp. 427–8; Ralph of Caen, p. 681.

71 Raymond of Aguilers, pp. 62, 146.

72 Raymond of Aguilers, pp. 53–4 (who commented that Bohemond said this simply for effect, although there is no reason to question the truth of Bohemond's statement: see Anna Comnena, *Alexiade*, ed. B. Leib (1937–76), 2, p. 232); Albert of Aachen, pp. 412, 427–8. See also Orderic Vitalis 5, p. 74.

73 Albert of Aachen, pp. 395–6.

74 Raymond of Aguilers, pp. 76–7.

75 Hagenmeyer, *Kreuzzugsbriefe*, p. 149.

76 Peter Tudebode, pp. 78–9, 81–2; Raymond of Aguilers, pp. 62–3, 100, 112, 146; 'Historia peregrinorum', p. 193; *Gesta Francorum*, p. 43; Albert of Aachen, pp. 428, 455.

77 Ralph of Caen, p. 651. See Raymond of Aguilers, pp. 54–5.

78 Vaissete, *Hist. gén. de Languedoc*, 3, p. 483.

79 *Gesta Francorum*, pp. 73–4, 83–4, 87–9; Peter Tudebode, pp. 115–16, 129, 134–6; Raymond of Aguilers, pp. 122–3, 141–2. Also Albert of Aachen, pp. 316, 422, 452.

80 Suger of St Denis, p. 36.

81 *Gesta Francorum*, p. 27; Peter Tudebode, p. 62.

82 Fulcher of Chartres, pp. 223–4; Raymond of Aguilers, p. 53. See Hagenmeyer, *Kreuzzugsbriefe*, p. 166; Albert of Aachen, p. 398; 'Gesta Ambaziensium dominorum', p. 101.

83 *Gesta Francorum*, pp. 56–7; Peter Tudebode, pp. 97–8; Raymond of Aguilers, p. 74; Fulcher of Chartres, pp. 246–7; Bartolf of Nangis, p. 502; Ralph of Caen, p. 662; Baldric of Bourgueil, p. 65 note; Albert of Aachen, pp. 414–15, 417, 482; Suger of St Denis, p. 36; 'Gesta Ambaziensium dominorum', p. 101.

84 *Gesta Francorum*, pp. 33, 66–7; Peter Tudebode, pp. 68, 108–9; Fulcher of Chartres, pp. 247–9; Raymond of Aguilers, p. 79; Albert of Aachen, pp. 420–1.

85 *Gesta Francorum*, pp. 33–4; Peter Tudebode, pp. 68–9; Albert of Aachen, pp. 414–15; Ralph of Caen, p. 650; Riley-Smith, 'The motives', p. 731.

86 Ralph of Caen, p. 662; Baldric of Bourgueil, p. 65 note; Albert of

Aachen, p. 410; Riley-Smith, 'The motives', pp. 729–30.

87 Hagenmeyer, *Kreuzzugsbriefe*, p. 144.
88 Hagenmeyer, *Kreuzzugsbriefe*, p. 160.
89 Hagenmeyer, *Kreuzzugsbriefe*, p. 152.
90 Hagenmeyer, *Kreuzzugebriefe*, p. 143; Raymond of Aguilers, pp. 46, 88, 90; For the shrine of St Faith at Conques, see Ward, *Miracles*, pp. 36–42.
91 Redon (A. de Courson, *Cartulaire de l'abbaye de Redon* (1863)), pp. 318–21; Aureil, p. 126.
92 Baldric of Bourgueil, p. 9.
93 Raymond of Aguilers, pp. 40–1; Peter Tudebode, pp. 45–6. Had the emperor changed his mind by the spring of 1099? See Raymond of Aguilers, p. 126.
94 Hagenmeyer, *Kreuzzugsbriefe*, p. 149; *Gesta Francorum*, p. 63; Peter Tudebode, pp. 104–5; Raymond of Aguilers, p. 77. See also Albert of Aachen, p. 312. For a discussion of the date of Stephen's election, see Hagenmeyer, *Kreuzzugsbriefe*, pp. 276–7. For a parallel in the election of captains in the armies of the first wave in Asia Minor, see *Gesta Francorum*, p. 3; Peter Tudebode, p. 34.
95 *Gesta Francorum*, p. 63; Peter Tudebode, pp. 104–5; Raymond of Aguilers, p. 77; Fulcher of Chartres, p. 228; Hagenmeyer, *Kreuzzugsbriefe*, p. 166.
96 Raymond of Aguilers, pp. 99–100, 102, 112.
97 Hagenmeyer, *Kreuzzugsbriefe*, pp. 161–5. I have not included Eustace of Boulogne, who was listed among the authors of this letter, or Baldwin of Boulogne, whom Raymond of Aguilers (p.92) called a prince at a time when he had already seized Edessa.
98 Geoffrey Malaterra, 'De rebus gestis Rogerii Calabriae et Siciliae Comitis', *Rerum Italicarum Scriptores*, NS 5, 1, p. 102.
99 Raymond of Aguilers, pp. 62, 146.
100 Pflugk-Harttung, *Acta pont. Rom. inedita*, 2, p. 205; Fulcher of Chartres, pp. 740–1.
101 Ralph of Caen, pp. 649–50; *Gesta Francorum*, p. 72; Peter Tudebode, p. 115; Raymond of Aguilers, p. 93; Guibert of Nogent, 'Gesta', p. 254; Orderic Vitalis 5, pp. 270–2. Cf. R. Dussaud, *Topographie historique de la Syrie antique et médiévale* (1927) pp. 165–70, 229–31, 428–9, with whose identifications I have not always agreed. For Latakia, cf. Runciman, *Crusades*, 1, pp. 255–6 note.
102 See Raymond of Aguilers, p. 126; Albert of Aachen, pp. 300, 402; Riley-Smith, 'The motives', pp. 724–6, 730–3.
103 Ralph of Caen, p. 687.
104 For example, Raymond of St Gilles's *exercitus*: *Gesta Francorum*, pp. 73, 88; Peter Tudebode, pp. 115, 135.
105 Hagenmeyer, *Kreuzzugsbriefe*, p. 145. For his force, see Ralph of Caen, p. 681.
106 'Fragment d'une Chanson d'Antioche', pp. 474, 489. See also Raymond of Aguilers, p. 75.
107 Raymond of Aguilers, var. ms., F, *RHC Oc.* 3, p. 307.

108   *Gesta Francorum*, pp. 15–16; Raymond of Aguilers, p. 66; Hagen-
      meyer, *Kreuzzugsbriefe*, p. 159; Albert of Aachen, pp. 320, 363,
      365–6, 381, 407–8; Baldric of Bourgueil, p. 28.
109   *Gesta Francorum*, p. 92; Peter Tudebode, p. 141; Raymond of
      Aguilers p. 143.
110   *La Chanson d'Antioche*, 1, p. 441.
111   'Chronique de Zimmern', p. 24; Albert of Aachen, p. 277. For their
      use as rallying points, see William of Tyre, pp. 163–4.
112   *Gesta Francorum*, p. 40; Peter Tudebode, p. 74.
113   Raymond of Aguilers, pp. 51, 58; *Gesta Francorum*, p. 32; Peter
      Tudebode, p. 67.
114   Raymond of Aguilers, pp. 82, 119–20; 'Fragment d'une Chanson
      d'Antioche', pp. 492–3. Was this a *vexillum s. Petri*? See Fulcher of
      Chartres, p. 254.
115   Robert the Monk, p. 831; *La Chanson d'Antioche*, 1, pp. 426–7, 442.
      For his banner, see Anna Comnena 2, pp. 213–14.
116   For instance Raymond of Aguilers, p. 107; *Gesta Francorum*,
      pp. 91–2; Peter Tudebode, p. 141.
117   Raymond of Aguilers, pp. 137, 143. For the question whose banner
      should fly from the citadel of Antioch, see *Gesta Francorum*, p. 71;
      Peter Tudebode, p. 113. For rights of conquest, see Fulcher of
      Chartres, p. 304.
118   For instance Albert of Aachen, pp. 315–17, 422; Baldric of Bourgueil,
      pp. 27–8, 33–4; William of Tyre, p. 263.
119   Raymond of Aguilers, p. 41; Peter Tudebode, p. 46.
120   *Acta sanctorum. Aprilis*, 3, pp. 824–5.
121   William of Tyre, pp. 106, 263.
122   Baldric of Bourgueil, pp. 28, 33; Orderic Vitalis 5, pp. 34, 54, 58. See
      also Stumpf-Brentano, *Die Reichskanzler*, 3, 88.
123   William of Tyre (old. French tr.), p. 118; *La Chanson d'Antioche*, 1,
      pp. 77–8.
124   See Riley-Smith, 'The motives', p. 729.
125   *Gesta Francorum*, p. 8; Baldric of Bourgueil, p. 21; Orderic Vitalis 5,
      p. 36; Hagenmeyer, *Kreuzzugsbriefe*, p. 156; 'Fragment d'une Chan-
      son d'Antioche', pp. 478, 494.
126   Orderic Vitalis 5, pp. 168–70; Eadmer, *Historia novorum in Anglia*,
      ed. M. Rule (1884), pp. 179–81.
127   Hagenmeyer, *Kreuzzugsbriefe*, p. 156.
128   Albert of Aachen, p. 362; William of Tyre, p. 164.
129   Baldric of Bourgueil, p. 21 note; Robert the Monk, p. 833.
130   Albert of Aachen, pp. 304–5; William of Tyre, p. 80; Robert the
      Monk, p. 833.
131   Albert of Aachen, p. 427. But cf. Albert of Aachen, p. 322, which may
      suggest that he was already attached to Godfrey of Bouillon during the
      siege of Nicaea.
132   Riley-Smith, 'The motives', pp. 730–1, 736.
133   Hagenmeyer, 'Étude', pp. 68–74.
134   Albert of Aachen, pp. 281, 283, 286, 288 (where wrongly reported

killed). For his brother, see Raymond of Aguilers, p. 64.

135 'Chronique de Zimmern', p. 29; Riley-Smith, 'The motives', p. 725.

136 Albert of Aachen, pp. 357, 442, 446; Riley-Smith, 'The motives', pp. 730–1. He may have served with Bohemond for a time. See Raymond of Aguilers, p. 64; Robert the Monk, pp. 799–800; Ralph of Caen, p. 654; Orderic Vitalis 5, p. 90.

137 With Hugh: *Gesta Francorum*, p. 5. With Raymond: *Gesta Francorum*, pp. 88–9; Peter Tudebode, p. 135; Raymond of Aguilers, p. 141; Albert of Aachen, pp. 468–9.

138 With Hugh: Albert of Aachen, p. 424. With Raymond: *Gesta Francorum*, pp. 85; Peter Tudebode, p. 131; Fulcher of Chartres, p. 270; Raymond of Aguilers, pp. 108–9; Ralph of Caen, pp. 680–1.

139 Baldric of Bourgueil, p. 21 note; 'Gesta Ambaziensium dominorum', p. 101.

140 Raymond of Aguilers, pp. 85, 128; Riley-Smith, 'The motives', p. 732.

141 *Gesta Francorum*, pp. xi–xvi, 73, 82–92 *passim*.

142 See *Gesta Francorum*, p. 11; Ralph of Caen, p. 607; Baldric of Bourgueil, p. 24.

143 Raymond of Aguilers, pp. 100, 102, 112; Albert of Aachen, pp. 471, 479.

144 See Peter Tudebode, pp. 78, 110.

145 With Raymond: Peter Tudebode, p. 78; William of Tyre, p. 96. With Godfrey: Albert of Aachen, pp. 462–3; Raymond of Aguilers, pp. 145–6; *Gesta Francorum*, p. 92; Peter Tudebode, p. 141.

146 Riley-Smith, 'The motives', pp. 728–9.

147 St Benignus of Dijon (G. Chevrier and M. Chaume, *Chartes et documents de Saint-Bénigne de Dijon* (1943) 2, p. 167; Guibert of Nogent, 'Gesta', pp. 232–3; Orderic Vitalis 4, p. 119, 5, pp. 34, 208–10, 264–6.

148 Albert of Aachen, pp. 327–8.

149 Raymond of Aguilers, p. 119; William of Tyre, pp. 274–5; Chamalières, p. 54; Maurice of Neufmoustier, 'Albrici Trium Fontium chronica a monacho novi monasterii Hoiensis interpolata', *MGHS* 23, p. 824.

150 William of Tyre, p. 423; Guibert of Nogent, 'Gesta', pp. 182–3, 251; Albert of Aachen, pp. 370–1, 375–6.

151 *Chronicon sancti Petri Vivi Senonensis*, pp. 184–8; Fulcher of Chartres, pp. 163–203 *passim*, 206, 215; Guibert of Nogent, 'Gesta', p. 250.

152 Raymond of Aguilers, p. 108.

153 Raymond of Aguilers, pp. 72, 89–92, 97–100, 102, 104–5, 111, 119–21, 124, 128, 135, 146, 153.

154 Hagenmeyer, *Kreuzzugsbriefe*, p. 156; 'Historia peregrinorum', pp. 176–7, 189, 216; 'Chronica monasterii Casinensis', p. 477; Ralph of Caen, p. 683; Raymond of Aguilers, p. 152; *Gesta Francorum*, pp. 93–4. The 'Historia peregrinorum' and the 'Chronica monasterii Casinensis' refer also to a bishop of Roscignolo, although no such diocese appears to have existed. The bishop of Martirano must have

gone to Jerusalem with Tancred.

155 *Gesta Francorum*, p. 93; Peter Tudebode, p. 142; Raymond of
      Aguilers, pp. 153–4; Guibert of Nogent, 'Gesta', p. 232–3; Ralph of
      Caen, p. 604; Albert of Aachen, pp. 461, 489–90; *Chronicon sancti
      Petri Vivi Senonensis*, pp. 184–6; William of Tyre, pp. 304, 313;
      Orderic Vitalis 5, p. 34. For Robert of Normandy and the kingdom of
      Jerusalem, see below p. 122.

156 Hagenmeyer, *Kreuzzugsbriefe*, p. 145; Raymond of Aguilers,
      pp. 131–2; 'Historia peregrinorum', p. 181.

157 Fulcher of Chartres, p. 741.

158 Raymond of Aguilers, p. 89.

159 Cf. J.H. and L.L. Hill, 'Contemporary Accounts and the Later Reputa-
      tion of Adhémar, Bishop of Puy', *Medievalia et Humanistica*, 9
      (1955), pp. 30–8.

160 *Chronicon sancti Petri Vivi Senonensis*, pp. 184–6. See J. Richard,
      'Quelques textes sur les premiers temps de l'église latine de Jérusalem',
      Recueil de travaux offerts à M. Clovis Brunel, 2 (1955), pp. 420–3.

161 William of Tyre, pp. 365–6; Raymond of Aguilers, pp. 91–2, 97–100,
      102, 104–5, 111, 120–1, 124, 128, 146, 152–3; Peter Tudebode,
      pp. 117, 131 note, 138; *Gesta Francorum*, p. 75; Ralph of Caen,
      pp. 673, 681–3; Albert of Aachen, pp. 470–1.

162 See Riley-Smith, 'Death on the First Crusade', p. 19.

163 Kehr, *Italia pontificia*, 6, 2, p. 323.

164 Raymond of Aguilers, p. 152.

165 *Acta sanctorum. September*, 7, p. 523. It is not certain that St Peter of
      Anagni took part in the crusade. Porges, 'The Clergy', p. 23.

166 Raymond of Aguilers, p. 118.

167 See the gloss on *Gesta Francorum*, p. 75, in Robert the Monk, p. 840;
      also B. Hamilton, *The Latin Church in the Crusader States. The
      Secular Church* (1980), p. 23.

168 Guibert of Nogent, 'Gesta', pp. 232–3; Ralph of Caen, pp. 604,
      665–6, 683; Robert the Monk, p. 870; Albert of Aachen, p. 470;
      C.W. David, *Robert Curthose, Duke of Normandy* (1920), pp. 217–
      20; R. Foreville, 'Un chef de la première croisade: Arnoul de Male-
      couronne', *Bulletin philologique et historique du comité des travaux
      historiques et scientifiques* (1953–4), pp. 377–90. See the reference
      to his '*supplicationes mellifluas*' in Hagenmeyer, *Kreuzzugsbriefe*,
      p. 176.

169 Hagenmeyer, intr. to Fulcher of Chartres, pp. 49–65.

170 Raymond of Aguilers, pp. 153–4; Guibert of Nogent, 'Gesta', p. 233;
      William of Tyre, pp. 304, 365. See Hamilton, *The Latin Church*,
      pp. 12–13.

171 Raymond of Aguilers, pp. 152, 154; Ralph of Caen, p. 683.

172 Albert of Aachen, pp. 370–1.

173 Chamalières, p. 54. For an earlier illness at Antioch, see Raymond of
      Aguilers, p. 119.

174 See Baldric of Bourgueil, p. 17; Wiederhold, 'Papsturkunden',
      pp. 313–14; Kehr, *Italia pontificia*, 5, p. 156.

175 Guibert of Nogent, 'Gesta', p. 182. He was '*quemdam praedicatissimi omnium coenobii monachum*'.

176 Ekkehard of Aura, 'Hierosolymita', p. 19; Albert of Aachen, pp. 291, 295; Bernold of St Blasien, p. 464; Guibert of Nogent, 'Gesta', pp. 182–3, 250–1; Bar Simson, p. 27; Baldric of Bourgueil, p. 17; Raymond of Aguilers, p. 102; Fulcher of Chartres, pp. 169–70; 'Historia de translatione sanctorum magni Nicolai ... ejusdem avunculi alterius Nicolai, Theodorique ... de civitate Mirea in monasterium S. Nicolai de Littore Venetiarum', *RHC Oc*. 5, p. 255; Orderic Vitalis 5, p. 30.

177 Guibert of Nogent, 'Gesta', pp. 182–3, 251. See William of Tyre, p. 423.

178 See Hill, 'Contemporary Accounts', p. 32; J.A. Brundage, 'Adhémar of Puy; the Bishop and his Critics', *Speculum*, 34 (1959), pp. 201–12; J. Richard, 'La papauté et la direction de la première croisade', *Journal des savants* (1960), pp. 52–8; H.E. Mayer, 'Zur Beurteilung Adhémars von Le Puy', *Deutsches Archiv*, 16 (1960), pp. 547–52.

179 Anna Comnena 2, pp. 218–19.

180 Guibert of Nogent, 'Gesta', p. 182. See Fulcher of Chartres, p. 252.

181 Ralph of Caen, p. 673.

182 Peter Tudebode, p. 138; Albert of Aachen, pp. 470–1; Raymond of Aguilers, p. 145.

183 *Gesta Francorum*, pp. 67–8; Peter Tudebode, p. 110.

184 *Gesta Francorum*, p. 94. See also *Gesta Francorum*, p. 4; Raymond of Aguilers, pp. 54, 111, 128, 134.

185 Hagenmeyer, *Kreuzzugsbriefe*, pp. 144, 160, 167; Fulcher of Chartres, pp. 196–7; *Gesta Francorum*, pp. 67–8; Peter Tudebode, p. 110; Raymond of Aguilers, pp. 79, 109, 157; Ralph of Caen, p. 681; Albert of Aachen, pp. 422, 492.

186 'Fragment d'une Chanson d'Antioche', p. 493.

187 Albert of Aachen, p. 433; 'Historia peregrinorum', p. 195. For other references to purification ceremonies, see Fulcher of Chartres, p. 306; *Gesta Francorum*, p. 75.

188 Fulcher of Chartres, pp. 196–7, 252–3; Hagenmeyer, *Kreuzzugsbriefe*, p. 167; Raymond of Aguilers, p. 81; Albert of Aachen, pp. 492–3. See Peter Tudebode, pp. 145–6.

189 *Gesta Francorum*, p. 68; Hagenmeyer, *Kreuzzugsbriefe*, p. 167; Fulcher of Chartres, pp. 252–3; Raymond of Aguilers, p. 81.

190 'Historia peregrinorum', pp. 204–5.

191 *Gesta Francorum*, pp. 78–9; Raymond of Aguilers, p. 97 (on the orders of SS Peter and Andrew transmitted by a visionary).

192 Ralph of Caen, pp. 692–3; 'Historia peregrinorum', p. 221.

193 *Gesta Francorum*, p. 94; Peter Tudebode, pp. 144–5; Raymond of Aguilers, p. 155.

194 See, for instance, Raymond of Aguilers, pp. 54, 101, 120, 127; Fulcher of Chartres, p. 238; Peter Tudebode, p. 108; Bartolf of Nangis, p. 499.

195 *Gesta Francorum*, p. 58; Raymond of Aguilers, p. 73.

196 Raymond of Aguilers, p. 76; also p. 128.

197   Guibert of Nogent, 'Gesta', p. 183. See Orderic Vitalis 5, p. 28.
198   Raymond of Aguilers, pp. 81 (he was in the battle lines himself), 125.
199   Raymond of Aguilers, pp. 54, 102, 137, 144–5, 151, 155; Hagen-
        meyer, *Kreuzzugsbriefe*, pp. 167, 171; *Gesta Francorum*, pp. 67–8,
        81, 90, 92, 94; Peter Tudebode, pp. 110, 126, 137–8, 144–5; Albert
        of Aachen, pp. 470–1; Fulcher of Chartres, p. 305. Baldric of Bour-
        gueil (p. 97) reported that those crusaders who were not on armed
        duty removed their shoes at the first sight of Jerusalem.
200   Raymond of Aguilers, pp. 71, 142–3, 153; Fulcher of Chartres,
        p. 319.
201   Gilo, 'Historia de via Hierosolymitana', *RHC Oc.* 5, p. 731; Raymond
        of Aguilers, pp. 54, 127, 144; Peter Tudebode, pp. 110, 142; 'Narratio
        Floriacensis', p. 360; Bartolf of Nangis, p. 499; Hagenmeyer, *Kreuz-
        zugsbriefe*, p. 167; *Gesta Francorum*, pp. 67, 90; Fulcher of Chartres,
        pp. 238, 247; Caffaro, p. 106; Albert of Aachen, p. 470.
202   Caffaro, pp. 106–7. See Raymond of Aguilers, p. 41; Guibert of
        Nogent, 'Gesta', p. 205. For the Muslims' knowledge of the crusaders'
        fasts and of their starvation, see Ibn al-Qalanisi, p. 46; Ibn al-Athir 1,
        pp. 194–5.
203   See Albert of Aachen, p. 274.
204   *La Chanson d'Antioche*, 1, p. 98; Fulcher of Chartres, pp. 218, 223;
        Gesta Francorum, p. 59; Raymond of Aguilers, pp. 74, 136.
205   Fulcher of Chartres, pp. 202–3; Ralph of Caen, p. 676; Albert of
        Aachen, p. 339.
206   Raymond of Aguilers, pp. 52, 78, 105; Ralph of Caen, pp. 651,
        675–6. For the distinguishing of Franks from Burgundians, see
        Grenoble, pp. 136–7, 154.
207   See, for example, Raymond of Aguilers, p. 98.
208   *Gesta Francorum*, pp. 58–9, 75–6; Peter Tudebode, pp. 100, 118–19;
        Albert of Aachen, p. 381.
209   *Gesta Francorum*, p. 75; Peter Tudebode, p. 118; Raymond of
        Aguilers, p. 93.
210   Hagenmeyer, *Kreuzzugsbriefe*, p. 145; *Gesta Francorum*, pp. 65–6;
        Raymond of Aguilers, p. 79; 'Historia peregrinorum', p. 181.
211   *Gesta Francorum*, pp. 30, 35–6, 39, 75–6, 80–1; Peter Tudebode,
        pp. 65, 70–1, 73, 114, 125; Raymond of Aguilers, pp. 64, 92–3,
        99–100, 124.
212   *Gesta Francorum*, p. 30; Peter Tudebode, p. 65.
213   *Gesta Francorum*, p. 87; Peter Tudebode, p. 134. See Raymond of
        Aguilers, p. 136.
214   *Gesta Francorum*, pp. 58–9; Peter Tudebode, p. 100.
215   *Gesta Francorum*, pp. 44, 75–6; Peter Tudebode, pp. 84, 118–19;
        Raymond of Aguilers, p. 93.
216   *Gesta Francorum*, pp. 76, 84; Peter Tudebode, p. 119; Raymond of
        Aguilers, pp. 42, 55.
217   Hagenmeyer, *Kreuzzugsbriefe*, p. 149. See *Gesta Francorum*, p. 63;
        Peter Tudebode, pp. 104–5.
218   *Gesta Francorum*, pp. 75–6; Peter Tudebode, pp. 118–19, 142;

Fulcher of Chartres, p. 308; Raymond of Aguilers, pp. 143, 152–3.
219 Raymond of Aguilers, pp. 91–2.
220 Albert of Aachen, pp. 449–50; Peter Tudebode, pp. 132, 137; Raymond of Aguilers, pp. 136, 144.
221 See, for instance, Raymond of Aguilers, pp. 62–3.
222 Raymond of Aguilers, p. 73. See also 'Chronicon monasterii sancti Petri Aniciensis', ed. C.U.J. Chevalier, *Collection de cartulaires dauphinois*, 8, 1 (1884), pp. 163–4.
223 Albert of Aachen, p. 440; Raymond of Aguilers, p. 84.
224 Baldric of Bourgueil, p. 28.
225 Albert of Aachen, pp. 378–9. See Guibert of Nogent, 'Gesta', p. 182.
226 *Gesta Francorum*, p. 58; Peter Tudebode, p. 99; Raymond of Aguilers, pp. 51, 54, 96–7; Guibert of Nogent, 'Gesta', p. 182; Fulcher of Chartres, p. 223; Bartolf of Nangis, pp. 498–501. See also Albert of Aachen, p. 365; Baldric of Bourgueil, p. 17. On the laws of pilgrimage, see J.A. Brundage, 'Prostitution, Miscegenation and Sexual Purity in the First Crusade', *Crusade and Settlement*, pp. 57, 61–2, but cf. Baldric of Bourgueil, p. 28.
227 Raymond of Aguilers, p. 84.
228 Raymond of Aguilers, pp. 97, 115–16. See also Peter Tudebode, p. 122.
229 Raymond of Aguilers, p. 79.
230 Guibert of Nogent, 'Gesta', pp. 241–2; *La Chanson d'Antioche*, 1, pp. 169–70, 218–21, 228, 318, 407, 438–9, 475–6. L.A.M. Sumberg ('The "Tafurs" and the First Crusade', *Mediaeval Studies*, 21 (1959), pp. 224–46) and Rouche ('Cannibalisme sacré', pp. 33–6) seem to me to make the evidence provided by the *Chanson d'Antioche* carry more weight than it can bear.
231 Raymond of Aguilers, p. 111.
232 Raymond of Aguilers, pp. 93–4, 99–102; Albert of Aachen, pp. 449–50; Robert the Monk, p. 855.

Chapter 4   The ideas of the crusaders

1 Hagenmeyer, *Kreuzzugsbriefe*, p. 142.
2 Hagenmeyer, *Kreuzzugsbriefe*, p. 147.
3 For example, Hagenmeyer, *Kreuzzugsbriefe*, pp. 168–74.
4 Fulcher of Chartres, p. 117. For a similar reaction from an eastern Christian, see Matthew of Edessa, p. 40.
5 Fulcher of Chartres, pp. 116–17, 227; Raymond of Aguilers, pp. 53, 152; Hagenmeyer, *Kreuzzugsbriefe*, p. 148.
6 Fulcher of Chartres, pp. 203–5 (who reported that the comet appeared while the crusaders were at Ereghli, which is impossible: it was visible from 2 to 25 October), 224; Raymond of Aguilers, pp. 54, 74–5; *Gesta Francorum*, p. 62; Peter Tudebode, p. 103; Albert of Aachen, pp. 447–8, 461 (with wrong date); 'Narratio Floriacensis', p. 358; Matthew of Edessa, pp. 34–5, 43–4; Ibn al-Qalanisi, p. 43; Hagenmeyer, *Chronologie*, p. 189.

7   Orderic Vitalis 5, pp. 8–9; Guibert of Nogent, 'Gesta', pp. 246–7; 'Historia monasterii Aquicinctini', *MGHS* 14, p. 592; 'Genealogiae comitum Flandriae', *MGHS* 9, p. 323.

8   Ralph of Caen, p. 665; Foreville, 'Un chef', pp. 383–5. See also the story of the prophesying hermit at Jerusalem. Raymond of Aguilers, p. 139.

9   *Gesta Francorum*, pp. 53–5; Peter Tudebode, pp. 93–6.

10 Vaissete, *Hist. gén. de Languedoc*, 3, p. 562; J.H. and L.L. Hill, *Raymond IV de Saint-Gilles 1041 (ou 1042)–1105* (1959), pp. 1, 19, 140. For Raymond's devotion to St Robert, see *Acta sanctorum. Aprilis*, 3, p. 330.

11 'Fragment d'une Chanson d'Antioche', p. 491; *Acta sanctorum. Junius*, 1, pp. 87–107.

12 Raymond of Aguilers, pp. 69, 127–8, 130; Hagenmeyer, *Kreuzzugsbriefe*, pp. 160, 167; *La Chanson d'Antioche*, 1, pp. 357, 460; 'Anonymous Syriac Chronicle', p. 72.

13 Raymond of Aguilers, p. 145.

14 'Historia peregrinorum', p. 195.

15 Raymond of Aguilers, p. 155.

16 See J. Riley-Smith, 'Peace never established: the Case of the Kingdom of Jerusalem', *Transactions of the Royal Historical Society* 5th ser., 28 (1978), pp. 89–94.

17 Hagenmeyer, *Kreuzzugsbriefe*, p. 143.

18 'Narratio quomodo relliquiae martyris Georgii ad nos Aquicinenses pervenerunt', *RHC Oc.* 5, pp. 248–51; Walter of Thérouanne, 'Vita Karoli comitis Flandriae', *MGHS* 12, p. 540; 'Genealogiae breves regum Francorum', *MGHS* 13, p. 250; *La Chanson d'Antioche*, 1, p. 304.

19 Raymond of Aguilers, p. 90.

20 Raymond of Aguilers, pp. 131–4.

21 Orderic Vitalis 5, p. 170.

22 Raymond of Aguilers, pp. 68–72, 75–6, 118–19; Hagenmeyer, *Kreuzzugsbriefe*, pp. 159, 163, 166, 178; *Gesta Francorum*, pp. 59–60, 65; Peter Tudebode, pp. 100–1, 107–8; Fulcher of Chartres, pp. 235–7; Ralph of Caen, pp. 676–7. For eastern accounts, see Matthew of Edessa, pp. 41–2; Ibn al-Athir 1, p. 195; 'Anonymous Syriac Chronicle', p. 72.

23 Fulcher of Chartres, pp. 237–8; Albert of Aachen, p. 452; Raymond of Aguilers, p. 85; Ralph of Caen, pp. 677–9. For other accusations of avarice, see Raymond of Aguilers, p. 131.

24 Fulcher of Chartres, pp. 236–7; Raymond of Aguilers, pp. 72, 84–5, 89, 116–20, 127–8; Ralph of Caen, pp. 676–8; Bartolf of Nangis, p. 507.

25 Raymond of Aguilers, pp. 81–2; Caffaro, p. 108; Orderic Vitalis 5, p. 110. See 'Anonymous Syriac Chronicle', p. 72.

26 Hagenmeyer, *Kreuzzugsbriefe*, pp. 160, 167; *Gesta Francorum*, p. 68; Peter Tudebode, p. 110; Albert of Aachen, pp. 422, 426; Robert

the Monk, pp. 829, 834; Baldric of Bourgueil, p. 75; Guibert of Nogent, 'Gesta', p. 205; 'Historia peregrinorum', p. 205; Gilo, p. 773; *Chronique de Saint-Maixent*, p. 162.

27 Caffaro, p. 109; *La Chanson d'Antioche*, 1, pp. 384–91, 439.

28 Guibert of Nogent, 'Gesta' pp. 217–18, 252; 'Pancharta Caduniensis seu Historia sancti Sudarii Jesu Christi', *RHC Oc.* 5, pp. 299–301; Maurice of Neufmoustier, pp. 809, 824. See J. Riley-Smith, 'An Approach to Crusading Ethics', *Reading Medieval Studies*, 6 (1980), pp. 14–15. But cf C. Morris, 'Policy and Visions. The Case of the Holy Lance at Antioch', *War and Goverment in the Middle Ages. Essays in Honour of J.O. Prestwich* (1984), pp. 33–45.

29 Hagenmeyer, *Kreuzzugsbriefe*, pp. 163, 169–70, 174; Raymond of Aguilers, pp. 81–2; Guibert of Nogent, 'Gesta', p. 252; Albert of Aachen, p. 426.

30 Albert of Aachen, p. 435; *La Chanson d'Antioche*, 1, p. 473. See Guibert of Nogent, 'Gesta', p. 218.

31 See below pp. 116–17.

32 Raymond of Aguilers, pp. 88, 99, 116–20.

33 Raymond of Aguilers, p. 98.

34 Raymond of Aguilers, pp. 119–24, 128–9; Fulcher of Chartres, pp. 238–40; Peter Tudebode, p. 131 note; Albert of Aachen, p. 452; Ralph of Caen, p. 682; Guibert of Nogent, 'Gesta', pp. 217–18; *La Chanson d'Antioche*, 1, pp. 479–80.

35 Fulcher of Chartres, pp. 240–1; Ralph of Caen, pp. 682–3; Albert of Aachen, pp. 452, 475; 'Historia peregrinorum', p. 216.

36 Ralph of Caen, pp. 682–3; Fulcher of Chartres, p. 241; Raymond of Aguilers, pp. 71, 153, 156; Peter Tudebode, pp. 145–6.

37 Caffaro, p. 112; Albert of Aachen, p. 568; Matthew of Edessa, p. 47; Anselm of Gembloux, 'Sigeberti Gemblacensis Continuatio', *MGHS* 6, p. 379; Lambert of Ardres, p. 626.

38 Hagenmeyer, *Kreuzzugsbriefe*, p. 178; Fulcher of Chartres, pp. 309–10; Peter Tudebode, pp. 145–6; Raymond of Aguilers, p. 154; Albert of Aachen, pp. 488–9, 491–3; A. Frolow, *La Relique de la vraie croix* (1961), pp. 68–70, 286–90, 347–9; Riley-Smith, 'Peace never established', pp. 91–3.

39 Raymond of Aguilers, pp. 56–7, 82, 158.

40 Hagenmeyer, *Kreuzzugsbriefe*, p. 171; *Gesta Francorum*, p. 90; Peter Tudebode, p. 139; Fulcher of Chartres, p. 299.

41 *La Chanson d'Antioche*, 1, p. 211; Ralph of Caen, pp. 657–8; 'Historia peregrinorum', p. 216; Raymond of Aguilers, pp. 102, 130, 135–6, 158; Hagenmeyer, *Kreuzzugsbriefe*, pp. 172–3; Peter Tudebode, p. 146.

42 Albert of Aachen, p. 403; Raymond of Aguilers, pp. 62, 82; Ralph of Caen, p. 674; Hagenmeyer, *Kreuzzugsbriefe*, p. 173.

43 See Hagenmeyer, *Kreuzzugsbriefe*, pp. 142, 147.

44 Hagenmeyer, *Kreuzzugsbriefe*, pp. 138–40; and see pp. 144, 146, 148, 150, 157, 160, 166, 168, 176; also *Gesta Francorum*, pp. 11, 14,

16, 82, 86; Peter Tudebode, pp. 69, 79, 117, 126, 129, 131–2; Fulcher of Chartres, pp. 139, 215, 252, 308; Raymond of Aguilers, pp. 35, 37, 54, 59, 84, 100.

45 Fulcher of Chartres, p. 256. See *Gesta Francorum*, pp. 53–6; Peter Tudebode, pp. 94–6; Raymond of Aguilers, pp. 78, 134, 146; Hagenmeyer, *Kreuzzugsbriefe*, p. 150; Fulcher of Chartres, pp. 117, 227.

46 Raymond of Aguilers, pp. 35, 41, 45, 58, 62, 67, 73, 82–3, 97, 100, 127, 138–9, 144–5; Hagenmeyer, *Kreuzzugsbriefe*, pp. 147, 150–1, 159, 163–5, 167, 169; *Gesta Francorum*, pp. 15, 41, 58, 96; Peter Tudebode, p. 99; Fulcher of Chartres, pp. 118, 220–1, 230.

47 Raymond of Aguilers, pp. 57, 73; and see pp. 43, 60, 63–5, 67, 73, 88, 101, 108, 125, 139; *Gesta Francorum*, pp. 21, 40, 56, 96; Peter Tudebode, p. 146; Fulcher of Chartres, p. 198; Hagenmeyer, *Kreuzzugsbriefe*, pp. 142, 151.

48 Raymond of Aguilers, pp. 60, 94, 106, 124, 126–7, 148, 154, 157; Hagenmeyer, *Kreuzzugsbriefe*, pp. 169–70; Peter Tudebode, p. 138.

49 Hagenmeyer, *Kreuzzugsbriefe*, p. 170.

50 *Gesta Francorum*, pp. 53–4.

51 Raymond of Aguilers, p. 37; Fulcher of Chartres, p. 223; *Gesta Francorum*, p. 78; Peter Tudebode, p. 122. See also Raymond of Aguilers, pp. 58, 62.

52 Hagenmeyer, *Kreuzzugsbriefe*, p. 147.

53 Psalms 85:9 (the crusade on the march): Fulcher of Chartres, p. 162. Deuteronomy 11:24–5 (or Joshua 1:4–5) and Psalms 67:31 (the invincibility of the crusaders); *Gesta Francorum*, p. 54. Psalms 78:6 (God's punishment of the infidels): *Gesta Francorum*, p. 54; Peter Tudebode, p. 94. Psalms 131:7 (the liberation of the Holy Sepulchre): Fulcher of Chartres, p. 162. Raymond of Aguilers also made reference to an unidentifiable promise by Christ to Our Lady and the apostles that he would raise the kingdom of the Christians and throw down the rule of the pagans and to prophecies in an apocryphal Gospel of St Peter. Raymond of Aguilers, pp. 78, 118, 130. Matthew of Edessa (pp. 24, 44) saw the crusade as the fulfilment of a prophecy of the fourth-century Armenian saint, Nerses. See also *Gesta Francorum*, p. 55; Peter Tudebode, p. 95.

54 Hagenmeyer, *Kreuzzugsbreife*, p. 168.

55 Hagenmeyer, *Kreuzzugsbriefe*, p. 178.

56 Raymond of Aguilers (pp. 95, 144) called them *legati*.

57 Raymond of Aguilers, pp. 46, 68–9; Hagenmeyer, *Kreuzzugsbriefe*, p. 142.

58 Hagenmeyer, *Kreuzzugsbriefe*, p. 142; *Gesta Francorum*, pp. 58–9; Peter Tudebode, p. 100; Raymond of Aguilers, pp. 74, 118–9.

59 I have not included two very dubious ones. Fulcher of Chartres, who was not an Antioch at the time, reported (pp. 231–2) that before 2 June 1098 a captain called Firuz had been ordered to surrender the city in three separate visions. This story, or variants of it, found its way into later accounts (Bartolf of Nangis, p. 499; Robert the Monk, pp. 796–8; *La Chanson d'Antioche*, 1, pp. 290–1), but was not

reported by those who ought to have known (*Gesta Francorum*, pp. 44–8; Peter Tudebode, pp. 82–8; Ralph of Caen, p. 652) and was considered doubtful by Guibert of Nogent ('Gesta', p. 251). Even more unlikely was a message supposedly sent by Christ to Godfrey of Bouillon in the spring of 1099, urging him to push on to Jerusalem. *La Chanson d'Antioche*, 1, p. 481. For another dubious vision, see *La Chanson d'Antioche*, 1, p. 287.

60 *Gesta Francorum*, pp. 57–8; Peter Tudebode, pp. 98–101, 110, 112; Raymond of Aguilers, pp. 72–4, 112, 118; Fulcher of Chartres, pp. 245–6; *La Chanson d'Antioche*, 1, pp. 354–5. *Congregati sunt* was an introit in a votive mass for times of war included in the Rheims Processional.

61 Raymond of Aguilers, pp. 112–16. For Peter's loss of his knowledge of letters, see Raymond of Aguilers, p. 76.

62 Raymond of Aguilers, p. 123.

63 Raymond of Aguilers, pp. 68–71, 75–6, 84–8, 90–1.

64 Raymond of Aguilers, pp. 112–13.

65 Raymond of Aguilers, pp. 89, 113, 119, 127, 131–2.

66 For Agatha: Raymond of Aguilers, p. 127. For Nicholas: Raymond of Aguilers, pp. 116–17. For Mark: Raymond of Aguilers, p. 118. We can ignore the references to the archangel Michael and St Denis, who play parts in *La Chanson d'Antioche* (1, pp. 211, 262–3; 'Fragment d'une Chanson d'Antioche', p. 477), perhaps because French audiences would have expected them. We can also put aside references to appearances by SS Maurice and Theodore. See J. Riley-Smith, 'The First Crusade and St Peter', *Outremer*, ed. Kedar, Mayer and Smail, p. 53.

67 Hagenmeyer, *Kreuzzugsbriefe*, p. 137.

68 See Raymond of Aguilers, pp. 51, 58; also *Gesta Francorum*, p. 32. Peter Tudebode, p. 67.

69 10 June 1098; Raymond of Aguilers, pp. 73–4; *Gesta Francorum*, pp. 57–8; Peter Tudebode, pp. 98–9; *La Chanson d'Antioche*, 1, pp. 354–6. Early April 1099: Raymond of Aguilers, pp. 123–4. Mid-April 1099; Raymond of Aguilers, pp. 127–8. For other references, see Raymond of Aguilers, pp. 78, 117, 134; 'Historia peregrinorum', pp. 204–5; *La Chanson d'Antioche*, 1, p. 184.

70 Hagenmeyer, *Kreuzzugsbriefe*, p. 164.

71 Riley-Smith, 'The First Crusade and St Peter', *passim*.

72 Raymond of Aguilers, pp. 45–6; Bartolf of Nangis, p. 496; 'Historia peregrinorum', pp. 173, 183. Note the development in 'Chronica monasterii Casinensis', p. 480.

73 Hagenmeyer, *Kreuzzugsbriefe*, p. 147.

74 Hagenmeyer, *Kreuzzugsbriefe*, p. 147; *Gesta Francorum*, p. 69; Peter Tudebode, pp. 100, 112; Metcalf, *Coinage*, p. 8; L. Réau, *Iconographie de l'art chrétien* (1955–8), 3, 2, p. 578. To Réau's list should be added two representations in the south of England, a wall-painting in Hardham church, Sussex, and a sculpted tympanum at Fordington church, Dorset. For the Battle of Antioch, see R.C. Smail, *Crusading*

Warfare (1097–1193) (1956), pp. 172–4. For an earlier and similar manifestation of St George in Sicily, see Erdmann, *The Origin*, pp. 134–5.

75 Raymond of Aguilers, pp. 131–4, 136; *Gesta Francorum*, p. 87; Peter Tudebode, pp. 133–4.

76 Raymond of Aguilers, pp. 69–70, 77–8, 86–8, 90–1, 95–8, 121–2, 124, 131. See Peter Tudebode, p. 122; *La Chanson d'Antioche*, 1, p. 479.

77 See Fulcher of Chartres, p. 136.

78 Raymond of Aguilers, p. 151.

79 Fulcher of Chartres, pp. 132–4; Raymond of Aguilers, p. 129.

80 Hagenmeyer, *Kreuzzugsbriefe*, pp. 141–2, 146–9, 164; Raymond of Aguilers, pp. 117–18. Cf. Lilie, *Byzanz*, pp. 36, 44–53.

81 Raymond of Aguilers, p. 38; Fulcher of Chartres, pp. 132–3; *Gesta Francorum*, pp. 13, 25; Peter Tudebode, pp. 47, 59.

82 Ibn al-Athir 1, p. 193. See also *Gesta Francorum*, p. 66; Peter Tudebode, p. 108; Hagenmeyer, *Kreuzzugsbriefe*, p. 160.

83 Hagenmeyer, *Kreuzzugsbriefe*, p. 164; Peter Tudebode, pp. 31–2, 40, 43, 60, 69, 79, 112, 114–15, 118–19, 125–6, 134–7, 146; Fulcher of Chartres, p. 306; Raymond of Aguilers, pp. 145, 155; *Gesta Francorum*, pp. 1, 7, 12, 26, 37, 40–1, 62, 64, 70, 72, 75–7, 80–1, 90, 97.

84 Hagenmeyer, *Kreuzzugsbriefe*, p. 154; Peter Tudebode, pp. 121, 125, 128, 130, 145; *Gesta Francorum*, p. 92; Raymond of Aguilers, p. 151; Geoffrey Grossus, 'Vita Beati Bernardi abbatis Tironiensis', *RHGF* 14, p. 167. But cf Dupront, 'La spiritualité', pp. 449–83.

85 Hagenmeyer, *Kreuzzugsbriefe*, pp. 171–2.

86 Raymond of Aguilers, pp. 131, 136; J. Richard, *The Latin Kingdom of Jerusalem* (1979), 1, pp. 20–1.

87 'Historia peregrinorum', p. 181; *Gesta Francorum*, pp. 66, 83; Peter Tudebode, pp. 108, 128.

88 S.D. Goitein, 'Geniza Sources for the Crusader Period: A Survey', *Outremer*, ed. Kedar, Mayer and Smail, p. 308, and see pp. 306–14; S.D. Goitein, 'Contemporary Letters on the Capture of Jerusalem by the Crusaders', *Journal of Jewish Studies*, 3 (1952), pp. 162–7; S.D. Goitein, *A Mediterranean Society* (1967–78), 3, p. 356.

89 Fulcher of Chartres, p. 227. See also the story in Albert of Aachen (p. 319) about the Muslim scout whose captors suspected that fear rather than conviction was responsible for his conversion.

90 Robert the Monk, p. 840; Raymond of Aguilers, pp. 91–2. See *Gesta Francorum*, pp. 74–5; Peter Tudebode, p. 117; also Baldric of Bourgueil, pp. 82–3; Guibert of Nogent, 'Gesta', p. 210; 'Historia peregrinorum', p. 207; Orderic Vitalis 5, p. 134; Riley-Smith, 'The First Crusade and the Persecution of the Jews', pp. 64–6.

91 *Gesta Francorum*, pp. 73–4; Peter Tudebode, pp. 115–16; Kamal ad-Din, 'Chronicle of Aleppo', *RHC Or.* 3, p. 584. See Robert the Monk, p. 838.

92 *Gesta Francorum*, p. 71; Peter Tudebode, pp. 113–14. For a correct distinction between the just war against pagans and the use of force

against heretics, see the letter from the leaders. Hagenmeyer, *Kreuzzugsbriefe*, p. 164.

93 *Gesta Francorum*, p. 21; Peter Tudebode, p. 55.
94 Peter Tudebode, pp. 54, 66–7; *Gesta Francorum*, pp. 22, 29, 62, 66–7, 73; Hagenmeyer, *Kreuzzugsbriefe*, pp. 150–1; Raymond of Aguilers, p. 43; Fulcher of Chartres, p. 318.
95 *Gesta Francorum*, pp. 66–7; Peter Tudebode, pp. 109, 137; Raymond of Aguilers, p. 155.
96 Fulcher of Chartres, p. 227; *Gesta Francorum*, p. 41.
97 *Gesta Francorum*, pp. 22, 32, 40, 62, 66, 96; Peter Tudebode, pp. 51, 55, 66, 74, 81, 103, 108, 114, 144–5; Hagenmeyer, *Kreuzzugsbriefe*, p. 150.
98 Fulcher of Chartres, p. 135; Hagenmeyer, *Kreuzzugsbriefe*, p. 171; *Gesta Francorum*, pp. 42, 75.
99 Raymond of Aguilers, p. 149.
100 Hagenmeyer, *Kreuzzugsbriefe*, p. 144; *Gesta Francorum*, pp. 9, 23–4, 29, 37, 40, 60, 66; Peter Tudebode, pp. 33, 44, 73, 104, 125; Raymond of Aguilers, pp. 37, 51, 137, 141, 148; Fulcher of Chartres, p. 141.
101 Hagenmeyer, *Kreuzzugsbriefe*, p. 144.
102 Hagenmeyer, *Kreuzzugsbriefe*, p. 150; *Gesta Francorum*, pp. 11, 18–19, 23–4, 33, 70, 73, 89, 96; Peter Tudebode, pp. 39, 44, 58, 69, 81, 112, 115, 123, 129, 134–5, 140, 145–6; Fulcher of Chartres, p. 136; Raymond of Aguilers, p. 60.
103 Hagenmeyer, *Kreuzzugsbriefe*, pp. 145–6; Fulcher of Chartres, pp. 118, 202–3.
104 Raymond of Aguilers, pp. 79, 83, 89.
105 Fulcher of Chartres, p. 116 and, of course, the title of the *Gesta Francorum*.
106 Raymond of Aguilers, pp. 79–80, 103; Fulcher of Chartres, pp. 118, 318.
107 Ekkehard of Aura, 'Hierosolymita', p. 19; Ralph of Caen, pp. 627, 633; 'Genealogiae comitum Flandriae', p. 308; 'Genealogia comitum Buloniensium', *MGHS* 9, pp. 300–1; 'Genealogiae Aquicinctinae', *MGHS* 14, pp. 620–2; William of Malmesbury 2, pp. 400, 431; Orderic Vitalis 5, pp. 118, 174; *Gesta Francorum*, p. 2; Peter Tudebode, p. 33; also Robert the Monk, p. 732. See K.F. Werner, 'Die Nachkommen Karls des Grossen bis um Jahr 1000', *Karl der Grosse*, ed. W. Braunfels and P.E. Schramm (1965–8), 4, pp. 403–79; R. Folz, *Le Souvenir et la légende de Charlemagne dans l'empire germanique médiéval* (1950), pp. 137–42.
108 Raymond of Aguilers, p. 154. See also Hagenmeyer, *Kreuzzugsbriefe*, pp. 148–9; Fulcher of Chartres, pp. 226–7, 306; Raymond of Aguilers, pp. 70, 103.
109 Raymond of Aguilers, p. 108.
110 *Gesta Francorum*, p. 64; Peter Tudebode, p. 106.
111 Hagenmeyer, *Kreuzzugsbriefe*, p. 157.
112 Hagenmeyer, *Kreuzzugsbriefe*, p. 169.

113 *Gesta Francorum*, pp. 34, 58, 74; Peter Tudebode, pp. 69, 99, 116; Raymond of Aguilers, pp. 35, 51, 54, 61–2, 68, 108, 141, 144, 155–6.
114 Fulcher of Chartres, p. 226. See *Gesta Francorum*, pp. 1–2; Peter Tudebode, p. 32; Raymond of Aguilers, p. 41.
115 Raymond of Aguilers, p. 138.
116 Forez 1, no. 1, p. 1; Hagenmeyer, *Kreuzzugsbriefe*, p. 142; Raymond of Aguilers, pp. 47, 134; *Gesta Francorum*, p. 7; Peter Tudebode, p. 40.
117 Fulcher of Chartres, pp. 115–17, 163, 203, 212; *Gesta Francorum*, pp.1, 74; Peter Tudebode, pp. 31, 46, 116; Hagenmeyer, *Kreuzzugsbriefe*, pp. 164, 178–9; Raymond of Aguilers, p. 117. For sadness at leaving wives and children, see Fulcher of Chartres, pp. 162–3; Guibert of Nogent, 'Gesta', p. 221; Baldric of Bourgueil, p. 17; *La Chanson d'Antioche*, 1, pp. 55. 303.
118 *Gesta Francorum*, pp. 15, 19–20, 31, 37, 40, 68, 70, 83; Peter Tudebode, pp. 72, 111–12, 129; Fulcher of Chartres, pp. 140–1.
119 Hagenmeyer, *Kreuzzugzbriefe*, pp. 142, 160, 165, 175–6; Robert the Monk, pp. 729–30; Bernold of St Blasien, p. 464; Guibert of Nogent, 'Gesta', p. 125.
120 Hagenmeyer, *Kreuzzugsbriefe*, p. 179; Fulcher of Chartres, p. 203.
121 Guibert of Nogent, 'Gesta', p. 179. See Fulcher of Chartres, p. 117; Peter Tudebode, pp. 80–1. *Cf.* H.E.J. Cowdrey, 'Martyrdom and the First Crusade', *Crusade and Setlement*, pp. 46–56.
122 Hagenmeyer, *Kreuzzugsbriefe*, pp. 164, 176; *Gesta Francorum*, p. 74; Peter Tudebode, pp. 116–17; Raymond of Aguilers, p. 84; Fulcher of Chartres, p. 258; Robert the Monk, p. 839; Guibert of Nogent, 'Gesta', p. 210; Baldric of Bourgueil, p. 82; Bartolf of Nangis, p. 506; Ralph of Caen, p. 673; 'Historia peregrinorum', p. 207. See also Albert of Aachen, p. 416.
123 Peter Tudebode, pp. 79–81; *La Chanson d'Antioche*, 1, pp. 205, 212–33, 2, pp. 198–9, 212–14. For other martyrs in this category, see *Gesta Francorum*, p. 4; Peter Tudebode, pp. 35–6, 138.
124 'Historia peregrinorum', p. 198. For other martyrs of this type, see Hagenmeyer, *Kreuzzugsbriefe*, pp. 150, 153–4, 176; *Gesta Francorum*, pp. 4, 17, 40, 85; Peter Tudebode, pp. 75, 131; Raymond of Aguilers, pp. 108–9, 119.
125 'Liber de poenitentia et tentationibus religiosorum', *PL* 213, col. 893. See Riley-Smith, 'Death on the First Crusade', pp. 20–2.
126 Baldric of Bourgueil, p. 15; Guibert of Nogent, 'Gesta', p. 138. For a later reference, see William of Malmesbury 2, p. 396.
127 Hagenmeyer, *Kreuzzugsbriefe*, pp. 145, 148, 150–1, 154; also pp. 153, 176. Note the promise made by Christ in the Greek patriarch's vision that labourers on the crusade would be crowned on the Last Day. Hagenmeyer, *Kreuzzugsbriefe*, p. 142.
128 Peter Tudebode, p. 100; Raymond of Aguilers, p. 78.
129 Fulcher of Chartres, pp. 246–7; Bartolf of Nangis, p. 502.
130 Raymond of Aguilers, pp. 84–6, 116–17, 119, 123–4, 127–8, 143–4, 151. Adhémar appeared to Peter Bartholomew, Bertrand of Bas, Stephen of Valence and Peter Desiderius.

131 Raymond of Aguilers, pp. 119–20. For his departure from France, see Chamalières, pp. 16–18.
132 Raymond of Aguilers, pp. 108–9; Ralph of Caen, pp. 680–1; 'Historia peregrinorum', p. 215.
133 Riley-Smith, 'The First Crusade and St Peter', pp. 58–63.
134 Anselm of Canterbury 3, p. 254; Hagenmeyer, *Kreuzzugsbriefe*, p. 164.
135 Wiederhold, 'Papsturkunden', p. 313; *Gesta Francorum*, p. 37.

Chapter 5   The crusade of 1101

1 *Gesta Francorum*, p. 72; Fulcher of Chartres, p. 258; Guibert of Nogent, 'Gesta', p. 208; Baldric of Bourgueil, pp. 79–80; Orderic Vitalis 5, p. 128.
2 Orderic Vitalis 5, pp. 268, 324.
3 Suger of St Denis, p. 36. See *Gesta Francorum*, pp. 56–7; Peter Tudebode, pp. 97–8; Ralph of Caen, p. 650; 'Historia peregrinorum', pp. 200–1; Guibert of Nogent, 'Gesta', p. 194; Baldric of Bourgueil, pp. 64–5; Orderic Vitalis 5, p. 98.
4 'Ex miraculis sancti Donatiani Brugensibus', *MGHS* 15, 2, p. 858. See 'Annales Blandinienses', p. 27.
5 'Gesta Ambaziensium dominorum', pp. 99–102; Marmoutier, pp. 40–1. See Baldric of Bourgueil, pp. 21 note, 33 note, 65 note.
6 Orderic Vitalis 5, p. 300; St Julian of Tours (L.J. Denis, *Chartes de St-Julien de Tours* (1912)), pp. 72–3.
7 Cluny 5, pp. 117–18; David, *Robert Curthose*, p. 226; Orderic Vitalis 4, p. 308.
8 Riley-Smith, 'The motives', p. 731 note 9; *Dictionnaire de biographie française*, 9, cols 867–8.
9 'Genealogiae comitum Flandriae', pp. 311, 323, 336 (and 306 with reference to Robert's father); 'Genealogiae breves regum Francorum', pp. 250, 257, 259; 'Annales Blandinienses', p. 27; Hermann, p. 313; Walter of Thérouanne, p. 540; Henry of Huntingdon, *Historia Anglorum*, ed. T. Arnold (1879), p. 238; 'Historia monasterii Aquicinctini', p. 586.
10 See for example Savigny (A. Bernard, *Cartulaire de l'abbaye de Savigny* (1853)) 1, p. 478; Vézelay (R.B.C. Huygens, *Monumenta Vizeliacensia* (1976)), p. 508. For the adoption of the cognomen by Hugh of Lusignan after the crusade of 1101, see abbé Cousseau, 'Mémoire historique sur l'église de Nôtre-Dame de Lusignan et ses fondateurs', *Mémoires de la société des antiquaires de l'Ouest* (1844), pp. 310–22, 401.
11 Lambert of Ardres, pp. 626–7.
12 William of Malmesbury 2, p. 461; Henry of Huntingdon, 'De captione Antiochiae a Christianis', *RHC Oc.* 5, p. 379.
13 Lambert of Ardres, p. 615. Or did these events occur before the crusade?

14   Fulcher of Chartres, pp. 301–5, 316–18; *Gesta Francorum*, pp. 91–2, 95, 97; Peter Tudebode, pp. 141, 148–9. See Ibn al-Athir 1, pp. 199, 202.

15   Fulcher of Chartres, pp. 302–3; Ralph of Caen, pp. 695–703; Ibn al-Athir 1, p. 199. See J. Prawer, *Crusader Institutions* (1980), pp. 85–101.

16   Orderic Vitalis 5, pp. 270–6; Albert of Aachen, pp. 499–504.

17   Suger of St Denis, p. 38. See Albert of Aachen, p. 563. For another crusader bringing home relics after the 1101 crusade, see *Chronicon sancti Petri Vivi Senonensis*, pp. 184–8.

18   Hagenmeyer, *Kreuzzugsbriefe*, pp. 142–3; 'Historia monasterii Aquicinctini', p. 586; 'Annales Aquicinctini', *MGHS* 16, p. 503; 'Sigeberti Gemblacensis chronica auctarium Aquicinense', p. 395; 'Narratio quomodo', pp. 248–52; 'Genealogiae comitum Flandriae', p. 323; Orderic Vitalis 5, p. 170; *Chronique de Saint-Maixent*, p. 170; *Liber memorandorum ecclesie de Bernewelle*, ed. J.W. Clark (1907), pp. 46–7, 54, 55; Redon, pp. 318–21; Lambert of Ardres, p. 626; Maurice of Neufmoustier, pp. 815, 821; Giles of Orval, 'Gesta episcoporum Leodiensium', *MGHS* 25, p. 93; 'Historia de translatione', pp. 260–81; 'Qualiter reliquiae B. Nicolai episcopi et confessoris ad Lotharingiae villam, quae Portus nominatur, delatae sunt', *RHC Oc. 5*, pp. 293–4. For Pagan Peverel, see S. Edgington, 'Pagan Peverel: An Anglo-Norman Crusader', *Crusade and Settlement*, pp. 90–93. For Peter the Hermit, see H. Hagenmeyer, *Peter der Eremite* (1879), pp. 280–91.

19   Aureil, p. 126; Redon, p. 318; 'Gesta Ambaziensium dominorum', p. 101.

20   Cluny 5, p. 152; St Andrew of Vienne, pp. 207–8; Gilbert 'Chronicon Hanoniense', *MGHS* 21, p. 504.

21   See 'Chronicon sancti Andreae castri Cameracesii', *MGHS* 7, p. 545; Brinkmann, *Entstehungsgeschichte*, pp. 71–2. For the dating of charters by these events, see Grenoble, pp. 80, 112, 136–7, 154.

22   W. Wattenbach, 'Handschriftliches', *Neues Archiv*, 7 (1881–2), pp. 625–6. See also Hehl, *Kirche und Krieg*, pp. 13–20; P. Knoch, 'Kreuzzug und Siedlung. Studien zum Aufruf der Magdeburger Kirche von 1108', *Jahrbuch für die Geschichte Mittel- und Ostdeutschlands*, 23 (1974), pp. 1–33.

23   Kehr, *Italia pontificia*, 6, 1, p. 54; Riant, 'Inventaire', pp. 192–3, 195; Landulf the Younger, p. 22.

24   Paschal II, 'Epistolae et Privilegia', *PL* 163, col. 108. See Hehl, *Kirche und Krieg*, pp. 13–14; N. Housley, 'Crusades Against Christians: their origins and early development, c.1000–1216', *Crusade and Settlement*, p. 20.

25   J. Goñi Gaztambide, *Historia de la Bula de la Cruzada en España* (1958), pp. 64–6.

26   Hagenmeyer, *Kreuzzugsbriefe*, pp. 178–9.

27   Hagenmeyer, *Kreuzzugsbriefe*, pp. 174–6; Hugh of Flavigny, p. 487; Orderic Vitalis 5, pp. 322–4.

28 Molesme 2, pp. 63–5, 84.
29 For Simon and William, see Orderic Vitalis 5, pp. 29, 39, 346. For the deaths of the two Walters, see Orderic Vitalis 5, pp. 29, 31, 39; Fulcher of Chartres, p. 159; Albert of Aachen, p. 288.
30 Orderic Vitalis 5, pp. 268, 280, 322.
31 *Chronique de Saint-Maixent*, p. 172.
32 Hugh of Flavigny, p. 487. For his preparations for departure, see Savigny 1, pp. 433–4.
33 William of Malmesbury 2, p. 447. See J.L. Cate, 'The Crusade of 1101', *A History of the Crusades*, ed.-in-chief K.M. Setton, 2nd edn (1969), 1, pp. 346–51.
34 Landulf the Younger, p. 22.
35 Hagenmeyer, *Kreuzzugsbriefe*, pp. 175–6; Geoffry of Châlard, 'Dictamen de primordiis ecclesiae Castaliensis', *RHC Oc.* 5, p. 348.
36 Cluny 5, pp. 87–8.
37 St Benignus of Dijon 2, p. 171.
38 Cluny 5, p. 108.
39 Cluny 5, p. 89; St Benignus of Dijon 2, p. 172; 'Chronica prioratus de Casa-Vicecomitis', ed. P. Marchegay and É. Mabille, *Chroniques des églises d'Anjou* (1869), p. 341.
40 Gellone (P. Alaus, L. Cassan and E. Meynial, *Cartulaire de Gellone* (1898)), p. 248. For the death of Bernard Raymond of Béziers, see Raymond of Aguilers, p. 51.
41 Albert of Aachen, pp. 563, 568, 573. For the death of Raynald of Broyes, see Albert of Aachen, p. 288.
42 'Gesta Ambaziensium dominorum', pp. 102–3. For the death of her husband Aimery of Courron, see 'Gesta Ambaziensium dominorum', p. 101.
43 Baldric of Bourgueil, p. 15.
44 Orderic Vitalis 5, pp. 324, 346; Albert of Aachen, pp. 563, 568, 573; Suger of St Denis, p. 38. Miles had already been on the First Crusade. Orderic Vitalis 5, p. 30.
45 'Historia Welforum Weingartensis', *MGHS* 21, p. 462.
46 St Benignus of Dijon 2, pp. 174–6 (and see p. 180). See St Martin of Pontoise (J. Depoin, *Cartulaire de l'abbaye de Saint-Martin de Pontoise* (1895)), p. 21; also Cate, 'The Crusade of 1101', pp. 349–50.
47 Landulf the Younger, p. 22; Geoffrey of Châlard, p. 349.
48 Orderic Vitalis 5, pp. 280, 324; *RHGF* 11, pp. 157–8; St Laon of Thouars (H. Imbert, *Cartulaire de l'abbaye de Saint-Laon de Thouars* (Niort, n.d.)), p. 32. William of Aquitaine may have renounced his claims to Toulouse in exchange for cash from Raymond of St Gilles. See Robert of Torigni, *Chronica*, ed. R. Howlett (1889), p. 202.
49 St Benignus of Dijon 2, p. 172; Marcigny (J. Richard, *Le Cartulaire de Marcigny-sur-Loire* (1957), pp. 164–5.
50 Molesme 2, pp. 13, 18, 40–3, 143 (and see p. 12); Cluny 5, p. 89; Gellone, p. 248.
51 'Chronica prioratus de Casa-Vicecomitis', p. 341. See also St Benignus of Dijon 2, p. 172.

52 'Narratio Floriacensis', p. 360.
53 Orderic Vitalis 5, p. 322.
54 Fulcher of Chartres, p. 432; Albert of Aachen, pp. 572, 577–8.
55 Orderic Vitalis 5, pp. 328–34.
56 Albert of Aachen, p. 563. See Anna Comnena 3, pp. 36–7.
57 Guibert of Nogent, 'Gesta', p. 244; Albert of Aachen, p. 568.
58 See Albert of Aachen, p. 563; also 'Notae sanctae Mariae Mediolan-
    enses', *MGHS* 18, p. 385; Anna Comnena 3, p. 36; 'Anonymous Syriac
    Chronicle', p. 74.
59 Ekkehard of Aura, 'Hierosolymita', p. 30.
60 Albert of Aachen, p. 580; 'Chronica prioratus de Casa-Vicecomitis',
    p. 342; 'Narratio Floriacensis', p. 361; Matthew of Edessa, pp. 56,
    59–60. See Orderic Vitalis 5, p. 270.
61 For Corba, see 'Gesta Ambaziensium dominorum', pp. 102–3.
62 Orderic Vitalis 5, p. 340; Fulcher of Chartres, pp. 432–3, 436–7. See
    William of Malmesbury 2, p. 448.
63 'Chronica prioratus de Casa-Vicecomitis', pp. 342–3.
64 Guibert of Nogent, 'Gesta', pp. 244–5; Albert of Aachen, p. 544;
    Orderic Vitalis 5, pp. 350–2.
65 Otto of Freising, *Chronica*, ed. A. Hofmeister (1912), p. 317.
66 See my forthcoming 'The Venetian Crusade of 1122–24'.
67 Urban II, cols 288, 332, 370; also col. 380.
68 Baldric of Bourgueil, p. 71.
69 Baldric of Bourgueil, p. 82.
70 Orderic Vitalis 5, p. 132.
71 Fulcher of Chartres, p. 433.
72 Geoffrey of Breuil, p. 430.
73 Baldric of Bourgueil, p. 95; Orderic Vitalis 5, p. 154.

Chapter 6   Theological refinement

1   It has been suggested that Robert the Monk visited the East, but it is
    very unlikely that he did so.
2   *RHC Oc.* 3, pp. xli–lv; Knoch, 'Kreuzzug und Siedlung', pp. 10–21.
3   *RHC Oc.* 4, pp. xv–xx; E.-R. Labande, intr. to Guibert of Nogent, *De
    vita sua*, pp. ix–xv; J. Chaurand, 'La conception de l'histoire de Guibert
    de Nogent', *Cahiers de civilisation médiévale*, 8 (1965), pp. 381–6.
4   *RHC Oc.* 4, pp. iii–xiv; *Dictionnaire de biographie française*, 5, cols
    903–4. On Robert, Guibert and Baldric, cf. L. Boehm, ' "Gesta Dei per
    Francos" – oder "Gesta Francorum". Die Kreuzzüge als historio-
    graphisches Problem', *Saeculum*, 8 (1957), pp. 43–81.
5   Orderic Vitalis 5, pp. 376, 378, 6, pp. 68–70 (and see p. 102, where
    Orderic suggested that there was no heavenly inspiration for this
    crusade, only greed); Ralph of Caen, pp. 713–14; 'Historia peregri-
    norum', pp. 228–9; Bartolf of Nangis, p. 538; Guibert of Nogent,
    'Gesta', p. 134; William of Malmesbury 2, p. 454; *Acta sanctorum.
    Novembris*, 3, pp. 160–8; *Chronique de Saint-Maixent*, p. 178; Suger

of St Denis, pp. 44–8; 'Chronicon Vindocinense seu de Aquaria', ed. P. Marchegay and É. Mabille, *Chroniques des églises d'Anjou* (1869), pp. 171–2; Holtzmann, 'Zur Geschichte', pp. 280–2.

6 Robert the Monk, pp. 721–2.
7 Guibert of Nogent, 'Gesta', pp. 119–20.
8 Baldric of Bourgueil, p. 10.
9 See G.T. Evans, *The Mind of St Bernard of Clairvaux* (1983), pp. 38–41.
10 Guibert of Nogent, 'Gesta', p. 124.
11 Baldric of Bourgueil, pp. 15, 19, 34–6, 52, 63, 66, 78–9, 92, 95, 103–4, 108–10; Guibert of Nogent, 'Gesta', pp. 138, 140, 154, 177, 195, 197, 204; Robert the Monk, pp. 747, 763–4, 771–2, 776–8, 780, 792, 801, 812, 836, 845, 854–5, 858, 866, 873, 876, 882.
12 Robert the Monk, p. 723.
13 Robert the Monk, pp. 765, 877–8; and see also pp. 788, 812–13.
14 Robert the Monk, p. 797.
15 Robert the Monk, p. 763.
16 Robert the Monk, p. 723.
17 Guibert of Nogent, 'Gesta', p. 250.
18 Guibert of Nogent, 'Gesta', p. 123.
19 Guibert of Nogent, 'Gesta', p. 241.
20 Guibert of Nogent, 'Gesta', p. 221.
21 Guibert of Nogent, 'Gesta', pp. 138, 207, 221; and see also pp. 120, 162, 192–4, 225, 232.
22 Guibert of Nogent, 'Gesta', pp. 138, 194, 207, 226, 232, 241, 247; Robert the Monk, pp. 728, 731, 747, 779, 812; Baldric of Bourgueil, pp. 14–16, 19, 28, 43, 64.
23 He referred only twice to prophecies: Psalms 44:4 (the invincibility of the crusaders); Canticles 1:4 (the march of the crusaders). Baldric of Bourgueil, pp. 15, 28.
24 Guibert of Nogent, 'Gesta', pp. 237–40. For other references to prophecies, see Guibert of Nogent, 'Gesta', pp. 124–5, 139, 192, 216, 237–8.
25 Robert the Monk, pp. 764, 880, 882. For other references to prophecies, see Robert the Monk, pp. 739–40, 813, 852, 869, 880.
26 Guibert of Nogent, 'Gesta', p. 238.
27 Robert the Monk, p. 880.
28 Robert the Monk, pp. 739, 852.
29 Robert the Monk, p. 882. See also Ekkehard of Aura, 'Hierosolymita', p. 38.
30 Guibert of Nogent, 'Gesta', pp. 138–9, 239. See McGinn, *Visions of the End*, p. 307 note 23; McGinn, 'Iter Sancti Sepulchri', pp. 47–8, 66–7. See above, pp. 34–5.
31 Baldric of Bourgueil, pp. 10, 17; Guibert of Nogent, 'Gesta', pp. 124, 223, 225, 229–30, 235; Robert the Monk, p. 741.
32 Robert the Monk, pp. 727, 734, 784, 828, 831, 869–71, 874, 876.
33 Robert the Monk, p. 812; and see p. 824; Guibert of Nogent, 'Gesta', pp. 192–3; Baldric of Bourgueil, p. 12.

34   Robert the Monk, p. 792.
35   Baldric of Bourgueil, p. 14.
36   Robert the Monk, p. 728; Guibert of Nogent, 'Gesta', pp. 139, 213; Baldric of Bourgueil, p. 9.
37   See above p. 110.
38   Guibert of Nogent, 'Gesta', p. 124. For another reference to right intention, see Guibert of Nogent, 'Gesta', p. 142.
39   Guibert of Nogent, 'Gesta', p. 138.
40   Baldric of Bourgueil, pp. 14, 34. See also perhaps Robert the Monk, p. 734.
41   Guibert of Nogent, 'Gesta', p. 178.
42   Robert the Monk, pp. 727–8, 792, 868; Guibert of Nogent, 'Gesta', pp. 131–2, 139–40; Baldric of Bourgueil, pp. 11–15.
43   For example, see Robert the Monk, pp. 743–4, 747, 749–50, 792; Guibert of Nogent, 'Gesta', pp. 133, 153–5; Baldric of Bourgueil, pp. 30–1.
44   Robert the Monk, pp. 758–9; and see p. 746.
45   Robert the Monk, pp. 747, 750–1; Guibert of Nogent, 'Gesta', pp. 132, 137.
46   Baldric of Bourgueil, pp. 12–13; and see also p. 74.
47   Robert the Monk, p. 792; and see p. 750; Guibert of Nogent, 'Gesta', p. 204; Baldric of Bourgueil, p. 74.
48   Guibert of Nogent, 'Gesta', p. 137–8; and see pp. 139–40, 237; Robert the Monk, pp. 881–2; Baldric of Bourgueil, pp. 14–15, 100.
49   Guibert of Nogent, 'Gesta', p. 138; Baldric of Bourgueil, p. 11.
50   Robert the Monk, pp. 729, 863; Baldric of Bourgueil, p. 11.
51   Baldric of Bourgueil, p. 14; Guibert of Nogent, 'Gesta', p. 137.
52   Guibert of Nogent, 'Gesta', pp. 137–8. See also Robert the Monk, pp. 729, 858–9, 863; Baldric of Bourgueil, pp. 13–14.
53   Robert the Monk, p. 728; and see pp. 727, 869–70, 882; Guibert of Nogent, 'Gesta', p. 138; Baldric of Bourgueil, pp. 9, 11–13, 40, 101, 103.
54   Baldric of Bourgueil, p. 101; and see pp. 14, 100; Robert the Monk, pp. 881–2.
55   Guibert of Nogent, 'Gesta', pp. 221, 225. See also Robert the Monk, p. 829.
56   Robert the Monk, pp. 723, 727, 882; Guibert of Nogent, 'Gesta', pp. 123, 192–3.
57   Robert the Monk, p. 741; and see pp. 765, 767, 792, 812, 855, 870; Guibert of Nogent, 'Gesta', pp. 174–5, 260; Baldric of Bourgueil, pp. 34, 46–7, 73, 91.
58   Robert the Monk, p. 723.
59   Baldric of Bourgueil, pp. 28–9.
60   Guibert of Nogent, 'Gesta', pp. 135–6; and see p. 125; Robert the Monk, p. 727.
61   Robert the Monk, p. 765.
62   Baldric of Bourgueil, p. 14. See also Robert the Monk, pp. 728, 748; Guibert of Nogent, 'Gesta', p. 138.

63 Guibert of Nogent, 'Gesta', p. 124.

64 Guibert of Nogent, 'Gesta', p. 221.

65 Guibert of Nogent, 'Gesta', p. 203.

66 Baldric of Bourgueil, pp. 28, 67; Robert the Monk, p. 781. See also Guibert of Nogent, 'Gesta', p. 243.

67 Guibert of Nogent, 'Gesta', pp. 124–5; and see pp. 123–4, 205–6; Robert the Monk, pp. 729–30, 739, 741, 747, 833, 882; Baldric of Bourgueil, pp. 9, 16.

68 Robert the Monk, pp. 728, 747, 850; Guibert of Nogent, 'Gesta', pp. 124, 141, 148–9, 161, 199, 201, 221, 235; Baldric of Bourgueil, p. 9.

69 Baldric of Bourgueil, p. 28.

70 Guibert of Nogent, 'Gesta', p. 221; and see pp. 123–4, 243; Robert the Monk, p. 829; Baldric of Bourgueil, pp. 9, 28–9, 45–6, 50, 54, 95; and also for other uses of the term 'brothers' for the participants by Baldric, pp. 19, 44, 67, 73, 79.

71 Baldric of Bourgueil, pp. 12–13, 15, 28, 44, 46.

72 Baldric of Bourgueil, p. 101, and see p. 16; Robert the Monk, p. 730; Guibert of Nogent, 'Gesta', p. 216. Ekkehard of Aura ('Hierosolymita', p. 39) was to state that they followed the way of the cross with Simon of Cyrene.

73 Guibert of Nogent, 'Gesta', p. 221; Baldric of Bourgueil, pp. 30, 44.

74 Robert the Monk, pp. 740, 792, 829–30; Guibert of Nogent, 'Gesta', pp. 161, 221.

75 Baldric of Bourgueil, pp. 15, 101; Guibert of Nogent, 'Gesta', p. 179.

76 Guibert of Nogent, 'Gesta', pp. 183–4. See also, for Matthew, Orderic Vitalis 5, p. 28.

Bibliography

Original sources

Acta sanctorum quotquot toto orbe coluntur, ed. Société des Bollandistes, 70 vols so far (1643 ff.).

J. Alberigo, P.-P. Joannou, C. Leonardi and P. Prodi, *Conciliorum Oecumenicorum Decreta* (1962).

Albert of Aachen, 'Historia Hierosolymitana', *RHC Oc.* 4.

Angers: C. Urseau, *Cartulaire noir de la cathédrale d'Angers* (1908).

Aniane: L. Cassan and E. Meynial, *Cartulaire d'Aniane* (1900).

Anna Comnena, *Alexiade*, ed. B. Leib, 4 vols (1937–76).

'Annales Altahenses maiores', *MGHS* 20.

'Annales Aquicinctini', *MGHS* 16.

'Annales Augustani', *MGHS* 3.

'Annales Blandinienses', *MGHS* 5.

'Annales Brunwilarenses', *MGHS* 1.

'Annales Casinenses', *MGHS* 19.

'Annales Corbeienses', *MGHS* 3.

'Annales Hildesheimenses', *MGHS* 3.

'Annales Parmenses minores', *MGHS* 18.

'Annales Pragenses', *MGHS* 3.

'Annales Rosenveldenses', *MGHS* 16.

'Annales Rotomagenses', ed. F. Liebermann, *Ungedruckte Anglo-Normannische Geschichtsquellen* (1879).

'Annales Sancti Albani Moguntini (Wirziburgenses), *MGHS* 2.

'Annales Sancti Dionysii Remenses', *MGHS* 13.

'Annales Sancti Disibodi', *MGHS* 17.

'Annales Sancti Pauli Virdunensis', *MGHS* 16.

'Annales Seligenstadenses', *MGHS* 17.

'Annalista Saxo', *MGHS* 6.

'Anonymi Florinensis brevis narratio belli sacri', *RHC Oc.* 5.

'Anonymous Syriac Chronicle', tr. A.S. Tritton, *Journal of the Royal Asiatic Society* (1933).

Anselm of Canterbury, *Opera omnia*, ed. F.S. Schmitt, 6 vols (1938–61).

Anselm of Gembloux, 'Sigeberti Gemblacensis Continuatio', *MGHS* 6.

Apt: N. Didier, H. Dubled and J. Barruol, *Cartulaire de l'église d'Apt* (1967),

Auch: C. Lacave la Plagne Barris, *Cartulaires du chapitre de l'église métropolitaine Sainte-Marie d'Auch* (1899).

Aureil: G. de Senneville, 'Cartulaire du prieuré d'Aureil', *Bulletin de la société archéologique et historique de Limousin*, 48 (1900).

Baldric of Bourgueil, 'Historia Jerosolimitana', *RHC Oc.* 4.

(Eliezer) Bar Nathan, 'Chronicle', tr. S. Eidelberg, *The Jews and the Crusaders* (1977).

(Solomon) Bar Simson, 'Chronicle', tr. S. Eidelberg, *The Jews and the Crusaders* (1977).

Bartolf of Nangis, 'Gesta Francorum Iherusalem expugnantium', *RHC Oc.* 3.

Bernold of St Blasien, 'Chronicon', *MGHS 5*.

Caffaro, 'De liberatione civitatum orientis', ed. L.T. Belgrano, *Annali Genovesi* (1890–1929), 1.

'Cantatorium Sancti Huberti', ed. Baron de Reiffenberg, *Monuments pour servir à l'histoire des provinces de Namur, de Hainault et de Luxembourg* (1844–74), 7.

'Catalogus imperatorum et pontificum Romanorum Cencianus', *MGHS 24*.

Chamalières: A. Chassaing, *Cartulaire de Chamalières-sur-Loire en Velay* (1895).

La Chanson d'Antioche, ed. S. Duparc-Quioc, 2 vols (1977–8).

'Chronica monasterii Casinensis', *MGHS 34*.

'Chronica monasterii de Hida juxta Wintoniam', ed. E. Edwards, *Liber monasterii de Hyda* (1866).

'Chronica prioratus de Casa-Vicecomitis', ed. P. Marchegay and É. Mabille, *Chroniques des églises d'Anjou* (1869).

'Chronicon monasterii sancti Petri Aniciensis', ed. C.U.J. Chevalier, *Collection de cartulaires dauphinois* (1884–91), 8, 1.

'Chronicon sancti Andreae castri Cameracesii', *MGHS 7*.

Chronicon sancti Petri Vivi Senonensis, ed. R.H. Bautier and M. Gilles (1979).

'Chronicon Vindocinense seu de Aquaria', ed. P. Marchegay and É. Mabille, *Chroniques des églises d'Anjou* (1869).

Chronique de Parcé, ed. H. de Berranger (1953).

La Chronique de Saint-Maixent, ed. J. Verdon (1979).

'Chronique de Zimmern', ed. H. Hagenmeyer, *AOL 2* (1884).

Cluny: A. Bernard and A. Bruel, *Recueil des chartes de l'abbaye de Cluny*, 6 . vols (1876–1903).

Cosmas of Prague, *Chronica Boemorum*, ed. B. Bretholz (1955).

L.V. Delisle, *Littérature latine et histoire du moyen âge* (1890).

G.M. Dreves *et al.*, *Analecta hymnica Medii Aevi*, 55 vols (1886–1922).

Eadmer, *Historia novorum in Anglia*, ed. M. Rule (1884).

Ekkehard of Aura, 'Chronicon universale', *MGHS 6*.

—— 'Hierosolymita', *RHC Oc. 5*.

'Ex miraculis sancti Donatiani Brugensibus', *MGHS 15*, 2.

Florence of Worcester, *Chronicon*, ed. B. Thorpe, 2 vols (1848–9).

Forez: G. Guichard, Comte de Neufbourg, E. Perroy and J.-E. Dufour, *Chartes du Forez*, 24 vols (1933–70).

'Fragment d'une Chanson d'Antioche en Provençal', ed. P. Meyer, *AOL* 2 (1884).

'Fragmentum historiae Andegavensis', ed. L. Halphen and R. Poupardin, *Chroniques des comtes d'Anjou et des seigneurs d'Amboise* (1913).

Fulcher of Chartres, *Historia Hierosolymitana*, ed. H. Hagenmeyer (1913).

Gallia christiana in provincias ecclesiasticas distributa, ed. Congregation of St Maur *et al.*, 16 vols (1715–1865).

Gellone: P. Alaus, L. Cassan and E. Meynial, *Cartulaire de Gellone* (1898).

'Genealogia comitum Buloniensium', *MGHS* 9.

'Genealogiae Aquicinctinae', *MGHS* 14.

'Genealogiae breves regum Francorum', *MGHS* 13.

'Genealogiae comitum Flandriae', *MGHS* 9.

Geoffrey Grossus, 'Vita Beati Bernardi abbatis Tironiensis', *RHGF* 14.

Geoffrey Malaterra, 'De rebus gestis Rogerii Calabriae et Siciliae Comitis', *Rerum Italicarum Scriptores*, NS 5, 1.

Geoffrey of Breuil, 'Chronica', *RHGF* 12.

Geoffrey of Châlard, 'Dictamen de primordiis ecclesiae Castaliensis', *RHC Oc*. 5.

Geoffrey of Vendôme, 'Epistolae', *PL* 57.

'Gesta Ambaziensium dominorum', ed. L. Halphen and R. Poupardin, *Chroniques des comtes d'Anjou et des seigneurs d'Amboise* (1913).

Gesta Francorum et aliorum Hierosolimitanorum, ed. R. Hill (1962).

'Gesta Treverorum', *MGHS* 8.

Gilbert, 'Chronicon Hanoniense', *MGHS* 21.

Giles of Orval, 'Gesta episcoporum Leodiensium', *MGHS* 25.

Gilo, 'Historia de via Hierosolymitana', *RHC Oc*. 5.

Göttweig: A.F. Fuchs, *Die Traditionsbücher des Benediktinerstiftes Göttweig* (1931).

Gratian, 'Decretum', ed. E. Friedberg, *Corpus Juris Canonici* (1879–81), 1.

Gregory VII, *Register*, ed. E. Caspar, 2 vols (1955).

Grenoble: J. Marion, *Cartulaires de l'église cathédrale de Grenoble* (1869).

Guibert of Nogent, *De vita sua*, ed. E.-R. Labande (1981).

—— 'Gesta Dei per Francos', *RHC Oc*. 4.

H. Hagenmeyer, *Die Kreuzzugsbriefe aus den Jahren 1088–1100* (1901).

Henry of Huntingdon, 'De captione Antiochiae a Christianis', *RHC Oc*. 5.

—— *Historia Anglorum*, ed. T. Arnold (1879).

Hermann, 'Liber de restauratione monasterii sancti Martini Tornacensis', *MGHS* 14.

'Historia de translatione sanctorum magni Nicolai ... ejusdem avunculi, alterius Nicolai, Theodorique ... de civitate Mirea in monasterium S. Nicolai de Littore Venetiarum', *RHC Oc*. 5.

'Historia monasterii Aquicinctini', *MGHS* 14.

'Historia monasterii novi Pictavensis', ed. I.M. Watterich, *Pontificum Romanorum vitae* (1862), 1.

'Historia peregrinorum euntium Jerusolymam', *RHC Oc*. 3.

'Historia Welforum Weingartensis', *MGHS* 21.

W. Holtzmann, 'Zur Geschichte des Investiturstreites (Englische Analekten II)', *Neues Archiv*, 50 (1935).
Hugh of Flavigny, 'Chronicon', *MGHS* 8.
Hugh of Fleury, 'Historia regum Francorum', *MGHS* 9.
Hugh of St Maria, 'Itineris Hierosolymitani compendium', *RHC Oc.* 5.

Ibn al-Athir, 'Sum of World History', *RHC Or.* 1–2.
Ibn al-Qalanisi, *The Damascus Chronicle*, extr. tr. H.A.R. Gibb (1932).
Ivo of Chartres, 'Decretum', *PL* 161.
—— 'Panormia', *PL* 161.

P. Jaffé, *Regesta pontificum Romanorum*, 2nd edn, 2 vols (1885–8).
Jumièges: J.J. Vernier, *Chartes de l'abbaye de Jumièges* (1916).

Kamal ad-Din, 'Chronicle of Aleppo', *RHC Or.* 3.
P.F. Kehr, *Papsturkunden in Spanien. I. Katalanien* (1926).
—— *Regesta pontificum Romanorum. Italia pontificia*, 10 vols (1906–75).

Lambert of Ardres, 'Historia comitum Ghisnensium', *MGHS* 24.
Lambert of Arras, 'De Atrebatensi episcopatu ab Urbano II restituto', *RHGF* 14.
Lambert Waterlos, 'Annales Cameracenses', *MGHS* 16.
Landulf the Younger of Milan, 'Historia Mediolanensis', *MGHS* 20.
Lawrence of Liége, 'Gesta episcoporum Virdunensium', *MGHS* 10.
'Leges Edwardi Confessoris', ed. F. Liebermann, *Die Gesetze der Angelsachsen* (1903–16), 1.
'Liber de poenitentia et tentationibus religiosorum', *PL* 213.
Liber memorandorum ecclesie de Bernewelle, ed. J.W. Clark (1907).
S. Löwenfeld, *Epistolae pontificum Romanorum ineditae* (1885).
Lupus Protospatarius, 'Annales', *MGHS* 5.

'Mainz Anonymous', tr. S. Eidelberg, *The Jews and the Crusaders* (1977).
J. Malbrancq, *De Morinis*, 3 vols (1639–54).
Marcigny: J. Richard, *Le Cartulaire de Marcigny-sur-Loire* (1957).
Marmoutier: C. Chantelou, *Marmoutier. Cartulaire Tourangeau* (1879).
Das Martyrologium des Nurnberger Memorbuches, ed. S. Salfeld (1898).
Matthew of Edessa, 'Chronicle', *RHC arm.* 1.
Maurice of Neufmoustier, 'Albrici Trium Fontium chronica a monacho novi monasterii Hoiensis interpolata', *MGHS* 23.
'Le memorbuch de Mayence', ed. A. Neubacher, *Revue des études juives*, 4 (1882).
Molesme: J. Laurent, *Cartulaires de l'abbaye de Molesme*, 2 vols (1907–11).
P.H. Morice, *Mémoires pour servir de preuves à l'histoire ecclesiastique et civile de Bretagne*, 3 vols (1642–6).

'Narratio Floriacensis de captis Antiochia et Hierosolyma', *RHC Oc.* 5.
'Narratio quomodo relliquiae martyris Georgii ad nos Aquicinenses pervenerunt', *RHC Oc.* 5.

'Notae sanctae Mariae Mediolanenses', *MGHS* 18.
'Notitiae duae Lemovicenses de praedicatione crucis in Aquitania', *RHC Oc.* 5.

Orderic Vitalis, *Historia aecclesiastica*, ed. M. Chibnall, 6 vols (1969–79).
Otto of Freising, *Chronica*, ed. A. Hofmeister (1912).
—— *Gesta Frederici I. Imperatoris*, ed. G. Waitz (1912).
H. and P. d'Outreman, *Histoire de la ville et comté de Valentiennes. Preuves* (1639).

'Pancharta Caduniensis seu Historia sancti Sudarii Jesu Christi', *RHC Oc.* 5.
Paray-le-Monial: C.U.J. Chevalier, 'Cartulaire du prieuré de Paray-le-Monial', *Collection de cartulaires dauphinois* (1869–1912), 8, 2.
Paschal II, 'Epistolae et Privilegia', *PL* 163.
Peter of Blois, 'De Hierosolymitano peregrinatione acceleranda', *PL* 207.
Peter Tudebode, *Historia de Hierosolymitano itinere*, ed. J.H. and L.L. Hill (1977).
J. von Pflugk-Harttung, *Acta pontificum Romanorum inedita*, 3 vols (1881–6).
'Primordia Windbergensia', *MGHS* 17.

'Qualiter reliquiae B. Nicolai episcopi et confessoris ad Lotharingiae villam, quae Portus nominatur, delatae sunt', *RCH Oc.* 5.

Ralph of Caen, 'Gesta Tancredi', *RHC Oc.* 3.
J. Ramackers *et al.*, *Papsturkunden in Frankreich*, 7 vols so far (1932–ff.).
Raymond of Aguilers, *Liber*, ed. J.H. and L.L. Hill (1969).
—— var. ms. in *RHC Oc.* 3.
Redon: A. de Courson, *Cartulaire de l'abbaye de Redon* (1863).
Reiner of St Lawrence of Liége, 'Triumphale Bulonicum', *MGHS* 20.
P. Riant, 'Inventaire critique des lettres historiques des croisades', *AOL* 1.
Richard of Poitiers, 'Chronicon', *RHGF* 12.
Robert of Torigni, *Chronica*, ed. R. Howlett (1889)
Robert the Monk, 'Historia Iherosolimitana', *RHC Oc.* 3.

St Andrew of Vienne: C.U.J. Chevalier, 'Cartulaire de l'abbaye de Saint-André-Le-Bas de Vienne', *Collection de cartulaires dauphinois*, 1 (1869).
St Benignus of Dijon: G. Chevrier and M. Chaume, *Chartes et documents de Saint-Bénigne de Dijon*, 2 vols (1943).
St Chaffre of Le Monastier: C.U.J. Chevalier, 'Cartulaire de l'abbaye de St.-Chaffre du Monastier', *Collection de cartulaires dauphinois* (1869–1912), 8, 1.
St George of Rennes: P. de la Bigne Villeneuve, *Cartulaire de l'abbaye de Saint-Georges de Rennes* (1875).
St Hubert in Ardenne: G. Kurth, *Chartes de l'abbaye de Saint-Hubert en Ardenne*, 1 (1903).
St Julian of Tours: L.J. Denis, *Chartes de St-Julien de Tours* (1912).
St Lambert of Liége: S. Bormans and E. Schoolmeesters, *Cartulaire de l'église*

Saint-Lambert de Liége, 6 vols (1893–1933).
St Laon of Thouars: H. Imbert, *Cartulaire de l'abbaye de Saint-Laon de Thouars* (Niort, nd).
St Maixent: A. Richard, 'Chartes et documents pour servir à l'histoire de l'abbaye de Saint-Maixent', *Archives historiques du Poitou*, 16, 18 (1886).
St Martin of Pontoise: J. Depoin, *Cartulaire de l'abbaye de Saint-Martin de Pontoise* (1895).
St Père of Chartres: B.E.C. Guérard, *Cartulaire de l'abbaye de Saint-Père de Chartres*, 2 vols (1840).
St Philibert of Tournous: R. Juënin, *Nouvelle histoire de l'abbaïe royale et collegiale de Saint Filibert*, 2 vols (1733).
St Victor of Marseilles: B.E.C. Guérard, *Cartulaire de l'abbaye de Saint-Victor de Marseille*, 2 vols (1857).
St Vincent of Le Mans: R Charles and S.M. d'Elbenne, *Cartulaire de l'abbaye de Saint-Vincent du Mans*, 2 vols (1886–1913).
St Vincent of Mâcon: M.-C. Ragut, *Cartulaire de Saint-Vincent de Mâcon* (1864).
Sauxillanges: H. Doniol, 'Cartulaire de Sauxillanges', *Mémoires de l'académie des sciences, belles-lettres et arts de Clermont-Ferrand*, NS 3 (1861).
Savigny: A. Bernard, *Cartulaire de l'abbaye de Savigny* (1853).
Sigebert of Gembloux, 'Chronica', *MGHS* 6.
'Sigeberti Gemblacensis chronica auctarium Aquicinense', *MGHS* 6.
R. Somerville, *The Councils of Urban II. 1: Decreta Claromontensia* (1972).
K.F. Stumpf-Brentano, *Die Reichskanzler*, 3 vols (1865–83).
Suger of St Denis, *Vita Ludovici Grossi regis*, ed. H. Waquet (1929).

Trinity of Vendôme: C. Metais, *Cartulaire de l'abbaye cardinale de la Trinité de Vendôme*, 2 vols (1893–4).
'Triumphus Sancti Lamberti de Castro Bullonio', *MGHS* 20.

Urban II, 'Epistolae et Privilegia', *PL* 151.

J. Vaissete, C. Devic and A. Molinier, *Histoire générale de Languedoc*, 16 vols (1872–1904).
A. Van Hasselt, 'Document inédit pour servir à l'histoire des croisades', *Annales de l'académie d'archéologie de Belgique*, 6 (1849).
F. Vercauteren, *Actes des comtes de Flandre 1071–1128* (1938).
Vézelay: R.B.C. Huygens, *Monumenta Vizeliacensia* (1976).

Walter of Thérouanne, 'Vita Karoli comitis Flandriae', *MGHS* 12.
W. Wattenbach, 'Handschriftliches', *Neues Archiv*, 7 (1881–2).
W. Wiederhold, 'Papsturkunden in Florenz', *Nachrichten von der Gesellschaft der Wissenschaften zu Göttingen. Phil.-hist. Kl.* (1901).
William of Malmesbury, *Gesta regum Anglorum*, ed. W. Stubbs, 2 vols (1887–9).
William of Tyre, 'Historia rerum in partibus transmarinis gestarum', *RHC Oc.* 1.

Secondary works

A.S. Abulafia, 'The interrelationship between the Hebrew chronicles on the first crusade', _Journal of Semitic Studies_, 27 (1982).

P. Alphandéry and A. Dupront, _La Chrétienté et l'idée de croisade_, 2 vols (1954–9).

A. Becker, _Papst Urban II (1088–1099)_, 1 (1964).

E.O. Blake, 'The Formation of the "Crusade Idea" ', _Journal of Ecclesiastical History_, 21 (1970).

M. Bloch, _Feudal Society_ (1961).

L. Boehm, ' "Gesta Dei per Francos" – oder "Gesta Francorum". Die Kreuzzüge als historiographisches Problem', _Saeculum_, 8 (1957).

H. Brinkman, _Entstehungsgeschichte des Minnesangs_ (1926).

J.A. Brundage, 'Adhemar of Puy: the Bishop and his Critics', _Speculum_, 34 (1959).

—— _Medieval Canon Law and the Crusader_ (1969).

—— 'The Army of the First Crusade and the Crusade Vow: some reflections on a recent book', _Mediaeval Studies_, 33 (1971).

—— 'Prostitution, Miscegenation and Sexual Purity in the First Crusade', _Crusade and Settlement_, ed. P.W. Edbury, (1985).

J.L. Cate, 'The Crusade of 1101', _A History of the Crusades_, ed.-in-chief K.M. Setton, 2nd edn, 4 vols so far (1969ff.), 1.

J. Chaurand, 'La conception de l'histoire de Guibert de Nogent', _Cahiers de civilisation médiévale_, 8 (1965).

M.-D. Chenu, _Nature, Man, and Society in the Twelfth Century_ (1968).

G. Constable, 'The Financing of the Crusades in the Twelfth Century', _Outremer_, ed. B.Z. Kedar, H.E. Mayer and R.C. Smail (1982).

abbé Cousseau, 'Mémoire historique sur l'église de Nôtre-Dame de Lusignan et ses fondateurs', _Mémoires de la société des antiquaires de l'Ouest_ (1844).

H.E.J. Cowdrey, 'Pope Gregory VII's "Crusading" Plans of 1074', _Outremer_, ed. B.Z. Kedar, H.E. Mayer and R.C. Smail (1982).

—— 'Pope Urban II's Preaching of the First Crusade', _History_, 55 (1970).

—— _The Cluniacs and the Gregorian Reform_ (1970).

—— 'The Peace and the Truce of God in the Eleventh Century', _Past and Present_, 46 (1970).

—— 'Martyrdom and the First Crusade', _Crusade and Settlement_, ed. P.W. Edbury, (1985).

C.W. David, _Robert Curthose, Duke of Normandy_ (1920).

E. Delaruelle, 'Essai sur la formation de l'idée de croisade', _Bulletin de littérature ecclésiastique_, 42 (1941), 45 (1944), 54–5 (1953–4).

Dictionnaire de biographie française, ed. J. Balteau _et al._, 14 vols so far (1933ff.).

G. Duby, _La Société aux XIe et XIIe siècles dans la région mâconnaise_ (1971).

—— *The Chivalrous Society* (1977).
—— *The Three Orders. Feudal Society Imagined* (1980).
A. Dupront, 'La spiritualité des croisés et des pélerins d'après les sources de la première croisade', *Convegni del Centro di Studi sulla spiritualità medievale*, 4 (1963).
R. Dussaud, *Topographie historique de la Syrie antique et médiévale* (1927).

S. Edgington, 'Pagan Peverel: An Anglo-Norman Crusader', *Crusade and Settlement*, ed. P.W. Edbury, (1985).
C. Erdmann, *The Origin of the Idea of Crusade* (1977).
G.R. Evans, *The Mind of St Bernard of Clairvaux* (1983).

A. Ferreiro, 'The Siege of Barbastro, 1064–5: a reassessment', *Journal of Medieval History*, 9 (1983).
A. Fliche, 'Urbain II et la croisade', *Revue d'histoire de l'église de France*, 13 (1927).
R. Folz, *Le Souvenir et la légende de Charlemagne dans l'empire germanique médiéval* (1950).
R. Foreville, 'Un chef de la première croisade: Arnoul Malecouronne', *Bulletin philologique et historique du comité des travaux historiques et scientifiques* (1953–4).
A. Frolow, *La Relique de la vraie croix* (1961).

P.J. Geary, *Furta Sacra* (1978).
A. Gieysztor, 'The Genesis of the Crusades: the Encyclical of Sergius IV (1009–1012)', *Medievalia et Humanistica*, 5–6 (1948).
J.T. Gilchrist, 'The Erdmann Thesis and the Canon Law, 1083–1141', *Crusade and Settlement*, ed. P.W. Edbury, (1985).
S.D. Goitein, *A Mediterranean Society*, 3 vols (1967–78).
—— 'Contemporary Letters on the Capture of Jerusalem by the Crusaders', *Journal of Jewish Studies*, 3 (1952).
—— 'Geniza Sources for the Crusader Period: A Survey', *Outremer*, ed. B.Z. Kedar, H.E. Mayer and R.C. Smail (1982).
J. Goñi Gaztambide, *Historia de la Bula de la Cruzada en España* (1958).
R.P. Grossman, 'The Financing of the Crusades' (Ph.D. Thesis, Chicago, 1965).
L.A.T. Gryting, *The Oldest Version of the Twelfth-Century Poem, La Venjance Nostre Seigneur* (1952).

H. Hagenmeyer, *Chronologie de la première croisade (1094–1100)* (1902).
—— 'Étude sur la Chronique de Zimmern', *AOL* 2.
—— *Peter der Eremite* (1879).
B. Hamilton, *The Latin Church in the Crusader States. The Secular Church* (1980).
E.-D. Hehl, *Kirche und Krieg im 12. Jahrhundert* (1980).
J.H. and L.L. Hill, 'Contemporary Accounts and the Later Reputation of Adhémar, Bishop of Puy', *Medievalia et Humanistica*, 9 (1955).
—— *Raymond IV de Saint-Gilles 1041 (ou 1042)–1105* (1959).

N. Housley, 'Crusades Against Christians: their origins and early development, *c*.1000–1216', *Crusade and Settlement*, ed. P.W. Edbury, (1985).

M. Keen, *Chivalry* (1984).
P. Knoch, 'Kreuzzug und Siedlung. Studien zum Aufruf der Magdeburger Kirche von 1108', *Jahrbuch für die Geschichte Mittel- und Ostdeutschlands*, 23 (1974).

R.-J. Lilie, *Byzanz und die Kreuzfahrerstaaten* (1981).
F. Lotter, *Die Konzeption des Wendenkreuzzugs* (1977).

B. McGinn, 'Iter Sancti Sepulchri: the Piety of the First Crusaders', *The Walter Prescott Webb Lectures: Essays in Medieval Civilization*, ed. R.E. Sullivan *et al.* (1978).
—— *Visions of the End* (1979).
H.E. Mayer, 'Zur Beurteilung Adhémars von Le Puy', *Deutsches Archiv*, 16 (1960).
—— *Mélanges dur l'histoire du royaume latin de Jérusalem* (1984).
D.M. Metcalf, *Coinage of the Crusades and the Latin East* (1983).
C. Morris, 'Policy and Visions. The Case of the Holy Lance at Antioch', *War and Government in the Middle Ages. Essays in Honour of J.O. Prestwich* (1984).
A. Murray, *Reason and Society in the Middle Ages* (1978).

J.W. Parkes, *The Jew in the Medieval Community* (1938).
W. Porges, 'The Clergy, the Poor, and the Non-Combatants on the First Crusade', *Speculum*, 21 (1946).
N.J.G. Pounds, *An Historical Geography of Europe 450BC–AD 1330* (1973).
J. Prawer, *Crusader Institutions* (1980).

L. Réau, *Iconographie de l'art chrétien*, 3 vols (1955–8).
J. Richard, 'La confrèrie de la croisade: à propos d'un épisode de la première croisade', *Mélanges E.-R. Labande* (1974).
—— 'La papauté et la direction de la première croisade', *Journal des savants* (1960).
—— 'Quelques textes sur les premiers temps de l'église latine de Jérusalem', *Recueil des travaux offerts à M. Clovis Brunel*, 2, (1955).
—— *The Latin Kingdom of Jerusalem*, 2 vols (1979).
J. Riley-Smith, 'An Approach to Crusading Ethics', *Reading Medieval Studies*, 6 (1980).
—— 'Crusading as an Act of Love', *History*, 65 (1980).
—— 'Death on the First Crusade', *The End of Strife*, ed. D.M. Loades (1984).
—— 'Peace never established: the Case of the Kingdom of Jerusalem', *Transactions of the Royal Historical Society*, 5th ser., 28 (1978).
—— 'The First Crusade and St Peter', *Outremer*, ed. B.Z. Kedar, H.E. Mayer and R.C. Smail (1982).

—— 'The First Crusade and the Persecution of the Jews', *Studies in Church History*, 21 (1984).

—— 'The motives of the earliest crusaders and the settlement of Latin Palestine, 1095–1100', *English Historical Review*, 98 (1983).

— *What were the crusades?* (1977).

L. and J. Riley-Smith, *The Crusades: Idea and reality, 1095–1274* (1981).

I.S. Robinson, *Authority and Resistance in the Investiture Contest* (1978).

—— 'Gregory VII and the Soldiers of Christ', *History*, 58 (1973).

M. Rouche, 'Cannibalisme sacré chez les croisés populaires', *La Religion populaire*, ed. Y.-M. Hilaire (1981).

P. Rousset, *Les Origines et les caractères de la première croisade* (1945).

S. Runciman, *A History of the Crusades*, 3 vols (1951–4).

R.C. Smail, *Crusading Warfare (1097–1193)* (1956).

R. Somerville, 'The Council of Clermont (1095) and Latin Christian Society', *Archivum historiae pontificiae*, 12 (1974).

—— 'The Council of Clermont and the First Crusade', *Studia gratiana*, 20 (1976).

A. Stickler, 'Il potere coattivo materiale della Chiesa nella Riforma Gregoriana secondo Anselmo di Lucca', *Studi gregoriani*, 2 (1947).

L.A.M. Sumberg, 'The "Tafurs" and the First Crusade', *Medieval Studies*, 21 (1959).

J. Sumption, *Pilgrimage* (1975).

M. Villey, *La Croisade: Essai sur la formation d'une théorie juridique* (1942).

B. Ward, *Miracles and the Medieval Mind* (1982).

K.F. Werner, 'Die Nachkommen Karls des Grossen bis um Jahr 1000', *Karl der Grosse*, ed. W. Braunfels and P.E. Schramm (1965–8), 4.

—— 'Liens de parenté et noms de personne. Un problème historique et méthodologique', *Famille et parenté dans l'occident médiéval*, ed. G. Duby and J. Le Goff (1977).

T. Wolff, *Die Bauernkreuzzüge des Jahres 1096* (1891).

Index

Abbreviations

Lightning Source UK Ltd.
Milton Keynes UK
UKOW020015240212

187795UK00009B/57/A